HOW TO USE

Microsoft®
Office 97

HOW TO USE

Microsoft®
Office 97

Kathy Ivens and Thomas E. Barich

Ziff-Davis Press
An imprint of Macmillan Computer Publishing USA
Emeryville, California

Publisher	Joe Wikert
Associate Publisher	Juliet Langley
Acquisitions Editor	Lysa Lewallen
Development/Copy Editor	Margo Hill
Technical Reviewer	Dick Hol
Production Editors	Ami Knox and Carol Burbo
Proofreader	Timothy Loughman
Book Design	Dan Armstrong and Bruce Lundquist
Page Layout	M. D. Barrera and Meredith Downs
Indexer	Valerie Robbins

Ziff-Davis Press, ZD Press, and the Ziff-Davis Press logo are trademarks or registered trademarks of, and are licensed to Macmillan Computer Publishing USA by Ziff-Davis Publishing Company, New York, New York.

Ziff-Davis Press imprint books are produced on a Macintosh computer system with the following applications: FrameMaker®, Microsoft® Word, QuarkXPress®, Adobe Illustrator®, Adobe Photoshop®, Adobe Streamline™, MacLink®Plus, Aldus® FreeHand™, Collage Plus™.

Ziff-Davis Press, an imprint of
Macmillan Computer Publishing USA
5903 Christie Avenue
Emeryville, CA 94608

PART OF A CONTINUING SERIES

All other product names and services identified throughout this book are trademarks or registered trademarks of their respective companies. They are used throughout this book in editorial fashion only and for the benefit of such companies. No such uses, or the use of any trade name, is intended to convey endorsement or other affiliation with the book.

ISBN 1-56276-564-7

Manufactured in the United States of America
10 9 8 7 6 5 4 3 2

This book was produced digitally by Macmillan Computer Publishing and manufactured using computer-to-plate technology (a film-less process) by GAC/Shepard Poorman, Indianapolis, Indiana.

This book is dedicated to Lysa Lewallen, with admiration, respect, and affection.
— Kathy Ivens,
Thomas E. Barich

ALL BOOKS REQUIRE the help and professional talents of a great many people, and this book faced a particularly complicated life from the day it was conceived until the moment it arrived at your book seller. There are more people to thank than will fit in the space allotted. And there really aren't sufficient words of praise to do an adequate job.

Lysa Lewallen, one of the best acquisition editors in the business, nursed the book, the authors, and the concept along, using her habitual humanity, efficiency, and humor. She suffers from chronic niceness.

Margo Hill and Pipi Diamond handled the details of production, editing, and tracking of manuscript pages with dispatch and efficiency, even as the project become more and more complicated. Dick Hol gets our thanks for checking the technical accuracy of every word we wrote. The art and production department personnel who produced the pages in their final form are a group of highly skilled professionals who have our deep respect and thanks.

T A B L E

Introduction xi

PART 1
Getting Started with Microsoft Office 97

How to Install Microsoft Office 97 2

How to Use Common Office Applications 4

How to Insert and Link Objects between Applications 6

How to Use the Binder 8

How to Get Help 10

How to Open, Save, Close, and Print Documents 12

PART 2
Microsoft Word

A Tour of the Word Window 16

How to Enter and Edit Text 18

How to Cut and Copy Using Cut-and-Paste 20

How to Use the Spelling and Grammar Checker 22

How to Create and Use AutoText Entries 24

How to Format Text 26

How to Copy Character Formatting 28

How to Change Fonts and Font Sizes 30

How to Change Line Spacing 32

How to Use Tabs 34

How to Create Numbered and Bulleted Lists 36

How to Create Tables 38

How to Add Borders and Shading 40

How to Change the Page Margins 42

How to Use Headers and Footers 44

How to Use the Document Map 46

How to Use Outline View 48

How to Use a Template 50

How to Modify a Template 52

How to Use a Wizard 54

How to Create a Mail Merge Document 56

How to Create the Mail Merge Data Source 58

How to Complete the Main Mail Merge Document 62

How to Run the Mail Merge 64

How to Insert a Graphic 66

How to Format a Graphic 68

PART 3
Microsoft Excel 97

How to Use the Excel Window 72

How to Enter Data 74

How to Enter a Formula 76

How to Sum Numbers 78

How to Enter Data Automatically 80

O F C O N T E N T S

How to Navigate around Worksheets 82

How to Insert Columns and Rows 84

How to Delete or Clear Cells 86

How to Move and Copy Data with Drag and Drop 88

How to Move and Copy Data with the Clipboard 90

How to Adjust Column Width 92

How to Format Numbers in Cells 94

How to Use Functions 96

How to Work with Absolute References 98

How to Name Ranges 100

How to Search for Data 102

How to Sort Data 104

How to Use the ChartWizard 106

How to Change the Chart Type 108

How to Work with Chart and Axis Titles 110

How to Change the Chart Data 112

How to Draw Shapes on a Chart 114

How to Use Multiple Worksheets 116

How to Plan a Database 126

How to Create a Table with the Table Wizard 128

How to Add, Delete, and Change Fields 130

How to Create a Form with the Form Wizard 132

How to Modify a Form in the Design View 134

How to Enter Data in the Database 136

How to Create a Report with the Report Wizard 138

How to Modify a Report in the Design View 140

How to Create a Switchboard Form 142

How to Dress Up the Switchboard Form 144

How to Sort Records 146

How to Apply Access Filters 148

How Use the Simple Query Wizard to Create a Query 150

How to Import Data 152

How to Export Data 154

How to Customize Access 156

PART 4

Microsoft Access 97

How to Understand Database Basics 120

How to Use the Database Wizard 122

How to Use the Switchboard to Enter Data 124

PART 5

Microsoft PowerPoint

How to Use the PowerPoint Toolbars 160

How to Use the AutoContent Wizard 162

How to Use a Template 164

How to Edit and Add Text on a Slide 166

How to Format and Align Text 168

How to Add Text Boxes 170

How to Add a Shape 172

How to Use Autoshapes 174

How to Use Fills, Shadows, and 3-D Effects 176

How to Add Clip Art, Pictures, Video, and Sound 178

How to Move, Size, and Rotate Objects 180

How to Layer Objects 182

How to Group and Ungroup Objects 184

How to Insert, Delete, and Reorder Slides 186

How to Create Speaker Notes 188

How to Create Handouts 190

How to Set Up a Slide Show 192

How to Run a Slide Show 194

How to Create a Self-Running Slide Show 198

How to Use Pack and Go 202

PART 6
Outlook 97

The Opening Window 206

How to Use the Personal Address Book 208

How to Compose and Send E-Mail 210

How to Attach a File to a Message 212

How to Open and Read E-Mail 214

How to Reply to and Forward Messages 216

How to Manage Received Attachments 218

How to Create an Appointment 220

How to Create a Recurring Appointment 222

How to Create Tasks Quickly 224

How to Create Contacts 226

How to Send E-Mail to a Contact 228

How to Autodial Contacts 230

How to Autorecord Journal Entries 232

How to Record Manual Journal Entries 234

How to Use AutoArchive 236

PART 7
Working with the Internet

How to Search the Web   *240*

How to Find Files on the Web   *242*

How to Download Files   *244*

How to Get Online Support   *246*

Make the Web Part of Your Office Document   *248*

PART 8
Office 97 Small Business Edition

How to Install the SBE Applications   *252*

How to Create Income Statements   *254*

How to Create Balance Sheets   *256*

How to Create a Trial Balance   *258*

How to Create a Cash Flow Report   *260*

How to Create a What-If Scenario   *262*

How to Find and Mark Locations in AutoMap   *264*

How to Highlight a Travel Route in AutoMap   *266*

PART 9
Microsoft Publisher 97

How to Install Publisher   *270*

How to Use the Publisher Toolbar   *272*

How to Use the Page Wizard   *274*

How to Create a Text Frame   *276*

How to Add Text to a Text Frame   *278*

How to Format Text   *280*

How to Insert Pages and Navigate Through Pages   *282*

How to Resize and Reposition Clip Art   *284*

How to Wrap Text around Clip Art   *286*

How to Flow Text between Text Frames   *288*

How to Recolor and Add a Drop Shadow to Text Frames   *292*

How to Add a Border to a Frame   *294*

How to Use Gradient Fills and Patterns   *296*

How to Layer Pictures for Special Effects   *298*

How to Group Objects   *300*

How to Insert Page Numbers and Dates   *302*

How to Use Design Gallery to Add Flair to Your Publication   *304*

How to Use the PageWizard for Special Elements   *306*

How to Use Shapes   *308*

Index   *310*

INTRODUCTION

THIS BOOK is written for users of Office 97 who don't qualify as propellerheads or computer weenies. The authors assume that the reader is new to one or more of the applications in the Office 97 suite.

We wrote this book to help you learn the basic functions and features of the Office 97 applications in a way that is clear, easy to understand, and straightforward.

Our goal is to make you self-sufficient and comfortable with all the basic tools for the software packages we've covered. The pictures, which match what you see on your own screen, add to the easy-to-learn presentation of facts we aimed for.

When you finish each section of this book you'll have the fundamental skills you need to accomplish two things: work productively in the software; and have enough understanding of the software to move on to more complicated tasks at your own pace.

We think you'll enjoy learning from this book, and we know you'll gain enough information to approach your Office 97 software with confidence.

P A R T 1

Getting Started with Microsoft Office 97

MICROSOFT OFFICE is a powerhouse of productivity tools, including Word, Excel, PowerPoint, Outlook, Access (Professional edition only) and more. Although it may seem a bit overwhelming at first glance, Office 97 is easily manageable once you understand the basics. That what this section is all about—giving you an overview of how the pieces fit together.

IN THIS SECTION YOU'LL LEARN

- How to Install Microsoft Office 97   2
- How to Use Common Office Applications   4
- How to Insert and Link Objects between Applications   6
- How to Use the Binder   8
- How to Get Help   10
- How to Open, Save, Close, and Print Documents   12

How to Install Microsoft Office 97

Installation procedures, once the bane of novice and experienced computer users alike, now provide a fairly quick and easy means of getting your software application up and running. To install Microsoft Office 97, simply insert the Office 97 CD into your CD-ROM drive and answer a few questions, and you're on your way.

If your CD-ROM drive autoinsert notification option is turned on (it probably is, since that is the default setting), the MS Office 97 Install screen automatically loads. Click Install to begin. If the installation screen does not automatically load (give it 15-20 seconds), open My Computer and double-click the CD-ROM drive icon. In the folder window that opens, find and double-click on setup.exe to start.

1 The Welcome dialog box not only greets you, but offers some valuable advice, as well. If you haven't already done so, use Alt+Tab or the Taskbar to close any other Windows applications that are running. Then click Continue to begin installation by filling out the Name and Organization Information dialog box.

● If the Office 97 installation process encounters an existing file on your system that is a duplicate of one that Office 97 installs, you will be offered a choice of retaining the original file or replacing it. You should always keep the newer (datewise) file of the two.

● If the MS Office 97 CD does not automatically load when you place it in your CD-ROM drive, your autoinsert notification option is probably turned off. To turn it on, click Start on the Windows 95 Taskbar and choose Settings, Control Panel to open the Control Panel folder window. Double-click the System icon to open the System Properties sheet. Click the Device Manager tab, double-click CDROM, then double-click the icon for your specific CD-ROM drive to open its property sheet. Click the Settings tab, and place a check (click) in the Auto Insert notification option box. Click OK until you return to Windows 95.

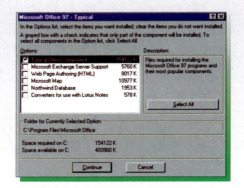

6 Review and confirm (or change) your choices when they're displayed, then click Continue to begin the actual installation of the Microsoft Office 97 software. A dialog box notifies you when the installation is successfully completed. Click OK to return to Windows 95. Now you're ready to begin using Office 97.

Name and Organization Information

Enter your full name in the box below. You may also enter the name of your organization. Setup will use this information for subsequent installations of the product.

Name: Tom Barich

Organization: Frameworx

[OK] [Exit Setup]

2 Windows automatically enters the name and organization information from your Windows 95 setup. You can change it if you wish or accept it as it is. Click OK to proceed to the Confirm Name and Organization Information dialog box. If the information is correct, click OK to open the CD Key dialog box; otherwise click Change and make the necessary changes.

Microsoft Office 97 Setup

Locate your 11-digit "CD Key" number and enter it in the space below. You can find this number on the sticker on the back of your CD case.

CD Key:

[   ]-[   ]

[OK] [Exit Setup]

3 On the back of the jewel case containing your Office 97 CD you'll find an 11-digit CD key code. Enter it in the CD Key space. There's no need to enter the hyphen—just type the 11 digits. Double-check to be sure you entered the correct number and click OK.

Microsoft Office 97 Setup

Microsoft Office 97 Professional

Welcome to Microsoft Office 97

Get the most out of Microsoft® Office 97 by registering your software. If you register online, you will be eligible to access exclusive content for Office 97 users at the Microsoft Office Web site.

To register with a modem, click the online registration button after you have finished installing Office 97. If you do not have a modem, fill in and mail the registration card included with your Office product.

Microsoft **Office 97**

Microsoft Office Setup: Disk 1

Destination File:
C:\...\Microsoft Office\Office\ACCFIL80.ODE

1%

[Cancel]

Microsoft Office 97 Setup

Setup will install Microsoft Office Professional in the following destination folder.

To install to this folder, click OK.

To install to a different folder, click the Change Folder button.

You can choose not to install Microsoft Office Professional, or change its destination folder later during Setup.

Folder:
C:\Program Files\Microsoft Office   [Change Folder...]

[OK] [Exit Setup]

4 Setup automatically installs Office 97 in the \Program Files\Microsoft Office folder unless you instruct it otherwise. If you prefer another location for the installation, click Change Folder and indicate the new folder; otherwise click OK to continue.

5 Next you must decide whether to do a typical installation, a custom install, or a minimal install (in which you run the software from a CD-ROM). If you're familiar with previous Office versions and know exactly which elements you want to install, choose Custom. If you are short on disk space, choose the CD-ROM installation. Otherwise, select the Typical installation option. Remember, you can always add or remove any of the Office 97 components at a later time, as the need arises.

Microsoft Office 97 Setup

To choose the installation you want, click one of the following buttons.

Typical
Recommended for most users. Installs all Office applications and popular components. (Approx. 121 MB)

Custom
Recommended for expert users. Includes Typical installation and the option to add and remove components. (Max. 191 MB)

Run from CD-ROM
Install Office to run from the CD-ROM. Shared components will be copied to your local hard disk. (Approx. 60 MB)

Folder:
C:\Program Files\Microsoft Office

[Exit Setup]

How to Use Common Office Applications

In addition to Word, Excel, Access, PowerPoint, and Outlook, Microsoft Office 97 includes several smaller applications whose sole purpose is to enhance your finished Office documents. The most popular of these miniapplications are WordArt, Microsoft Clip Gallery, and Microsoft Graph.

WordArt enables you to transform words or short phrases into works of art by converting them to drawing objects and adding special effects. The Microsoft Clip Gallery offers an extensive selection of clip art, photos, sound files, and video clips to dress up your forms, letters, memos, and other documents. Microsoft Graph breathes life into listless reports and workbooks through eye-catching and informative charts.

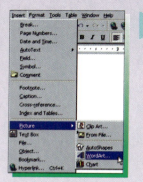

1 To access WordArt from Word, Excel, or PowerPoint, choose Insert, Picture, WordArt from the menu bar. Don't panic if you can't find WordArt in Access. The reason is simple: It's not available in Access.

- If you performed a typical install when first setting up Microsoft Office 97, the Chart feature will not be available in Access. To utilize the Chart feature, run the Microsoft Office 97 setup again, select Add/Remove, and highlight Microsoft Access. Click the Change Option button and select Advanced Wizards by placing a checkmark in the box to the left. Click OK to return to the Microsoft Office 97 - Maintenance dialog box, then click Continue to complete the setup.

- To edit or manipulate an inserted chart, clip art item, or piece of WordArt, place your mouse pointer over the object and right-click to display an option menu.

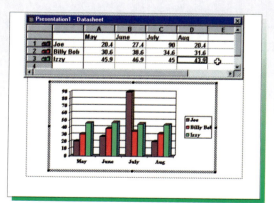

7 The Chart feature in Word, PowerPoint, and Access inserts a sample chart and data table into your document. As you enter your own information into the sample data table, the chart changes to reflect the new input.

2 Select a style from the WordArt Gallery and click OK. Type your text, choose a font and font size, add bold or italic if you wish, and click OK to create your masterpiece.

3 To add visual or audio clips to your document, place your cursor at the location in the document where you want the clip inserted. Then choose Insert, Picture, Clip Art to activate the Microsoft Clip Gallery.

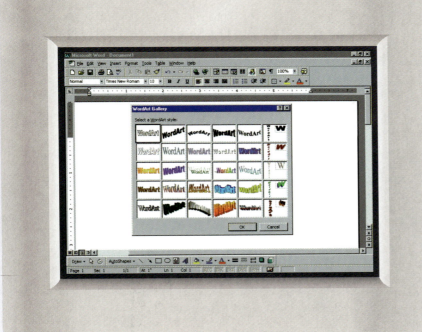

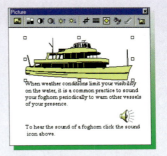

4 Select a category, choose a file from the display window, and click Insert. Voila! The selected clip appears in your document at the cursor. Nothing to it. Note that when you choose a piece of clip art or a photo, the picture toolbar also appears, providing formatting options.

6 In Excel the Chart Wizard walks you through the four steps needed to create a chart: chart type, data source range to use, chart options to apply, and chart location in an existing document or as a new document.

5 Methods of accessing Microsoft Graph vary depending on the Office application you're using. Since graphs (charts) are most often used in conjunction with spreadsheets, the standard Excel toolbar contains a Chart Wizard button. In Word, you would select Insert, Picture, Chart. In PowerPoint and Access the Chart option is in the Insert menu.

How to Insert and Link Objects between Applications

The reason you work with different Office applications is to create different types of documents. However, it is often advantageous to include all or part of one document within a document of another type. For example, submitting a PowerPoint budget presentation that includes spreadsheet figures to back up your fiscal plan packs a lot more punch.

Office provides two methods of sharing data between applications: linking and embedding, each with its own advantages and disadvantages. Both methods insert a copy of the object in the target document (such as a range of Excel cells into a Word document). The difference is in the inserted object's role after it is inserted. A linked object retains a conne«ction with the original file and reflects all changes made to the original file. An embedded object, on the other hand, becomes part of the target file and is completely isolated from the original file. Changes made to the embedded object or to the original file have no effect on one another.

FYI

● If you use the Paste Special command to embed a portion of an Excel spreadsheet in your document, be advised that it pastes only the information that is visible within the defined limits of the individual cells. In other words, if you copy a cell that has a long string of text that exceeds the bounds of the cell width and height, the text will be truncated when you paste it into your document.

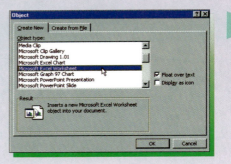

1 To insert a new Office document within your current Office document, select Insert, Object from the menu bar to open the Object dialog box. Choose an object type from the Create New tab and click OK. Note that since links can be created only between existing objects, this new object will be embedded.

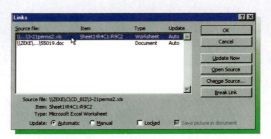

6 Some circumstances, such as moving or deleting a source file, frequently necessitate changing links or the manner in which links are updated. Link options include changing the source file, breaking the link, performing a manual update, and determining the update mode. To edit links select Edit, Links from the menu bar. In the Links dialog box highlight the link to edit and click the appropriate button or change the desired setting, then click OK to effect the changes and return to your document.

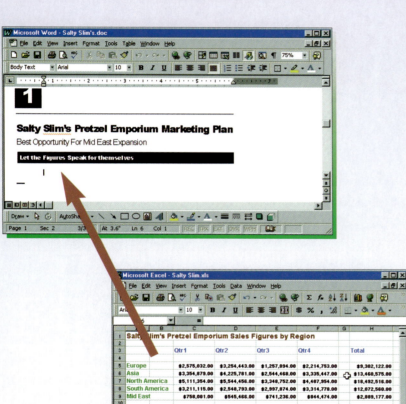

2 Enter the necessary information in the new document that opens. When you finish, move the mouse pointer to an area outside the new object and click once to embed it in your document.

3 You can either link or embed a previously created document in the current document. Select Insert, Object to open the Object dialog box, then click the Create from File tab. In the File Name text box, type the path and file name of the document you want to insert, or click the Browse button to locate and choose a file. To embed the selected file click OK. To link the selected file rather than embed it, place a checkmark in the Link to File box and then click OK.

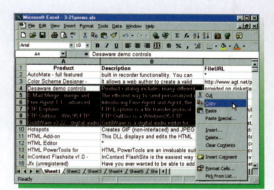

4 To insert only a selected portion of an existing Office document rather than the entire document, open the existing document in its native application, then copy the selection to the Clipboard.

5 Switch back to your original document and choose Edit, Paste Special from the menu bar. From the As display window in the Paste Special dialog box, highlight the format for the selection. To embed the selection click the radio button to the left of the word Paste. To link the selection click the radio button to the left of the phrase Paste Link. Click OK to insert the object in your document.

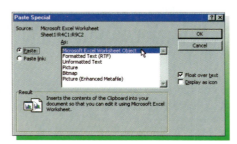

How to Use the Binder

Many projects you create using Microsoft Office 97 will probably comprise multiple documents, possibly of different types. You may use Word to generate proposals and memos, Excel to calculate and analyze the financial information, and PowerPoint to prepare the presentation.

Once you finish the project, you can use the Microsoft Office Binder to retain a complete record of the entire project in one place. By adding the various documents to the Microsoft Office Binder, you not only have an archive of the project but also the ability to print it as a single document.

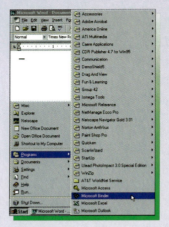

1 Select Start, Programs, Microsoft Binder from the Windows 95 Taskbar to open the Microsoft Office Binder and create a new binder. Every time you open Office Binder, it begins with a blank binder.

7 Since printing a multidocument project as a single print job is a primary reason for creating a binder, you should familiarize yourself with the print settings. Click the Print Settings tab in the Binder Page Setup dialog box to access the print settings. You have the option to print all sections or selected sections, and you can choose how to handle page numbering. When you're finished, click OK until you return to the binder.

FYI

● Since documents added to the binder are embedded, and therefore no longer connected to the original document, there is no way to make revisions to a section and reflect the changes in the original document. If you want to make changes that appear in both the binder section and the original document you must delete the section, open the original document, make the changes, save the document, and once again add it to the binder.

● Another way to add files to the binder is by opening the Windows Explorer and dragging files from the Explorer into the left pane of the Microsoft Office Binder.

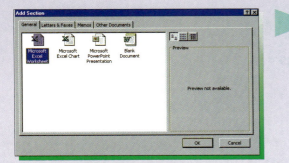

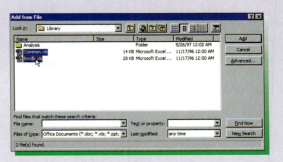

2 Microsoft Office Binder refers to each document in your binder as a *section*. Therefore, to add a new document to your binder choose Section, Add from the menu bar. Select the new document type from the Add Section dialog box. The associated application opens within Microsoft Office Binder, enabling you to create a new document that automatically becomes part of the binder.

3 To add an existing document to a binder, select Section, Add from File. Use the Add from File dialog box to locate and choose the existing file you want to include in your binder. Once you've highlighted the desired file(s), click Add to attach the file(s) and return to the binder.

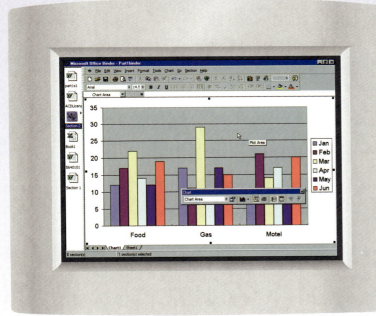

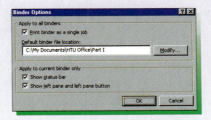

4 Select File, Binder Options from the menu bar to change the Office Binder's settings. From the Binder Options dialog box that appears, you can choose to print the binder as a single print job, change the default location of the binder file, and make some changes to the appearance of the binder window.

5 Before printing the binder, you might want to stop at Page Setup to add headers and footers or change the print settings. From the menu bar select File, Binder Page Setup.

6 Click the Custom button in either the Header or Footer section of the Binder Page Setup dialog box to create your own header or footer. Options include page number, section number, number of sections, section name, binder name, date, and time. After making your selections, click OK until you return to the binder.

How to Get Help

Every computer user, from novice to propeller head, needs help at one time or another. The folks at Microsoft figured this out and have provided an ample supply of help for Microsoft Office 97 users of all levels.

Microsoft Office 97 help comes in three basic flavors: the Office Assistant, the online Help system, and the What's This? help feature.

1 For friendly, and at times entertaining, help try the Office Assistant. Press the F1 function key or click the question mark icon on the standard toolbar to activate the Office Assistant. The animated assistant appears with a list of help topics, tips, and a search feature to aid you in your work.

7 A question mark attaches itself to the mouse pointer, indicating that What's This? help is active. Place the mouse pointer over the object for which you need help. Left-click to open the pop-up window with information on the object. Click anywhere on the screen to remove the pop-up window and return to your document.

FYI

● If you attempt to change the Office Assistant character, keep your Microsoft Office 97 CD handy. In order to conserve hard disk space, the characters are not copied from the CD during installation. Once you select the new character and click OK, Office prompts you to insert the CD in your CD-ROM drive.

● To obtain What's This? help in Office dialog boxes, point to the object you need help with and right-click. Click the small What's This? button that appears to view the pop-up help window.

6 For quick help on a menu item, toolbar icon, or application window area, use the What's This? help feature. To activate What's This? help, select Help, What's This? from the menu bar.

Click the Options button in the Office Assistant box to change the settings or even change the animated Office Assistant character itself. In the Office Assistant dialog box, select or deselect options in the Options tab to turn them on or off. Click the Gallery tab to choose a new Office Assistant character. Scroll through the available characters by using the Next and Back buttons. Click OK when done.

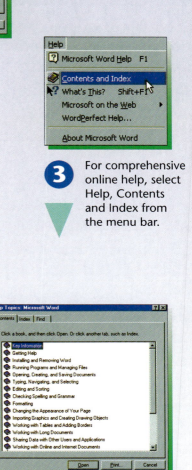

3 For comprehensive online help, select Help, Contents and Index from the menu bar.

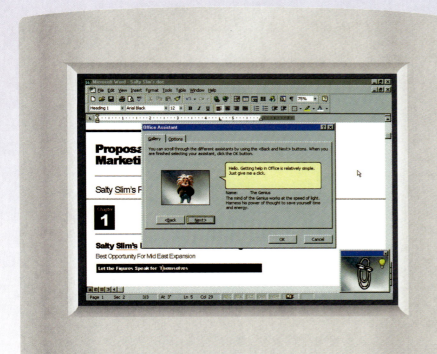

4 The Help Topics window contains three tabs, each providing a different type of help. The Contents tab is organized by subject, much like a book's table of contents. Double-click topics and subtopics to obtain help on the chosen subject.

 The Index tab is an alphabetical list of help topics, analogous to the index of a book. Double-click a topic to open the associated help file. The third tab, Find, provides a word search feature to find more specific help topics.

How to Open, Save, Close, and Print Documents

If you want to master the complexities of Microsoft Office 97, you must first take care of the basics, and you don't get much more basic than opening, saving, closing, and printing documents. Simple though these skills are, you'll be lost without them.

1 The quickest way to open an Office document is to press Ctrl+O from within any Office 97 application. From the ensuing Open dialog box, locate the file to open. If the document does not appear in the default folder (My Documents, unless you've changed it), use the Look In drop-down list to find the file you want. Highlight the file and click OK to open the document.

FYI

● You can open an Office document by locating the file in the Windows Explorer and double-clicking the icon to the left of the file name. It will even open the appropriate Office application if it is not already running.

● To quickly close an Office document, place your mouse pointer over the document icon at the left end of the menu bar (next to the word File) and double-click. You will be prompted to save the document if any changes have been made since the last save.

6 The Print dialog box opens, offering you several options for printing. From the Name drop-down list choose the printer you wish to use. In the Page Range section indicate the pages you wish to print. You can also print multiple copies of the document by changing the Number of Copies entry. When you finish selecting options, click OK to begin the print process.

2 Saving an existing Office document is as easy as pressing Ctrl+S. If the document has previously been named and saved, Office saves the current version of the document to your hard disk. However, if this is a new document or an old document that you want to save under a new name, select File, Save As from the menu bar to open the Save As dialog box.

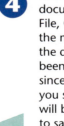

3 Type a descriptive name for the document in the File Name text box. From the Save In drop-down list choose the folder in which to save the document and then click OK. If you want to save the document as a different type (such as a format compatible with a competing product or earlier version of the Office application), open the Save as Type drop-down list and select from the available choices.

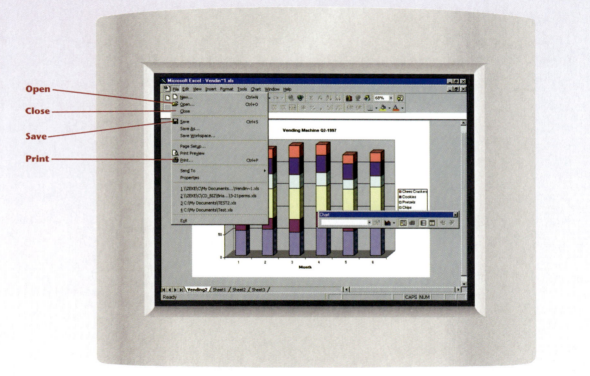

Open
Close
Save
Print

5 Printing an Office document requires that you have a printer connected to your computer, the appropriate printer driver (printer software) installed, and the printer turned on and online (ready to print). When you're ready to print, select File, Print from the menu bar.

4 To close an Office document select File, Close from the menu bar. If the document has been changed since the last time you saved it, you will be prompted to save it again.

P A R T 2

Microsoft Word

IF YOU USE NOTHING ELSE in Microsoft Office 97, chances are you will at least use Word. It's the world's most popular word processor for a good reason. It makes word processing a breeze for the novice and professional alike. While it has more features than you can shake a stick at, it also allows you to perform simple letter writing, list making, and report drafting without having to even know about all those other features. So, no matter what your needs, you will probably find them addressed somewhere within Word.

HERE'S WHAT YOU FIND IN THIS SECTION

- A Tour of the Word Window   16
- How to Enter and Edit Text   18
- How to Cut and Copy Using Cut-and-Paste   20
- How to Use the Spelling and Grammar Checker   22
- How to Create and Use AutoText Entries   24
- How to Format Text   26
- How to Copy Character Formatting   28
- How to Change Fonts and Font Sizes   30
- How to Change Line Spacing   32
- How to Use Tabs   34
- How to Create Numbered and Bulleted Lists   36
- How to Create Tables   38
- How to Add Borders and Shading   40
- How to Change the Page Margins   42
- How to Use Headers and Footers   44
- How to Use the Document Map   46
- How to Use Outline View   48
- How to Use a Template   50
- How to Modify a Template   52
- How to Use a Wizard   54
- How to Create a Mail Merge Document   56
- How to Create the Mail Merge Data Source   58
- How to Complete the Main Mail Merge Document   62
- How to Run the Mail Merge   64
- How to Insert a Graphic   66
- How to Format a Graphic   68

A Tour of the Word Window

When you start Word, the program window appears, named Microsoft Word, and one blank document window appears, named Document1. Usually, both windows are *maximized* (the program window fills the whole screen, and the document window fills the whole program window). When they are both maximized, two restore buttons (one for each window) are displayed in the set of buttons located in the upper-right corner of the screen (see the picture in the middle of the page). If you see a maximize button for either window, click on it. (The maximize button appears in place of the restore button; it looks like a single large square.) You'll probably find it preferable to keep both windows maximized, since it gives you more room to work.

Program name   **Document name**

W Microsoft Word - Document1

1 The title bar tells you what's in the window. When the document window is maximized, it has to share the title bar with the program window, so the title bar contains the names of both windows. If you restore the document window to a smaller size (by clicking its restore button), it gets its own separate title bar. Document1 is a temporary name for your document. When you save it for the first time, you replace that name with one of your choosing.

Page 1 out of 1 total in document

| Page 1 | Sec 1 | 1/1 | At 1" | Ln 1 | Col 1 |

9 The status bar indicates the current page, the total number of pages, and the location of your insertion point on the page. As you use Word, the status bar sometimes displays other information as well.

● If you don't see the Standard or Formatting toolbar, or if you see other toolbars you'd like to hide, choose View, Toolbars. In the Toolbars dialog box, mark the check boxes for the Standard and Formatting toolbars and clear the check boxes for other toolbars, and then click on OK.

● If either of your scroll bars or your status bar isn't showing, choose Tools, Options. Near the top of the Options dialog box, click on the View tab if it isn't already showing. Then, under Window, click on any option that isn't already marked—Status Bar, Horizontal Scroll Bar, and/or Vertical Scroll Bar—and then click on OK.

8 The Browse buttons (located in the lower-right corner of the document window) let you quickly jump from one part of your document to the next.

7 The View buttons (located in the lower-left corner of the document window) allow you to change the way your document is displayed on screen. By default, Word uses Normal view.

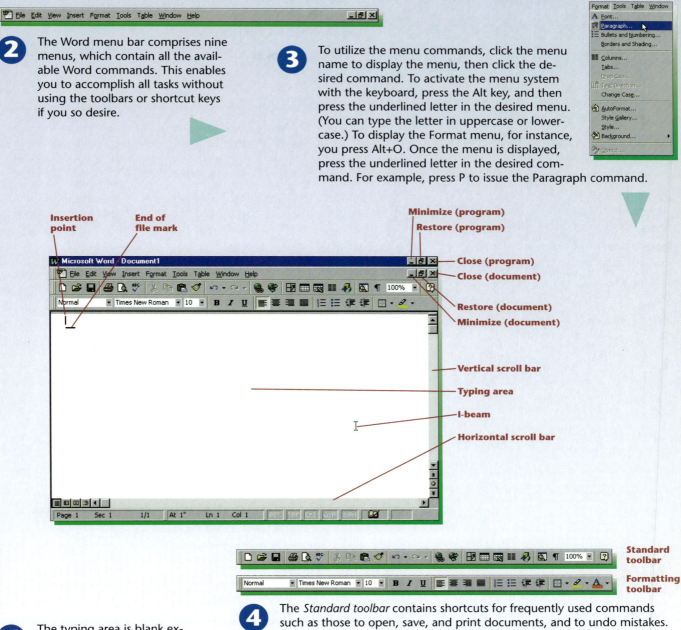

2 The Word menu bar comprises nine menus, which contain all the available Word commands. This enables you to accomplish all tasks without using the toolbars or shortcut keys if you so desire.

3 To utilize the menu commands, click the menu name to display the menu, then click the desired command. To activate the menu system with the keyboard, press the Alt key, and then press the underlined letter in the desired menu. (You can type the letter in uppercase or lowercase.) To display the Format menu, for instance, you press Alt+O. Once the menu is displayed, press the underlined letter in the desired command. For example, press P to issue the Paragraph command.

Insertion point

End of file mark

Minimize (program)

Restore (program)

Close (program)

Close (document)

Restore (document)

Minimize (document)

Vertical scroll bar

Typing area

I-beam

Horizontal scroll bar

Standard toolbar

Formatting toolbar

4 The *Standard toolbar* contains shortcuts for frequently used commands such as those to open, save, and print documents, and to undo mistakes. (You will likely memorize this one first!) The *Formatting toolbar* contains shortcuts for commands that change the appearance of the document.

6 The typing area is blank except for three symbols. The insertion point (also known as the cursor) shows you where the next character you type will appear. The end of file mark shows you where the document ends. You use the mouse pointer to select text and to move the insertion point. When the mouse pointer is in the typing area, it resembles an I-beam.

5 The ruler shows you where your margins are, and it lets you set tabs and indents. If you don't see the ruler, you can temporarily bring it into view by resting the tip of your mouse pointer on the gray horizontal line directly underneath the Formatting toolbar. With this method, the ruler disappears as soon as you move the mouse pointer to another part of the screen. To keep the ruler constantly in view, choose View, Ruler. You'll find out more about using the ruler later in this book.

How to Enter and Edit Text

Every great literary masterpiece began with a single blank page. In keeping with that time-honored tradition, Microsoft Word opens with a blank document window, ready for you to begin typing the next great American novel, short story, or interoffice memo.

The flashing insertion point indicates where the next character you type will appear. So, if you're ready to begin your journey on the road to literary fame and fortune, simply start typing.

Press Enter here.

Press Enter here.

Don't press Enter at the end of these lines.

Alice:

How about a company-wide party to celebrate the sale of our 100,000th lawn flamingo? Please check with your department heads and make sure Friday, July 15, at 3:00 p.m. is convenient for everyone.

1 Each time you press Enter, you insert a *paragraph mark* into your document. Press Enter to end short lines of text, to create blank lines, and to end paragraphs. Do not press Enter to start new lines within a paragraph. Word wraps the lines for you; if you later add or remove text in the paragraph, Word adjusts the line breaks accordingly.

Paragraph mark

Show/Hide button ¶

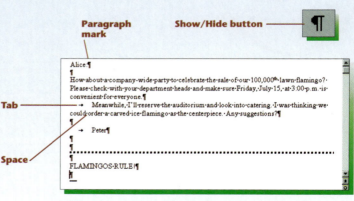

Tab

Space

FYI

● Until you have created some text, you cannot move the cursor in any direction. Once you've typed some characters you can use the arrow keys to move backward and forward, as well as up and down (you need more than one line of text to move up or down), through the newly created text. If you wish to start your document somewhere below the blinking cursor, press the Enter key to create new lines until you reach the desired starting point.

● If you accidentally type the wrong character, press the Backspace key (the left-pointing arrow above the Enter key) to delete it. Do the same if you accidentally press Enter, Tab, or the spacebar.

5 Click the Show/Hide button in the Standard toolbar to see where you pressed the spacebar, Tab, and Enter keys. A dot represents a space, an arrow represents a tab, and a paragraph mark indicates where you pressed Enter. You can use the Show/Hide button to check whether you accidentally typed an extra space between two words (you'd see two dots instead of one) or to see how many blank lines you have between paragraphs. To turn Show/Hide off, just click it again. You can delete extra spaces, tabs, and paragraph marks just as you'd delete regular characters.

Press Tab.

Alice:

How about a company-wide party to celebrate the sale of our 100,000th lawn flamingo? Please check with your department heads and make sure Friday, July 15, at 3:00 p.m. is convenient for everyone.

Meanwhile, I'll reserve the auditorium and look into catering. I was thinking we could order a carved ice flamingo as the centerpiece. Any suggestions?

Peter

2 Press the Tab key to indent the first line of a paragraph. If you keep pressing Tab, you shift the line toward the right one-half inch at a time. To indent all the lines in the paragraph instead of just the first one, highlight the paragraph, select Format, Paragraph from the menu bar, and reset the indentation settings.

LawnBirds, Inc.

Alice:

How about a company-wide party to celebrate the sale of our 100,000th lawn flamingo? Please check with your department heads and make sure Friday, July 15, at 3:00 p.m. is convenient for everyone.

Meanwhile, I'll reserve the auditorium and look into catering. I was thinking we could order a carved ice flamingo as the centerpiece. Any suggestions?

Peter

....

FLAMINGOS RULE!

Word converts three or more asterisks into a dotted line.

Alice:

How about a company-wide party to celebrate the sale of our 100,000th lawn flamingo? Please check with your department heads and make sure Friday, July 15, at 3:00 p.m. is convenient for everyone.

Meanwhile, I'll reserve the auditorium and look into catering. I was thinking we could order a carved ice flamingo as the centerpiece. Any suggestions?

Peter

....

3 To type the same character repeatedly, hold the key down. Word automatically converts some repeated characters into different types of lines. For example, if you type three or more asterisks (*) and press Enter, Word replaces them with a dotted line, as shown here. Use the equal sign (=) for a double line, the tilde (~)for a wavy line, the pound (#) symbol for a thick decorative line, the hyphen (-) for a thin single line, or the underscore (_) for a thick single line.

Press Caps Lock for easier uppercase typing.

Alice:

How about a company-wide party to celebrate the sale of our 100,000th lawn flamingo? Please check with your department heads and make sure Friday, July 15, at 3:00 p.m. is convenient for everyone.

Meanwhile, I'll reserve the auditorium and look into catering. I was thinking we could order a carved ice flamingo as the centerpiece. Any suggestions?

Peter

....

FLAMINGOS RULE!

4 To produce all uppercase letters without having to hold down the Shift key, press the Caps Lock key once before you begin typing. Press the Caps Lock key again when you're ready to switch this feature off. Caps Lock affects only the letter keys, not the number and punctuation keys. Thus, whether or not Caps Lock is on, you have to press Shift to type a character on the upper half of a number or punctuation key, such as * or %.

How to Cut and Copy Using Cut-and-Paste

Once you've tried cut-and-paste, you'll never go back to using any other method for your editing. If you've ever created a document using a typewriter and inadvertently left out an important step or paragraph, you know what I mean. You have to retype the whole thing! Not so with electronic word processing. Word enables you to easily pick up characters, words, sentences, paragraphs and more, and move them to a new location within your document by using the cut-and-paste feature.

Text to cut or copy

telemarketer who was pressured to meet quota.

As a result of this mix-up, we are rethinking our incentive policies. The telemarketer at fault has been reassigned.

On July 14 at noon, a LawnBirds, Inc. truck will arrive at your home to remove the 999

1 Select (highlight) the text you want to cut or copy by placing your cursor at the beginning of the text you wish to select. Then hold down the left mouse button and drag the cursor to the end of the text you want to highlight.

FYI

● The keyboard shortcuts for the Cut, Copy, and Paste commands are Ctrl+X for Cut, Ctrl+C for Copy, and Ctrl+V for Paste. These keyboard shortcuts are standard for all Windows-based programs.

● You can also cut or copy text to a document in another program which supports OLE (object linking and embedding). Cut or copy the desired text and switch to the other program (click on its button in the Windows taskbar at the bottom of the screen), open the document in which you want to insert the text, position the insertion point where you want the text to go, and issue the Paste command in that program.

● After you paste text, a copy of it remains in the Clipboard, so you can repeat steps 3 and 4 to insert more copies of the text elsewhere. The Clipboard contents are replaced only when you next issue the Cut or Copy command. The Clipboard empties when you exit Windows.

Cut Copy

2 To cut the text, click the Cut button in the Standard toolbar, or choose Edit, Cut from the menu bar. The text is deleted from your document, but it remains in a special Windows storage area called the *Clipboard*. To *copy* the text, click the Copy button in the Standard toolbar (or choose Edit, Copy). When you copy text, nothing appears to happen because the text remains in the original location, and a copy of the selected text is sent to the Clipboard.

Destination

> The flamingo you keep
>
> We very much apprecia
>
> Sincerely yours,

3 Place the cursor at the point where you want to insert the text. If necessary, you can open another document or switch to another already open document to insert text there. (To switch to another open document, click the Window menu, then click the document name at the bottom of the menu.)

LawnBirds, Inc.
8800 Industrial Way
Emeryville, CA 94608
(510) 555-2077

July 6, 1998

Morton L. Tashjian
333 Ellis Road
West Caldwell, NY 07006

Dear Mr. Tashjian:

Thank you for your letter dated June 21, 1998. We agree that our shipment of 1000 lawn flamingos exceeded your actual order by 999. We attribute this error to an overzealous telemarketer who was pressured to meet quota.

On July 14 at noon, a LawnBirds, Inc. truck will arrive at your home to remove the 999 extra flamingos. Your next credit card bill will reflect a credit for all 1000 flamingos. The flamingo you keep is free, with our apologies.

As a result of this mix-up, we are rethinking our incentive policies. The telemarketer at fault has been reassigned.

We very much appreciate your business and hope to serve you better in the future.

Sincerely yours,

Alice J. McCloskey
President

Paste

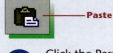
Paste

4 Click the Paste button in the Standard toolbar (or choose Edit, Paste).

Inserted text

> The flamingo you keep is free, with our apologies.
>
> As a result of this mix-up, we are rethinking our incentive policies. The telemarketer at fault has been reassigned.
>
> We very much appreciate your business and hope to serve you better in the future.

5 The text is pasted into the document beginning at the position of the insertion point. In a Cut operation such as the one shown on this page, the text is removed from the original location. If you perform a Copy operation, the text remains in its original location as well as being pasted into the new location.

How to Use the Spelling and Grammar Checker

The Spelling and Grammar Checker allows you to check the spelling and grammar of an entire document all at once. If your document is several pages long, this method is quicker than correcting words one by one. For additional grammar coaching as you check your document, display the Office Assistant. It gives you examples and advice relating to any grammatical problems the Word Grammar Checker finds.

 1 Click the Spelling and Grammar button on the Standard toolbar (or choose Tools, Spelling and Grammar). Word begins checking every word in your document against its dictionary and list of grammatical rules.

 8 Choose the Ignore button if you don't want to change the word or phrase; choose Ignore All to have Word ignore the same text if it appears elsewhere in your document. Word informs you when the spelling and grammar check is complete (either via the Office Assistant or a message box). Click OK to close the message box (or click outside the Office Assistant).

 7 When Word encounters a possible grammatical error, it displays the word and the surrounding text at the top of the dialog box and gives you a description of the problem—*Commonly Confused Words* in this example. If you see the correct version in the Suggestions list, click it and click the Change button. (If you don't see the correct version, edit the phrase in the upper part of the dialog box, and then click the Change button.)

 **FYI**

● To check the spelling and grammar of only a portion of the document, select that portion by highlighting it before starting the check. When Word finishes checking the selection, it asks if you want to check the rest of the document. Click the No button to end the check.

● To modify what Word looks for in a grammar check, choose Tools, Options, and click the Spelling & Grammar tab. In the Writing Style drop-down list, select the style—casual, technical, formal, and so on, that best describes your document. Optionally, you can hand pick which items Word checks by clicking on the Settings button. In the Grammar Settings dialog box, mark or clear check boxes for items such as wordiness, relative clauses, and passive sentences, make punctuation-related choices in the drop-down lists, and click OK.

Edit to correct the spelling.

None of the suggestions are correct.

 6 If the word is misspelled but the correct spelling is not in the Suggestions list, double-click the misspelled word at the top of the dialog box to select it, and type over it with the correct spelling. Then click the Change button.

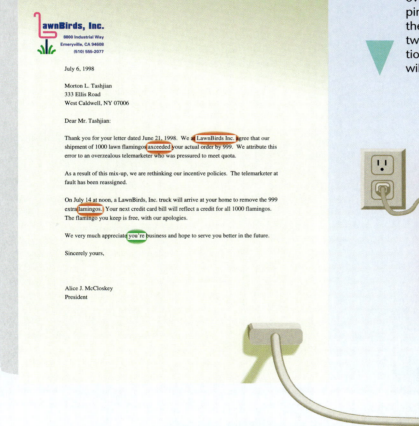

2 Word presents the Spelling and Grammar dialog box when it encounters a word that is not in its dictionary or does not conform to a grammatical rule.

3 If the problem is spelling-related, Word displays the word and its surrounding text in a text box labeled Not in Dictionary. If the word is spelled correctly but you don't expect to use it often, click the Ignore button to skip over the word. To prevent Word from stopping on other instances of the same word in the document, click Ignore All. Because these two buttons do not add the word to the dictionary, the Spelling and Grammar Checker will question the word in other documents.

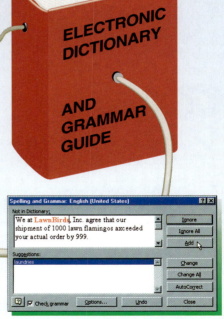

5 If the word is misspelled and you see the correct spelling in the Suggestions list, click the spelling you want, and click the Change button to correct the word. (Click the Change All button to have Word correct all instances of this misspelled word in your document.)

4 If the word is correctly spelled and you plan to use it frequently in other documents, click the Add button. This adds the word to the dictionary so that Word won't question it when you run spelling and grammar checks on other documents.

How to Create and Use AutoText Entries

The Word AutoText feature can save you time by inserting a long string of text each time you enter a short AutoText entry. For example, you could create a letter closing entry which would insert your name and title each time you type *Regards,*. AutoText entries can be of any length, from a short sentence to an entire letter. Word organizes AutoText entries according to the style of the first paragraph in the entry. (A *style* is a collection of formatting codes that has been assigned a name). The default style in Word documents is *Normal,* so unless you use other styles, all your AutoText entries will be stored with the Normal style.

FYI

● You can print a list of AutoText entries to help you remember what text each entry contains. Choose File, Print, and display the Print What list in the lower-left corner of the Print dialog box. Click AutoText Entries, and then click OK.

● Unless you indicate otherwise, Word makes your AutoText entries accessible to all documents. It does this by saving your entries in the Normal template, also known as the Blank Document template.

● To modify the text of an AutoText entry, first insert it in your document, then make your changes. Select the text again, being sure to include all the text you want in the entry, not just the part you modified. Click the New button in the AutoText toolbar, type the name of the existing entry, and click OK. When Word asks if you want to redefine the AutoText entry, click Yes.

 1 If the AutoText toolbar isn't already displayed, choose View, Toolbars, AutoText to bring it into view.

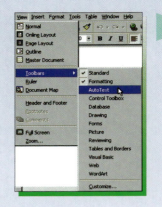

8 To delete an AutoText entry, click the AutoText button at the left edge of the AutoText toolbar to display the AutoText tab of the AutoCorrect dialog box. Click the entry, click the Delete button, and click OK.

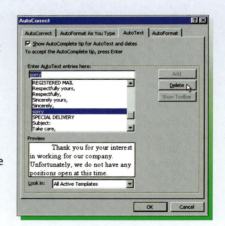

7 You can also insert AutoText entries from the AutoText toolbar. Click the All Entries button to display a list of categories of AutoText entries. Many of these categories contain entries that come with Word. The ones you have created will be listed under Normal (and possibly other style names, depending on what entries you have created). Point to the style name, and then click the desired entry in the submenu.

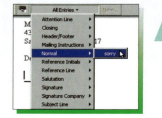

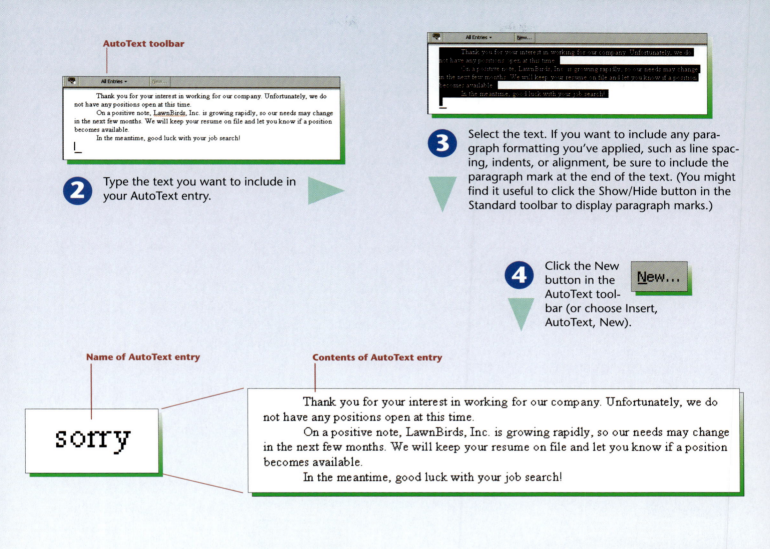

AutoText toolbar

2 Type the text you want to include in your AutoText entry.

3 Select the text. If you want to include any paragraph formatting you've applied, such as line spacing, indents, or alignment, be sure to include the paragraph mark at the end of the text. (You might find it useful to click the Show/Hide button in the Standard toolbar to display paragraph marks.)

4 Click the New button in the AutoText toolbar (or choose Insert, AutoText, New).

New...

Name of AutoText entry

Contents of AutoText entry

sorry

Thank you for your interest in working for our company. Unfortunately, we do not have any positions open at this time.

On a positive note, LawnBirds, Inc. is growing rapidly, so our needs may change in the next few months. We will keep your resume on file and let you know if a position becomes available.

In the meantime, good luck with your job search!

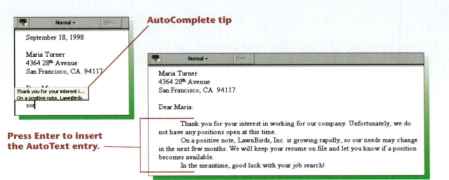

AutoComplete tip

Press Enter to insert the AutoText entry.

5 In the Create AutoText dialog box, type a name for the entry in the text box labeled Please Name Your AutoText Entry, and click OK. It's best to choose a name that's short and easy to type (although Word allows AutoText names that are more than one word long).

6 To use the entry, click at the desired location in your document and begin typing the name. After you type the first three characters, an AutoComplete tip appears with a snippet of the entry. Press Enter to insert the entry in your document. (You can also type the entry's name and press F3.)

How to Format Text

Formatting refers to all the techniques that enhance the appearance of your document. In Word, you can roughly divide formatting techniques into three categories: character, paragraph, and page.

Character formatting includes all the features that can affect individual characters. The primary character formatting features are boldface, italic, underline, font, and font size. Paragraph formatting includes line spacing, indents, alignment, tabs, and so on. The third category, page formatting, includes margins, page breaks, and paper size.

The most commonly used formatting features are Boldface, Italicize and Underline text. As a matter of fact, they are so frequently used that they have had their own toolbar buttons since the early days of Word.

- To remove boldface, italics, or underline, select the text, and then click the appropriate button again.

- If you don't feel like reaching for your mouse, you can apply font styles by selecting the text, then using one of the following keyboard shortcuts: Ctrl+B for boldface, Ctrl+I for italics, Ctrl+U for underline, or Ctrl+Shift+D for double underline. You can also type asterisks before and after a word to boldface it (as in *poodle*) or type underscore characters before and after a word to underline it (as in _poodle_). As soon as you type the next word, Word deletes the asterisks or underscores and applies the formatting.

- If you want to boldface, italicize, or underline a single word, you don't have to select the word first. Just click anywhere in the word, and then apply the formatting using any of the methods described on this page.

AGENDA
Meeting of the Homeowners Association
Plaza Heights Condominium

1 To boldface text, select the text and then click the Bold button on the Formatting toolbar.

OK

8 When you've made your selections, click the OK button to close the dialog box and apply the changes to the selected text.

Preview

Meeting of the Homeowners Association

This is a TrueType font. This font will be used on both printer and screen.

7 You can preview your choices in the Preview area at the bottom of the dialog box.

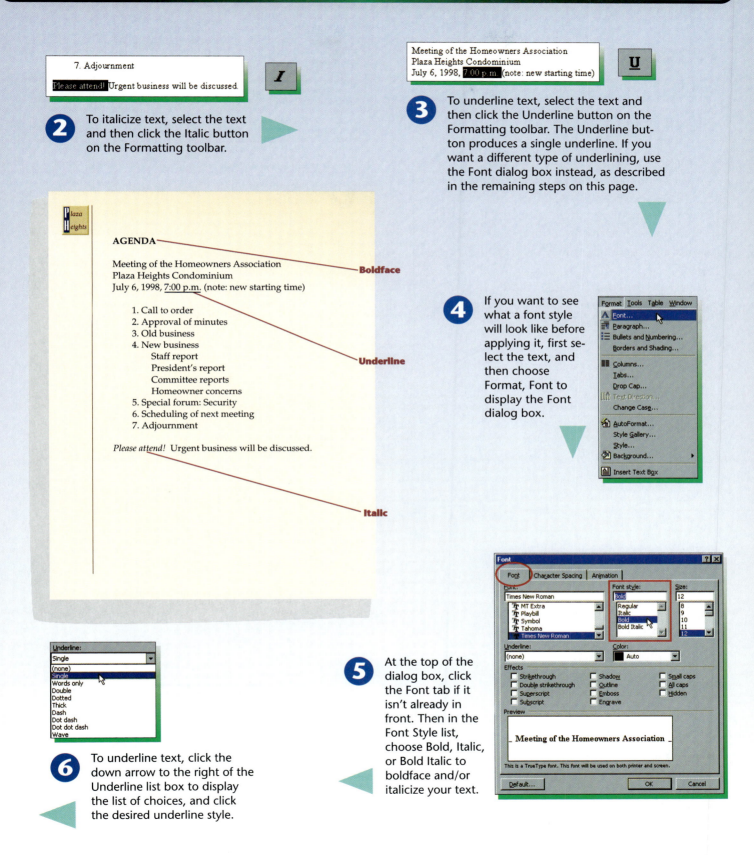

7. Adjournment

Please attend! Urgent business will be discussed.

I

2 To italicize text, select the text and then click the Italic button on the Formatting toolbar.

Meeting of the Homeowners Association
Plaza Heights Condominium
July 6, 1998, 7:00 p.m. (note: new starting time)

U

3 To underline text, select the text and then click the Underline button on the Formatting toolbar. The Underline button produces a single underline. If you want a different type of underlining, use the Font dialog box instead, as described in the remaining steps on this page.

Plaza Heights

AGENDA

Meeting of the Homeowners Association
Plaza Heights Condominium
July 6, 1998, 7:00 p.m. (note: new starting time)

Boldface

1. Call to order
2. Approval of minutes
3. Old business
4. New business
    Staff report
    President's report
    Committee reports
    Homeowner concerns
5. Special forum: Security
6. Scheduling of next meeting
7. Adjournment

Underline

Please attend! Urgent business will be discussed.

Italic

4 If you want to see what a font style will look like before applying it, first select the text, and then choose Format, Font to display the Font dialog box.

Format Tools Table Window
Font...
Paragraph...
Bullets and Numbering...
Borders and Shading...
Columns...
Tabs...
Drop Cap...
Text Direction...
Change Case...
AutoFormat...
Style Gallery...
Style...
Background...
Insert Text Box

Underline:
Single
(none)
Single
Words only
Double
Dotted
Thick
Dash
Dot dash
Dot dot dash
Wave

5 At the top of the dialog box, click the Font tab if it isn't already in front. Then in the Font Style list, choose Bold, Italic, or Bold Italic to boldface and/or italicize your text.

Font | Character Spacing | Animation

Font:
Times New Roman
MT Extra
Playbill
Symbol
Tahoma
Times New Roman

Font style:
Bold
Regular
Italic
Bold
Bold Italic

Size:
12
8
9
10
11
12

Underline:
(none)

Color:
Auto

Effects
☐ Strikethrough
☐ Double strikethrough
☐ Superscript
☐ Subscript
☐ Shadow
☐ Outline
☐ Emboss
☐ Engrave
☐ Small caps
☐ All caps
☐ Hidden

Preview

Meeting of the Homeowners Association

This is a TrueType font. This font will be used on both printer and screen.

Default... | OK | Cancel

6 To underline text, click the down arrow to the right of the Underline list box to display the list of choices, and click the desired underline style.

How to Copy Character Formatting

If you've applied several different character formats—such as a font, a font size, and a font style (bold, italic, underline)—to a block of text in your document, and then later decide you'd like to apply the same formatting to another block of text, you don't have to apply those formats one by one to the new location. Instead, you can use the Format Painter button to take all the formats from the original block of text and "paint" them across the new text.

This text is formatted in an 18-point, boldface, italic Footlight MT Light font.

When
October 25, 1998 from 1:00 p.m. to 5:00 p.m.

Where
Green Meadow park, by the duck pond (maps and parking directions are available at the front desk)

1 Select the text that has the formatting you want to copy.

When
October 25, 1998 from 1:00 p.m. to 5:00 p.m.

Where
Green Meadow park, by the duck pond (maps and parking directions are available at the front desk)

Activities
Barbecue, volleyball, horseshoes, games for the kids, and an all-age lawn birds dress up contest

What to Bring
Friends and family (including the four-footed!), a sweater in case it gets breezy, and cold drinks

6 To copy the same formatting across several blocks of text at one time, *double-click* the Format Painter button. Word keeps the Format Painter feature turned on so you can drag across multiple blocks of text. For example, you could paint across all the headings in the document shown here. When you're finished, click the Format Painter button again to turn the feature off.

● Another way to create the same look for headings and other text elements in your documents is to use styles.

2 Click the Format Painter button in the Standard toolbar.

3 Your mouse pointer changes to an I-beam with an attached paintbrush.

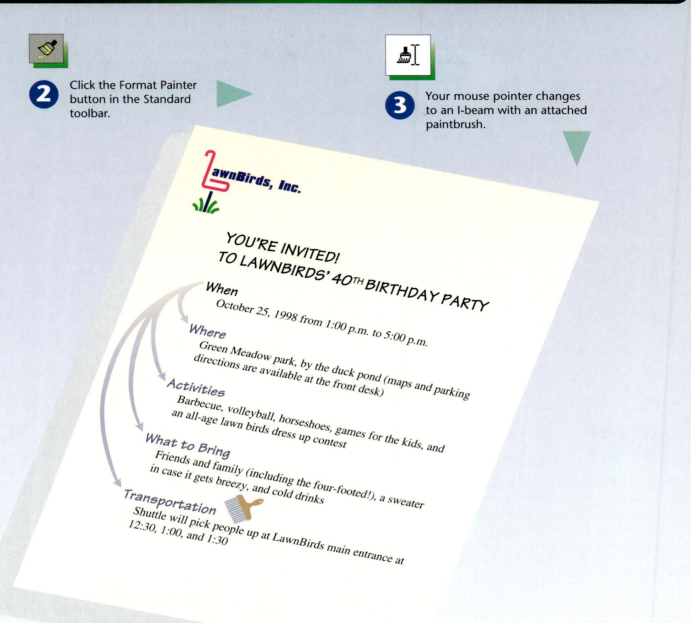

When
October 25, 1998 from 1:00 p.m. to 5:00 p.m.

Where
Green Meadow park, by the duck pond (maps and parking directions are available at the front desk)

When
October 25, 1998 from 1:00 p.m. to 5:00 p.m.

Where
Green Meadow park, by the duck pond (maps and parking directions are available at the front desk)

4 Drag the cursor across the text to be formatted.

5 Release the mouse. The text takes on the formatting of the original location. You can then click once to deselect the newly formatted text.

How to Change Fonts and Font Sizes

For many people, fiddling with fonts is one of the more entertaining aspects of word processing. However, it's easy to go overboard and format the document to the point that it becomes excessively busy and difficult to read. Resist this temptation! Two fonts per document is usually enough.

AGENDA

Meeting of the Homeowners Association
Plaza Heights Condominium
July 6, 1998, 7:00 p.m. (note: new starting time)

1 Select the text whose font you want to change.

FYI

● The number and type of available fonts can vary from one computer to the next, but most computers have a wide selection of TrueType fonts. They're displayed in font lists with a TT symbol next to their names. TrueType fonts are good ones to use because they look the same on screen as they do when printed out.

● If you want to spice up the appearance of a heading, try some of the special effects in the Effects area of the Font dialog box. Shadow, Outline, Emboss, and Engrave can all add a nice decorative touch to small blocks of text.

● The settings in the Formatting toolbar—for font, font size, font style, and so on—show you the formatting at the location of the insertion point. This behavior comes in handy when you aren't sure what font is applied to a particular block of text. All you have to do is click in the text to place the insertion point there, and then look at the Formatting toolbar to see what settings are in effect.

● The keyboard shortcut to display the Font dialog box is Ctrl+D.

6 Scroll if necessary to find the size you want, and then click on it to apply it to the selected text.

2 Click the down arrow to the right of the Font list box in the Formatting toolbar to display a list of your available fonts.

3 Scroll through the list to find the font you want, and then click it to apply it to the selected text. Note that Word places the fonts you use frequently above a double line at the top of the list. Below the double line is an alphabetical list of all the fonts.

AGENDA

Meeting of the Homeowners Association
Plaza Heights Condominium
July 6, 1998, 7:00 p.m. (note: new starting time) ——————— **Arial**

    1. Call to order
    2. Approval of minutes
    3. Old business
    4. New business ——————— **Times New Roman**
        Staff report
        President's report
        Committee reports
        Homeowner concerns
    5. Special forum: Security
    6. Scheduling of next meeting ——————— **Arial**
    7. Adjournment

Please attend! Urgent business will be discussed.

4 Once you've chosen a font, you may find that for emphasis or other reasons you wish to make it larger or smaller. Select the text whose size you want to change.

5 Click on the down arrow to the right of the Font Size list in the Formatting toolbar to display the list of font sizes.

How to Change Line Spacing

Line spacing is the amount of space between lines within a paragraph. Word assumes single spacing, which provides just enough space between lines so that letters don't overlap. Double spacing is good for rough drafts of documents, because it gives you extra room to write in edits by hand. One-and-a-half spacing makes text easier to read by separating lines with an extra half a line of blank space.

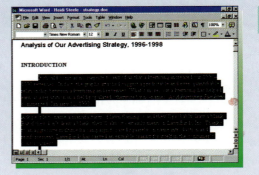

1 To change the line spacing of several adjacent paragraphs, select them first. In the example shown here, all the body text is selected. (If you want to change the line spacing of only one paragraph, see steps 7 and 8.)

● For a line spacing other than those offered, skip steps 3 and 4. Instead, in the Paragraph dialog box, click in the At text box (to the right of the Line Spacing list) and type a line-spacing value. For example, type 3 for triple spacing. (As soon as you type in the At box, Word changes the Line Spacing setting to Multiple.)

● A new paragraph takes on the formatting of the preceding one. Therefore, if you are typing in a double-spaced paragraph and you press Enter to start a new paragraph, the new paragraph too will be double-spaced. You can change the line spacing of the new paragraph—or of any paragraph—by following the steps on these pages.

Ask people to name a manufacturer of lawn flamingos and they'll probably draw a blank. But if they don't draw a blank, they'll almost certainly mention LawnBirds, Inc. Thanks to an aggressive multimedia campaign focused squarely on name introduction and reinforcement, LawnBirds has carved an enviable cranny for itself in the consumer's consciousness.

8 The line spacing for this paragraph was changed to one-and-a-half.

Ask people to name a manufacturer of lawn flamingos and they'll probably draw a blank. But if they don't draw a blank, they'll almost certainly mention LawnBirds, Inc. Thanks to an aggressive multimedia campaign focused squarely on name introduction and reinforcement, LawnBirds has carved an enviable cranny for itself in the consumer's consciousness.

7 To change the line spacing of a single paragraph, you don't need to select it first. Just place the insertion point anywhere in the paragraph and follow steps 2 through 5.

2 Choose Format, Paragraph to display the Paragraph dialog box.

3 At the top of the Paragraph dialog box, click the Indents and Spacing tab if it's not already in front. Then display the Line Spacing list by clicking on the down arrow to its right.

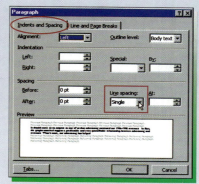

 LawnBirds, Inc.

Analysis of Our Advertising Strategy, 1996–1998

INTRODUCTION

It should come as no surprise to any of us that advertising increased our 1996–1998 revenues. In fact, the graphs attached suggest a predictable and even quantifiable relationship. What's more, our advertising has helped earn us a reputation in a field populated otherwise by no-names. As *Advertising Punditry* commented (January 12, 1998):

Ask people to name a manufacturer of lawn flamingos and they'll probably draw a blank. But if they don't draw a blank, they'll almost certainly mention LawnBirds, Inc. Thanks to an aggressive multimedia campaign focused squarely on name introduction and reinforcement, LawnBirds has carved an enviable cranny for itself in the consumer's consciousness.

The question, then, is not *whether* advertising sells lawn flamingos. It does. The question is *how many* lawn flamingos advertising sells. Do the increased revenues make up our costs? If they have so far, will they continue to? Do the economics call for increasing our ad budget, stabilizing it, decreasing it, or shifting it among the different media?

This analysis attempts to point our advertising in the right direction for the immediate future. However, we must note one obvious constraint: Any hindsight as to what our revenues and profits would have been without advertising is little more than guesswork. The most we can do is project our growth from our preadvertising years and factor in those marketplace changes that we understand and that are quantifiable.

Why did we start advertising in the first place? It's worthwhile occasionally to

Double spacing

One-and-a-half spacing

4 Click the desired line spacing: Single, 1.5 Lines, or Double.

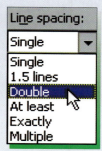

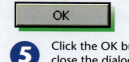

5 Click the OK button to close the dialog box.

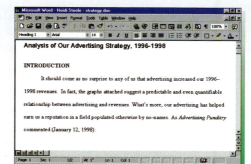

6 The new line spacing is applied to the paragraphs you selected.

How to Use Tabs

Default tabs in Word are positioned at every half inch across the ruler. Each time you press the Tab key, your insertion point moves to the next tab stop, pushing over any text to the right of the insertion point. In regular body text, these default tabs work just fine. When you want to create a list with two or more columns of text, however, it's easier if you replace the default tabs with custom tabs at the exact locations where you want to line up your text.

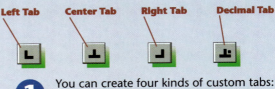

Left Tab   **Center Tab**   **Right Tab**   **Decimal Tab**

1 You can create four kinds of custom tabs: left, center, right, and decimal. Word uses the symbols shown here to represent the different types. Use left tabs to align text on the left, right tabs to align text on the right, center tabs to center text across the tab, and decimal tabs to align numbers on the decimal point. (See the sample document in the middle of the page for examples of all four types.)

● To delete a custom tab, point to it on the ruler, drag straight down into the text area of the document window, and then release the mouse.

● To see what custom tabs are in effect for a certain paragraph, click anywhere in the paragraph, and then look at the ruler.

● To restore the default tabs below a paragraph that contains custom tabs, click in the paragraph where you'd like the default tabs to begin, and simply drag the custom tabs off the ruler (see the first tip). The default tabs will automatically reappear.

● If you accidentally press the Tab key too many times, delete the extra tabs by pressing Backspace if the insertion point is just past the tabs, or Del if the insertion point is just before them.

● You can also set custom tabs in the Tabs dialog box (choose Format, Tabs). This method allows you to create *bar* tabs, which you can use to add vertical lines to your document, and tabs with dot leaders.

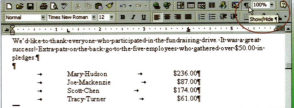

8 When you're working with custom tabs, it's often helpful to click the Show/Hide button on the Standard toolbar. When Show/Hide is enabled, Word displays arrows to show where you pressed the Tab key and paragraph marks (¶) to show where you pressed Enter.

7 If you decide to shift the position of one of the custom tabs, select all the lines in your list first. Then point to the tab, and drag it along the ruler.

Tab Alignment button   **Default tabs**

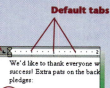

2 Place your cursor at the point in the paragraph where you want the custom tabs to begin. Before you add any custom tabs, you'll see faint gray tick marks spaced one-half inch apart on the ruler. These are the default tabs.

awnBirds, Inc.

MEMORANDUM

Date: March 10, 1998
To: All Employees
From: Daycare Center Fundraising Committee
Re: Fundraising Drive

We'd like to thank every one who participated in the fundraising drive. It was a great success! Extra pats on the back go to the five employees who gathered over $50.00 in pledges:

Mary Hudson $236.00
Joe Mackenzie $87.00
Scott Chen $174.00
Tracy Turner $61.00

We'll keep you posted on plans for the next drive. Any ideas or suggestions would be more than welcome. Thanks again for all your hard work.

Here are the final group assignments for the brainstorming sessions discussed in the memo last week:

Group 1   **Group 2**   **Group3**
Jan Lao   Travis Jones   Deb Larkin
Marcus Lerner   Elizabeth Montoya   Jefferson Hunter
Sue Johnson   Robin Taylor   Henry Forbes
Pete Chen   Joshua Ng   Pat Smith

3 Use the Tab Alignment button to tell Word which type of custom tab you want to create. When you click the button repeatedly, you cycle through the symbols representing each of the four tabs. The left tab symbol is showing by default, so you only need to click the Tab Alignment button if you want to create a center, right, or decimal tab. In this example, the column of names is created with a left tab.

We'd like to thank eve[Left Tab]who participated in the fundraising drive. It was a great success! Extra pats on the back go to the five employees who gathered over $50.00 in pledges:

4 Create the custom tab by clicking at the desired position on the ruler. The symbol for the tab appears on the ruler, and all the default tabs to the left of the custom tab disappear.

We'd like to thank everyone who participated in the fundra[Decimal Tab]It was a great success! Extra pats on the back go to the five employees who gathered over $50.00 in pledges:

5 Repeat steps 3 and 4 to add additional custom tabs if necessary. In this example, a decimal tab is added to the right of the left tab. This tab will be used to line up the dollar amounts in the list.

We'd like to thank everyone who participated in the fundraising drive. It was a great success! Extra pats on the back go to the five employees who gathered over $50.00 in pledges:

Mary Hudson $236.00
Joe Mackenzie $87.00
Scott Chen $174.00
Tracy Turner $61.00

6 To use the custom tabs, press the Tab key to move out to the first custom tab stop, and type your text (in this example, an employee's name). If you've created another custom tab, press Tab again to move to that tab stop, and type the text (in this example, a dollar amount). Press Enter after typing the last block of text on each line.

How to Create Numbered and Bulleted Lists

Word's Numbered and Bulleted List features automatically add numbers or bullets when you're typing a list, and they indent the text so that it doesn't wrap underneath the numbers or bullets (see the sample document). What's more, when you type the first item in a list and press Enter, Word automatically turns on the feature for you. (If it doesn't, see the second item in the FYI list on this page.)

1 To create a numbered list, type **1.** followed by a space, type the text for the first item, and press Enter. Word turns on the Numbered List feature (the Numbering button on the Formatting toolbar now looks like it's pushed in), inserts a *2.* on the next line, and creates a hanging indent so that the text in items that take up more than one line won't wrap under the number.

● When you cut and paste to change the order of items in a numbered list, Word keeps the numbering sequential.

● To turn the Automatic Bulleted Lists or Automatic Numbered Lists feature on or off, choose Tools, AutoCorrect, and then click the AutoFormat As You Type tab. Mark or clear the Automatic Bulleted Lists and Automatic Numbered Lists check boxes, and then click OK. If you disable these features, you can still turn numbered or bulleted lists on manually by clicking the Numbering or Bullets toolbar buttons.

● You can change the appearance of the numbers or bullets in your list. Select the list first, then choose Format, Bullets and Numbering, and experiment with the options in the Bullets and Numbering dialog box.

● Discuss the ostrich proposal.

● Set a date for the training session. This is important because the consultants are already lined up and waiting for us to finalize the plans.

● Make a final decision on a new position for the department.

● Review the report on customer satisfaction. It's about time we put the less than satisfactory results of the customer survey out on the table.

● Eat bagels and drink good coffee!

7 If you want to separate each item in a list with a blank line, press Shift+Enter, Enter at the end of each item. When you press Shift+Enter, Word inserts a *line break character,* which breaks the line of text without ending the paragraph (thus creating a blank line). Pressing Enter then ends the paragraph and inserts the next number or bullet. (To see where you have pressed Shift+Enter, click on the Show/Hide button on the Standard toolbar. Word represents line break characters with the ¿ symbol.)

2 To create a bulleted list, type an asterisk (*) followed by a space, type the text for the first item, and then press Enter. Word turns on the Bulleted List feature (the Bullets button on the Formatting toolbar looks pushed in); it changes the asterisk to a bullet, inserts another bullet on the next line, and creates a hanging indent.

Peter:

Here's a list of things I think we should cover at tomorrow's meeting. Please let me know if there's anything you want to add.

1. Discuss the ostrich proposal.
2. Set a date for the training session. This is important because the consultants are already lined up and waiting for us to finalize the plans.
3. Make a final decision on a new position for the department.
4. Review the report on customer satisfaction. It's about time we put the less than satisfactory results of the customer survey out on the table.
5. Eat bagels and drink good coffee!

Talk to you soon,

JoAnne

3 Continue typing items, pressing Enter at the end of each one.

4 After you type the last item, press Enter twice to turn the Numbered or Bulleted List feature off.

5 If you want to change the numbers to bullets (or vice versa), select the entire list, and then click the Bullets or Numbering button on the Formatting toolbar.

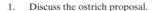

6 In this example, the numbered list has been changed to a bulleted list.

How to Create a Table

If you want to create a complex list or chart, the best option is to use a Word table. A table is a grid of rows and columns, and each box in a table is called a cell. Tables are incredibly flexible. You can use them to create anything from simple charts to invoices, employee lists, or resumes.

Word lets you create tables in two ways: You can use the Table, Insert Table command (or the Insert Table button on the Standard toolbar) to specify how many rows and columns you want, and Word then creates an empty table for you. Alternatively, you can use the Draw Table button on the Tables and Borders toolbar to draw the table with your mouse. This method is the more flexible, so it's the one you'll learn here. Regardless of how you insert the table, you can easily adjust the number of rows and columns at any time (see the next page).

- If you want to create a large table, it's faster to use the Insert Table command than to draw the table with the mouse. Choose Table, Insert Table, type the number of rows and columns you want in the Insert Table dialog box, and click OK. (You can also click the Insert Table button in the Standard toolbar and drag across the desired number of rows and columns in the grid that drops down.)

- To insert a tab in a cell, press Ctrl+Tab; pressing the Tab key by itself moves the insertion point from cell to cell.

- If you inserted a table at the very top of a document and later decide you want to type text above the table, click at the very beginning of the upper-left cell in the table and press Enter. Word inserts a blank line above the table and places your insertion point in it so you can start typing.

1 Choose View, Page Layout to switch to Page Layout view.

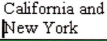

— Pressing Enter here forced text down to the next line.

8 The Enter key functions the same way in a table as it does in ordinary text. Each time you press it, you insert a paragraph mark, forcing any text to the right of the insertion point down to the next line. If you want to see where you've pressed Enter in a table, click the Show/Hide button in the Standard toolbar. As with normal text, you use Backspace or Delete to remove paragraph marks.

	Flamingo	Great Egret	Roseate Spoonbill
Selling Points	Looks good in small flocks	Especially attractive with vines trailing up its legs	Maintains color very well
Flaws	Frequently develops cracks in its tail	Has been known to scare dogs and small children	Tends to lean to one side in windy areas
Best-Selling Regions	Florida and the Northwest	New England and the Midwest	California and New York

7 Enter text into the cells. If the entry in a cell is too wide to fit, Word automatically wraps the text to the next line and increases the row height to accommodate the text.

Draw table Line style Line weight Border color

2 Click the Tables and Borders button on the Standard toolbar.

3 Word displays the Tables and Borders toolbar floating over the document window. Click the Draw Table button if it isn't already selected, then use the Line Style, Line Weight, and Border Color lists to choose the type of line you want to use for the outside border of your table.

Word's Draw Table button makes it easy to create complex tables.

COLOR AVAILABILITY
NOVEMBER 1998

Lawn Bird	Flamingo			Great Egret			Roseate Spoonbill		
Size	S	M	L	S	M	L	S	M	L
Aqua	✓	✓	✓	✓		✓	✓	✓	✓
Fuchsia		✓			✓	✓	✓	✓	
Rose	✓	✓		✓	✓	✓		✓	✓
Sienna		✓	✓	✓		✓	✓	✓	✓

(Color)

Release the mouse when the table is the desired size.

4 Move the mouse into the document window, and notice that when the Draw Table button is selected, the mouse pointer becomes a small pencil. Starting at the upper-left corner of where you want the table to go, drag diagonally down and to the right, releasing the mouse when the outline of the table is approximately the right size.

6 You can navigate in a table by clicking in the desired cell with your mouse. You can also use the four arrow keys, although if a cell contains text, the right and left arrow keys move the insertion point character by character within the cell. Lastly, you can press Tab to move cell by cell to the right, and Shift+Tab to move to the left. When a cell contains text, pressing Tab or Shift+Tab selects the contents of the cell you move into.

5 Select a different type of line if desired (see step 3), and draw the lines for the rows and columns. As you drag, a dashed line shows you where the line will be inserted. Release the mouse as the line extends across the entire width or height of the table. You can draw a simple table such as the one shown here, or a complex one such as the one in the middle of the page.

How to Add Borders and Shading

You don't have to know anything about graphics to add attractive borders and shading to headings and paragraphs of body text, and you can even create a decorative border around the entire page. The steps on this page tell you how to work with the Borders and Shading dialog box. However, you can also issue most of the commands with the Tables and Borders toolbar (choose View, Toolbars, Tables and Borders).

MEMORANDUM

1 Click anywhere within the paragraph to which you want to add borders and shading, or select adjacent paragraphs if you want to add borders and shading to all of them.

9 Word creates the border around every page in your document.

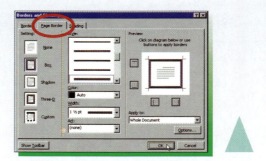

8 To create a border around your page, click the Page Border tab in the Borders and Shading dialog box, specify the type of border you want, and click OK.

FYI

● If you don't want the right and left borders on a paragraph to extend all the way to the margins, indent the paragraph an equal amount from the left and right.

● To quickly add a single-line horizontal border, click the line where you want the border to go, type - - - (three hyphens) and press Enter. To create a double-line border, type === (three equal signs) and press Enter. To enable/disable this feature (it's turned on by default), choose Tools, AutoCorrect, click the AutoFormat As You Type tab, mark or clear the Borders check box, and then click OK.

7 To change the distance between the top and bottom borders and the paragraph text, simply point to the border you want to adjust, drag it up or down, and then release the mouse.

2 Choose Format, Borders and Shading to display the Borders and Shading dialog box.

3 Click the Borders tab if it isn't already in front. If you see an option under Setting that closely matches the type of border you want to add, click it.

LawnBirds, Inc.

MEMORANDUM

Date: March 10, 1998
To: All Employees
From: Daycare Center Fundraising Committee
Re: Fundraising Drive

We'd like to thank every one who participated in the fundraising drive. It was a great success! Extra pats on the back go to the five employees who gathered over $50.00 in pledges:

Mary Hudson	$236.00
Joe Mackenzie	$87.00
Scott Chen	$174.00
Tracy Turner	$61.00

We'll keep you posted on plans for the next drive. Any ideas or suggestions would be more than welcome. Thanks again for all your hard work.

4 To customize the style of the lines in your border, scroll through the Style list, and click the desired style. You can also use the Color and Width drop-down lists to change the color and width of the lines. If you want to design a border from scratch, choose Custom under Setting, select the desired style, color, and width options for one of the lines, and then click the line in the sample box under Preview. Repeat this process to create the remaining three lines.

OK

6 When you've made all of your selections in the Borders and Shading dialog box, click the OK button.

5 To add shading, click the Shading tab at the top of the dialog box, and then click the desired color under Fill.

How to Change the Page Margins

The default margins in Word are 1 inch on the top and bottom of the page and 1.25 inches on the left and right. These margins are fine for most documents, but like all features in Word, they are by no means mandatory. Larger margins can give the page a more spacious feel, and narrower margins can come in handy when you're trying to fit text onto one page. For example, in the document on this page, all the introductory text of a business report fits on one page thanks to some rather narrow margins.

1 Choose File, Page Setup. (It doesn't matter where the insertion point is resting, and you shouldn't have any text selected.)

● If you want to see what the margins will look like before you print, use Print Preview or Page Layout view.

● Rather than type a margin setting in steps 4 and 5, you can click the up and down arrows next to the text boxes to adjust the setting in increments of one-tenth of an inch.

● If your company uses margin settings on all its documents that differ from Word's default margins, you can set the default margins to match those used by your company. This way, you won't have to change the margins each time you start a new document. To do this, follow steps 1 through 5 on this page, but before you click the OK button in step 6, click the Default button. Word asks if you want to change the default settings for page setup. Click the Yes button, then click OK. If you later want to change the default margins to something else, just repeat these steps.

Page Setup

Margins | Paper Size | Paper Source | Layout

Top: | 1"
Bottom: | 1"
Left: | 1.25"
Right: | 1.25"
Gutter: | 0"

From edge
Header: | 0.5"
Footer: | 0.5"

Preview

Apply to: | Whole document

☐ Mirror margins

Default... | OK | Cancel

2 In the Page Setup dialog box, click the Margins tab if it is not already active.

Top: | 1"
Bottom: | 1"
Left: | 1.25"
Right: | 1.25"

3 The content of the Top text box is selected when the dialog box is first displayed. If you want to change the top margin first, go on to the next step. To begin with the bottom, left, or right margin, first select the existing setting in the appropriate text box by double-clicking on it or by pressing the Tab key to move to it.

awnBirds, Inc.   **We Can Do Better**

Report to the President on Customer Service Mishaps

January through June, 1998

Rarely do we get such a cluster of major service mishaps in a six-month period. As one irate customer wrote to us just last week:

I am in shock. Utter shock. That you double-billed me is bad enough. But that you sent your collections people after me when I refused to pay the second bill--even though your own records showed only one flamingo shipment--even though I wrote to you immediately to report the problem--is just intolerable. The long-time customer with a flawless payment record--is just intolerable. The many flamingos on my lawn used to spark in me a sense of pride in my beautiful home. Now they trigger only queasiness as I recall my unfortunate dealings with your wretched firm.

A scathing indictment, but not without merit. Overzealous telemarketers, problems with the billing system, personnel turnover, and the infamous "beige flamingo" incident conspired to make the first half of the year a service nightmare.

Happily, we have turned the corner, and this report will detail the steps we have taken to restore LawnBirds to its distinguished position as the service leader in the lawn flamingo industry. Our market research suggests that flamingo purchasers are a loyal group that will stick with a company as it goes through hard times--as long as that company makes a strong effort to improve. Let us hope our market research is right and we can win back the many valued customers we alienated during the Dark Days of early 1998.

The first part of this report presents, in gory detail, each major area of service defect we have experienced this year. The second part outlines the personnel, product, and procedure changes we have launched to attack each defect.

Narrow margins help fit all the text on one page.

Top: | .5
Bottom: | 1"
Left: | 1.25"
Right: | 1.25"

4 Type a new setting in inches. (Typing the inch symbol is optional.) The number you type replaces the existing setting.

Top: | .5
Bottom: | .5
Left: | 1
Right: | 1

5 Change any other margins you want to reset.

OK

6 Click the OK button to close the dialog box and apply the change.

How to Use Headers and Footers

A header appears at the top of every page, and a footer appears at the bottom of every page. You might want to use headers and footers to display the document title, your name, the name of your organization, and so on. You can also place fields in headers and footers. (A *field* is a holding place for information that Word updates automatically, such as the current date.) Finally, Word offers several AutoText entries specially designed for headers and footers.

① 1 To add headers and footers, choose View, Header and Footer. It doesn't matter where the insertion point is located because headers and footers automatically appear on every page in a predetermined position (which can be adjusted by using Page Setup options).

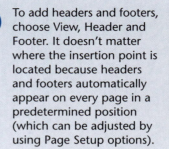

 FYI

● If you need to delete a field in a header or footer, first select it and then press Delete. When you click a field, it turns a light shade of gray. The field isn't actually selected, however, until you double-click it or drag across it with the mouse pointer.

● If you want different headers or footers on odd and even pages of your document (this is common for documents that will be bound), choose File, Page Setup, click the Layout tab, mark the Different Odd and Even check box, and click OK. You can then use the Show Next and Show Previous buttons in the Header and Footer toolbar to navigate between the headers and footers for odd and even pages.

● If you want different headers and footers in different portions of your document, insert *next page section breaks* to divide your document into two or more sections. By default, Word carries the same header and footer across all sections of your document. To allow the headers and footers to vary, click in each section, and click the Same As Previous button in the Header and Footer toolbar to turn off the feature. You can use the Show Next and Show Previous buttons in the toolbar to display the header and footer areas for each different section.

⑧ 8 Click the Close button in the Header and Footer toolbar to return to viewing the document text. Headers and footers aren't visible in Normal view, but you can see them in both Page Layout view and in Print Preview. (In fact, you can activate the header and footer areas from Page Layout view by simply double-clicking on them.)

Date field

Header
Report to the President   7/06/98

Filename and Path AutoText entry   **Page X of Y AutoText entry**

Footer
D:\My Documents\Reports\mishaps report.doc   Page 1 of 9

⑦ 7 In this example, the header includes regular text on the left margin, and the date field on the right. The footer contains two AutoText entries, Filename and Path on the left, and Page X of Y on the right. After you've typed your text (and inserted any fields or AutoText entries), you can select it and format it in the usual ways. For example, you may want to decrease the font size to make the header and footer text less prominent.

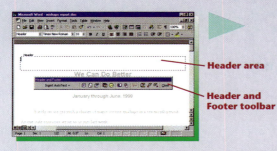

Header area

Header and Footer toolbar

2 Word switches to Page Layout view, places the insertion point in the header area, and displays the Header and Footer toolbar, which contains buttons that access special commands for working with headers and footers.

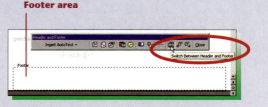

Footer area

3 If you want to add a footer, click the Switch Between Header and Footer button to place the insertion point in the footer area. You can go back to the header area by clicking on this button again.

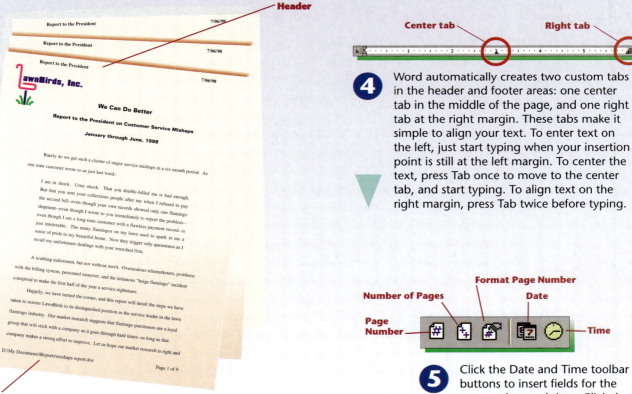

Header

Footer

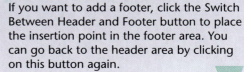

Center tab

Right tab

4 Word automatically creates two custom tabs in the header and footer areas: one center tab in the middle of the page, and one right tab at the right margin. These tabs make it simple to align your text. To enter text on the left, just start typing when your insertion point is still at the left margin. To center the text, press Tab once to move to the center tab, and start typing. To align text on the right margin, press Tab twice before typing.

Number of Pages

Format Page Number

Date

Page Number

Time

5 Click the Date and Time toolbar buttons to insert fields for the current date and time. Click the Page Number button to insert the page number, and the Number of Pages button to insert the total number of pages.

6 Clicking the Insert AutoText button in the Header and Footer toolbar displays a list of AutoText entries. Most of them insert a combination of text and fields. The first entry inserts the page number surrounded by dashes (-1-). The second and third entries use commas to show you where the text will be placed—on the left margin, in the center of the page, or on the right margin. If you insert an entry you don't want to keep, select it and press the Delete key.

How to Use the Document Map

The Document Map gives you a bird's-eye view of your headings as you're working. It shows you where you are in a long document, and you can use it to quickly jump from section to section. The Document Map works best if you format your headings with heading styles, as shown in the examples on this page, or outline levels. If Word doesn't find heading styles or outline levels, it searches for paragraphs that look like headings (for example, short lines formatted in a larger font size), applies outline levels to them, and then displays them in the Document Map.

1 Click the Document Map button in the Standard toolbar.

8 To adjust the width of the Document Map pane, point to the boundary between the Document Map and the document, and when you see the Resize ScreenTip, drag to the desired spot and release the mouse. To close the Document Map, either double-click the boundary or click the Document Map button on the Standard toolbar again.

● If the Document Map is blank, it means that Word couldn't find any paragraphs formatted with heading styles or outline levels, or paragraphs that looked like headings. If this happens, follow the directions in the first two topics of the next chapter to apply heading styles or outline levels to your headings, and then redisplay the Document Map.

● If you need to change the levels of some of your headings or move headings around in your document, use Outline view instead of the Document Map.

7 In this example, clicking on Heading 2 in the context menu collapsed the Document Map to display only headings formatted with the Heading 1 and Heading 2 styles.

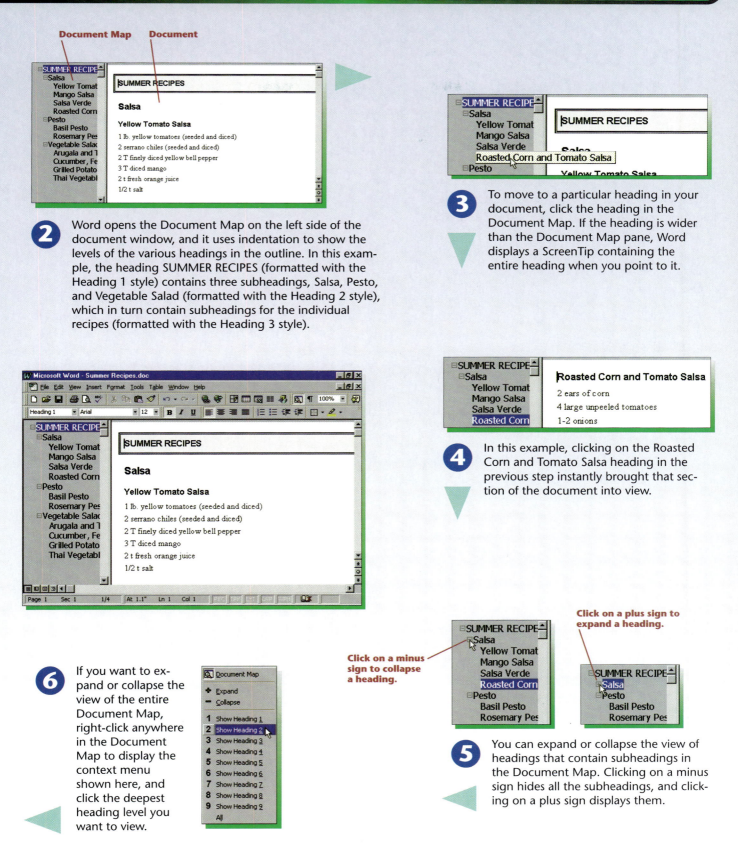

Document Map   **Document**

2 Word opens the Document Map on the left side of the document window, and it uses indentation to show the levels of the various headings in the outline. In this example, the heading SUMMER RECIPES (formatted with the Heading 1 style) contains three subheadings, Salsa, Pesto, and Vegetable Salad (formatted with the Heading 2 style), which in turn contain subheadings for the individual recipes (formatted with the Heading 3 style).

3 To move to a particular heading in your document, click the heading in the Document Map. If the heading is wider than the Document Map pane, Word displays a ScreenTip containing the entire heading when you point to it.

4 In this example, clicking on the Roasted Corn and Tomato Salsa heading in the previous step instantly brought that section of the document into view.

6 If you want to expand or collapse the view of the entire Document Map, right-click anywhere in the Document Map to display the context menu shown here, and click the deepest heading level you want to view.

Click on a minus sign to collapse a heading.

Click on a plus sign to expand a heading.

5 You can expand or collapse the view of headings that contain subheadings in the Document Map. Clicking on a minus sign hides all the subheadings, and clicking on a plus sign displays them.

How to Use Outline View

Outline view is similar to the Document Map, but it's intended to help you modify the structure of your outline instead of simply helping you navigate. In Outline view, you can move headings—and any body text or subheadings they contain—-using drag-and-drop, and you can adjust heading levels by clicking on toolbar buttons. You have to apply heading styles or outline levels to your headings before using Outline view.

1 Choose View, Outline (or click the Outline View button in the lower-left corner of the document window).

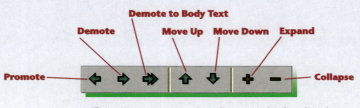

Demote to Body Text

Demote   Move Up   Move Down   Expand

Promote   Collapse

8 To promote a heading to a higher level or demote it to a lower level, select the heading, then click the Promote, Demote, or Demote to Body Text button. When you change the level of a heading, Word adjusts the level of all its subheadings accordingly.

● To move a heading up or down in the outline one line at a time, select the heading, and then click one or more times on the Move Up or Move Down toolbar button (see step 8).

● To expand or collapse the view of an individual heading, select the heading, and then click the Expand or Collapse toolbar button (see step 8).

● When you're done using Outline view, use the View menu or the View buttons in the lower-left corner of the document window to switch to Normal or Page Layout view.

● To view your headings in Outline view in plain unformatted text, click the Show Formatting button on the Outlining toolbar to turn it off.

This heading and its subheadings are now in a new location.

7 Word moves the heading and all its contents to the new location. Keep in mind that when you drag a heading in Outline view, you are potentially moving many pages of text in your document, depending on how many pages are contained in the heading and its subheadings.

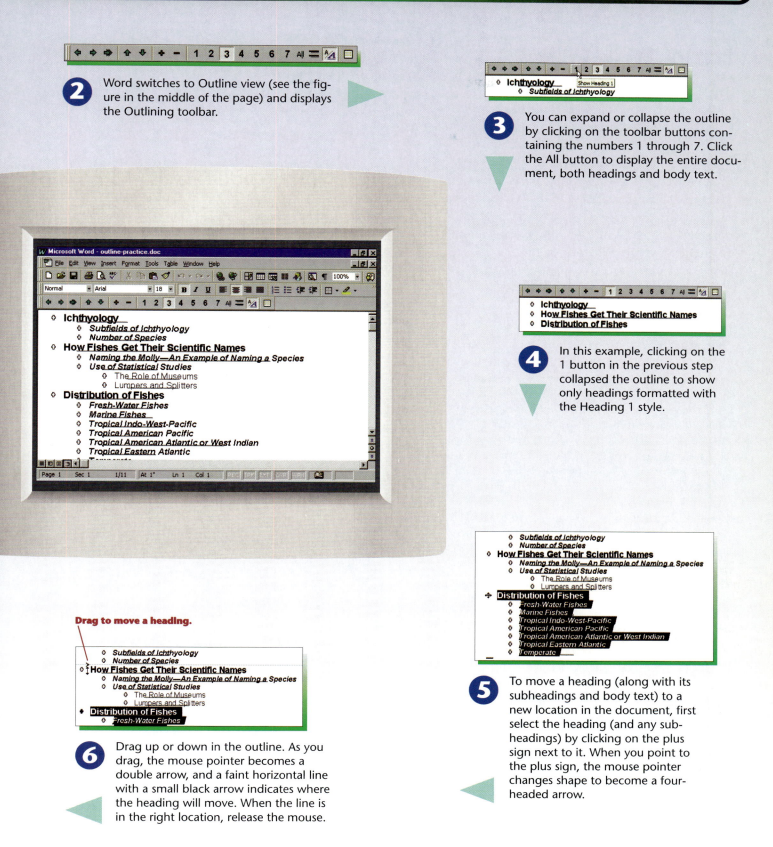

2 Word switches to Outline view (see the figure in the middle of the page) and displays the Outlining toolbar.

3 You can expand or collapse the outline by clicking on the toolbar buttons containing the numbers 1 through 7. Click the All button to display the entire document, both headings and body text.

4 In this example, clicking on the 1 button in the previous step collapsed the outline to show only headings formatted with the Heading 1 style.

5 To move a heading (along with its subheadings and body text) to a new location in the document, first select the heading (and any subheadings) by clicking on the plus sign next to it. When you point to the plus sign, the mouse pointer changes shape to become a four-headed arrow.

Drag to move a heading.

6 Drag up or down in the outline. As you drag, the mouse pointer becomes a double arrow, and a faint horizontal line with a small black arrow indicates where the heading will move. When the line is in the right location, release the mouse.

How to Use a Template

Word templates are well-designed and easy to use. A paint-by-numbers approach to document creation, templates show you exactly what type of text to enter where. In fact, you may notice fancy formatting in some templates that you don't quite understand and wouldn't know how to create yourself. Don't worry about it. The beauty of using a template is that you can let Word handle the formatting for you.

● The advantage of using a template instead of an ordinary document to store text and formatting you want to reuse is that you can't accidentally overwrite a template. When you start a document based on a template, fill in the blanks, and save, Word saves the document separately from the template, leaving the template in its original form. In contrast, if you open a document you're using as a blueprint, revise it, and then accidentally use File, Save instead of File, Save As to save the filled-in version, you overwrite the original document and lose your blueprint.

● Some templates, such as the one on this page, include a sentence or two of instructions in the body of the document. Once you've read the instructions, simply select the text and type over it.

● Be sure to check the header and footer areas of the template. Many templates have dummy text in these areas that needs to be replaced.

● If necessary, you can attach a template to an existing document. Choose Tools, Templates and Add-Ins and click the Attach button. Select the desired template (it will be stored in the Templates folder or in one of its subfolders), and click OK. If you want the styles in the document to be updated to match the styles in the template you just attached, mark the Automatically Update Document Styles check box, and then click OK.

1 Choose File, New to display the New dialog box. In this situation, you can't use the New button on the Standard toolbar as a shortcut. (When you click the New button, Word assumes you want to start a new document based on the Normal template; it doesn't give you the chance to choose a different template.)

8 When you have completed the document, use the regular methods to save, print, and close it.

7 The text you typed replaces the "click here" text. Continue in the same fashion, replacing all the "click here" instructions with the text you want in the document.

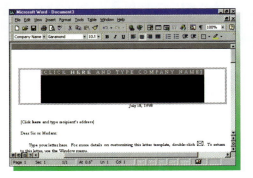

6 Click the first "click here" instruction to select it, and type your text.

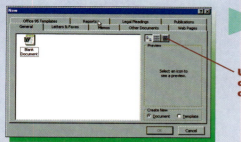

Use these buttons to change the display of template names.

2 The Normal (Blank Document) template is stored in the General tab. Click the other tabs at the top of the dialog box to see what additional templates are available. Depending on how Word was installed and whether anyone has created new templates, the tabs and templates you see may differ from those shown here. You can change the display of the template names by clicking on the Large Icon, List, and Detail buttons.

3 Try clicking on a few template names. When a template is selected, Word displays a preview of it on the right side of the dialog box (if a preview is available). Here, the Contemporary Report template in the Reports tab is selected.

Template   **Completed document**

[CLICK HERE AND TYPE COMPANY NAME]

July 18, 1998

[Click here and type recipient's address]

Dear Sir or Madam:

Type your letter here. For more details on customizing this letter template, double-click ✉. To return to this letter, use the Window menu.

Sincerely,

[Click here and type your name]
[Click here and type job title]

[STREET ADDRESS] • [CITY / STATE] • [ZIP / POSTAL CODE]
PHONE: [PHONE NUMBER] • FAX: [FAX NUMBER]

TROPICAL FISH EMPORIUM

July 18, 1998

Eliza Parker
Aquarium Hobbyist Newsletter
115 Browning Street
Philadelphia, PA 19119

Dear Eliza:

Thank you for your inquiry regarding the health of our fish. I'd like to assure you that the fish in our tanks are in excellent condition. Unlike some tropical fish stores, we take every fish casualty very seriously. Our tanks are monitored constantly to ensure steady temperature and pH levels, and our professional staff is well-equipped to recognize and isolate the occasional sickly fish that comes in from the wholesalers.

Please let me know when the article about our store will be published in your paper. I look forward to reading it! In the meantime, I'm available for further questions should you have any.

Sincerely,

Thea Noelle

Thea Noelle
General Manager

1050 TENTH STREET • PHILADELPHIA, PA • 19119
PHONE: 215-743-2647 • FAX: 215-743-2648

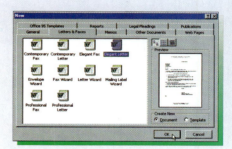

4 Some templates are called Wizards. *Wizards* are specialized templates that let you customize the document you create (see the next page). The Letters & Faxes tab shown here contains Wizards for creating envelopes, faxes, letters, and mailing labels. When you find the template you want to use (Elegant Letter in this example), click it, and then click the OK button.

5 Word creates a new document based on the template you chose. Many templates, including the one shown here, provide instructions to "Click here and type" to help you fill in your text. You may also see some cross-hatched boxes. Word uses these for formatting purposes only—they won't print out.

How to Modify a Template

After using a template for a while, you may notice some text or formatting that you want to change. While you can make the change in each document you base on that template, it's much more efficient to modify the template itself. Remember that changing a document based on the template does not in any way affect the underlying template. You must open the template itself and revise it.

1 Click the Open button in the Standard toolbar (or choose File, Open).

● Remember, you do not follow the steps described on this page if you simply want to use the template to create a document. If you do so accidentally, you'll end up overwriting the blank template with the filled-in version.

2 In the Open dialog box, choose Document Templates from the Files of Type list (located in the lower-left corner of the dialog box).

Revised letterhead

Tropical Fish Emporium
1050 Tenth Street • Philadelphia, PA 19119

September 18, 1998

[Type recipient's address here]

Dear [Type name here]:

[Type letter here]

Sincerely,

Thea Noelle
General Manager

Owned and Operated By Genuine Fish Fanatics

New footer

3 Double-click the folder in which the template is stored—either the Templates folder itself or a subfolder of Templates. (The Templates folder is usually a subfolder of the Microsoft Office folder. If you can't find it, ask your resident computer guru for help.)

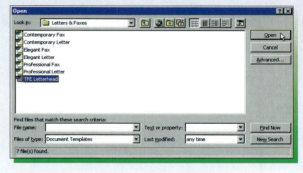

4 Click the template (TFE Letterhead in this example), and then click the Open button.

5 Make your changes to the text or formatting of the template. In this example, a box border is added to the letterhead, the address is reformatted to fit on one line, and a footer is added.

6 Save and close the template. When you use the template the next time, you'll see the modified version.

How to Use a Wizard

Wizards differ from standard templates in two ways: They offer a great deal of hand-holding, and they let you tailor the template to suit your preferences. Wizards typically ask you a series of questions about what text and formatting you want included in the document. When a Wizard has gathered all the information it needs, it presents you with a document that conforms to your requests. Wizard-generated documents look just like documents based on standard templates, complete with click-here instructions to help you fill in the text.

1 Choose File, New to display the New dialog box. Remember, you cannot use the New button on the Standard toolbar as a shortcut in this situation.

FYI

● If you've used a Wizard before and know that you want to keep all the default answers to the questions, you can click the Finish button on the Start page (see step 3) to complete the questionnaire without changing the default choices.

● Some Wizards display the document at a reduced zoom setting so that you can see more of it on your screen. If you want to enlarge the document to make it easier to read, display the Zoom Control list in the Standard toolbar, and click 100%. You may then need to use the horizontal scroll bar to scroll the right and left margins into view.

Interoffice Memo

Date: 7/1998
To: All Staff
From: Theo Noelle
RE: [Click here and type subject]

[Click here and type your memo text]

TN

Enc. 2

6 After a moment or two, Word displays a document in Page Layout view with the text and formatting you requested. Wherever you see click-here instructions, replace them with actual text. Then save, print, and close the document.

2 Click the tab that contains the Wizard you want to use, click the Wizard name, and click OK to start it. (This example uses the Memo Wizard in the Memos tab.)

3 Word displays the first page of the Wizard dialog box, called Start. As you progress through the Wizard, Word highlights the current step on the left side of the dialog box. Click the Next button to move to the next step.

Interoffice Memo

Date:	7/19/98
To:	All Staff
From:	Thea Noelle
RE:	Floaters

It has come to my attention that there have been a large number of floaters observed by customers in the tanks in recent weeks. This scares away customers and creates a horrible image for the store. Please do your utmost to a) keep them from dying in the first place, b) if they do die, remove them immediately!

For newer staff members, I'm enclosing two handouts that will help you spot the signs of a fish that isn't long for this world. Read them!

Your attention to this matter would be most appreciated. A bonus will be handed out at the end of the month to the staff of the area with the lowest number of reported floaters.

TN

Enc. 2

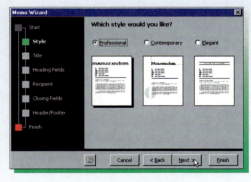

4 The Wizard presents the first question. In this example, it needs to know which style you prefer for your memo. Make your selection, and click Next again. Continue working your way through the steps. If you want to go back to a previous step, click the Back button one or more times.

5 When you reach the Finish step, click the Finish button to tell the Wizard to start generating the document.

How to Create a Mail Merge Document

You begin the mail merge process by telling Word which document you want to use as your main document. You can either create a new document (as shown on this page) or open an existing document you want to use as your form letter. If you're using a new document, you can type as much or as little of the text as you like at this stage. It's usually simplest to save the blank document without entering any text and move right into creating the data source. Then when you complete the main document, you'll enter both regular text and special merge codes telling Word where to insert each piece of information from the data source.

1 Close any open documents, and start a new document. (See the FYI list if you want to use an existing document.)

● If you want to use a letter on your disk as your main document, open it, remove all the personal information—such as the name, address, and salutation—and save the document under a new name. Then continue with step 2 on this page.

● If you plan on running a lot of merges, it's a good idea to create a separate folder to hold your main documents and data source files. In step 2 on this page, double-click the folder that will contain the new folder (so that it appears in the Save In list at the top of the Save As dialog box), and then click the Create New Folder button. Type a name for the folder and click OK. Finally, double-click the new folder (to display it in the Save In list) before saving the main document.

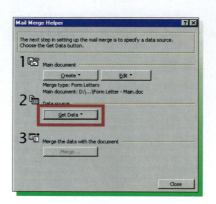

6 Word displays the name and location of the main document under Main Document and activates the Get Data button. You are now ready to perform the next step—creating the data source. Continue on to the next topic.

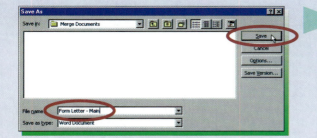

2 Save the blank document to disk. It's helpful to choose a name that will remind you that this is a main document, such as *Form Letter–Main* in this example. That way, when you're looking at a list of files on your disk, you'll be able to easily recognize this document as one that's designed for use in a mail merge. Select a folder for the document, and click the Save button.

3 Choose Tools, Mail Merge to display the Mail Merge Helper dialog box. (Make sure not to choose Tools, Merge Documents. Despite its name, this command has nothing to do with the mail merge feature.) The Mail Merge Helper will help guide you through the process of setting up and running the merge. All of the steps of a merge can be initiated from this dialog box, though you'll learn to use toolbar shortcuts instead where appropriate.

MAIN DOCUMENT

4 Under Main Document, click the Create button. Word displays a list of the different types of main documents you can create. Click Form Letters.

Address Book

5 Word asks what document you want to use as your main document. Since you've already started (or opened) yours, click the Active Window button.

How to Create the Mail Merge Data Source

Because a data source is a simple database, you need to understand two database-related terms to work with it: record and field. A *record* is all the information about one person in your data source. If you have names and addresses for 50 people in your data source, it would contain 50 records. A *field* is one category of information within each record. Typical fields include first name, last name, company, address, city, state, zip code, and so on. The first phase of creating a data source is defining the fields you want to use; the second phase is entering the data. Follow the steps on this page and the next to create your data source.

1 If you haven't done so yet, create your main merge document. Then click the Get Data button in the Mail Merge Helper dialog box.

8 In the example shown in step 7, the list of fields has been modified to include the following fields: FirstName, LastName, Company, Address1, City, State, PostalCode, and Salutation. If many of your addresses include building names or suite numbers, you may want to keep the Address2 field. The Salutation field is a nice one to add because it lets you use a name other than the first name or the last name after *Dear* in the salutation of a form letter.

(Continue to next page)

7 To change the position of a field in the list, click the field, then use a Move arrow to move it up or down the list. The field order in the Field Names in Header Row list doesn't affect the order in which you can place fields in your main document. Positioning them in a logical order now simply helps when you enter the actual data a little bit later on.

2 Word lets you create a new data source or open one from disk. If you already have a Word data source on disk, choose Open Data Source, select the file from the Open Data Source dialog box, and click the Open button.

3 If you're creating your data source from scratch, choose Create Data Source to display the Create Data Source dialog box (shown in the middle of the page), and continue with the next step.

Create Data Source

A mail merge data source is composed of rows of data. The first row is called the header row. Each of the columns in the header row begins with a field name.

Word provides commonly used field names in the list below. You can add or remove field names to customize the header row.

Field name:

Add Field Name ▸▸

Remove Field Name

Field names in header row:
Title
FirstName
LastName
JobTitle
Company
Address1
Address2

Move

MS Query...   OK   Cancel

4 The Create Data Source dialog box is the place where you define which fields you want to use in your data source. Word displays a list of the most typical fields under Field Names in Header Row. Your job is to remove the fields you don't need, add any new ones you want to use, and optionally change the order of the fields in the list.

Field name:

Add Field Name ▸▸

Remove Field Name

Field names in header row:
Title
FirstName
LastName
JobTitle
Company
Address1
Address2

Move

5 To remove a field, click it, and then click the Remove Field Name button.

Field name:
Salutation

Add Field Name ▸▸

6 To add a field, type the new field name in the Field Name text box (if a field name is currently in the box, select it and type over it), and click the Add Field Name button. Word adds the new field to the bottom of the list. No spaces are allowed in field names. You can also include fields that you want for reference purposes but don't intend to actually use in form letters, such as phone numbers or e-mail addresses.

How to Create the Mail Merge Data Source
(Continued)

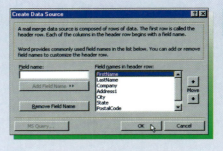

9 When you've finished defining your fields, click the OK button.

16 When you're finished entering records, click the OK button to close the Data Form. Congratulations! You've completed the most difficult part of the mail merge process. Proceed to the next page to complete the main document.

● If you already have a database of names and addresses in another database program, such as Access, Paradox, or FoxPro, you may be able to use that file as your data source. In step 2 of this topic, choose Open Data Source, and then in the Open Data Source dialog box, display the Files of Type list and click the appropriate file format. Locate and select your database file, and then click the Open button.

● The easiest way to edit the data source in the future is to open it through the main document. First open the main document (File, Open). Then click the Edit Data Source button at the far right end of the Mail Merge toolbar to display the Data Form. Make your revisions to the records, and then click OK to close the Data Form. Save the main document, and click Yes when Word asks if you want to save the data source attached to the main document.

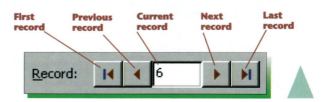

First record | Previous record | Current record | Next record | Last record

15 Word indicates which record you are on at the bottom of the Data Form. If you need to edit a previous record, you can use the red arrows to bring it into view. To delete a record, display it and then click the Delete button.

10 Word displays the Save As dialog box because it needs to save the data source before allowing you to start entering records. It's a good idea to choose a file name—such as *Mailing List–Data Source* in this example—that clearly indicates the document is a data source file. Select a folder for the document, and then click the Save button.

11 Word displays a message box informing you that your data source doesn't yet have any records in it. Click the Edit Data Source button to start adding the actual data. Depending on how many people are in your mailing list, this could be a time-consuming process. Luckily, you only have to do it once. (When you create other main documents in the future, you can use this same data source with them.)

12 Word displays the Data Form dialog box (shown in the middle of the page), which functions as an intermediary between you and the table Word uses behind the scenes to store your data source. The dialog box contains a text box for each field you defined in steps 5 and 6. Type the data for the first record, pressing Tab to move to the next field (or Shift+Tab to move to the previous field). The order in which you enter the records doesn't matter.

13 When you've finished typing the first record, click the Add New button. Be careful not to click the OK button at this point. If you do, Word closes the Data Form and displays the main document. To return to the Data Form if you closed it accidentally, click the Edit Data Source button at the far right edge of the Mail Merge toolbar just underneath the Formatting toolbar.

14 When you click Add New, Word empties the text boxes in the Data Form to let you enter the second record. Continue typing new records and pressing Add New in after each one.

How to Complete the Main Mail Merge Document

This is the fun part of setting up a mail merge. If your main document is blank at this point, you need to both type and format the text and insert the merge codes. If the main document already contains the text and formatting, you need only insert the codes (see steps 4 through 7).

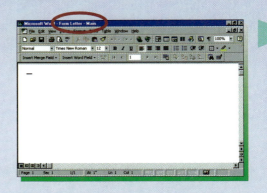

1 Open your completed (and saved) main document on screen.

Dear «Salutation»:

    We'd like to invite you to an open house on April 20 from 7:30 p.m. to 9:30 p.m. to celebrate our recent expansion into the office next door. Come admire our new 300 gallon tank and take home free guppies for the kids.
    There will be plenty of wine and cheese, and as usual, we'll be more than happy to answer all your fish-related questions. Hope to see you there!

Sincerely,

The Staff

8 Type the body of the letter and the closing. Then save the main document and go on to the next topic, which describes the final step in the mail merge process, running the merge.

April 5, 1998

«FirstName» «LastName»
«Company»
«Address1»
«City», «State» «PostalCode»

Dear «Salutation»

● From the main document, you can access the Data Form to edit the data source by clicking the Edit Data Source button at the far right end of the Mail Merge toolbar. Once you've made your changes in the Data Form, click the OK button to return to the main document.

● To delete a merge code, select it first, and then press the Delete key.

7 Repeat steps 4 and 5 to insert the remaining fields for the address block, pressing Enter and adding spaces and commas where necessary. If you have a Salutation field, insert it after the word *Dear*, and follow it with a colon or a comma. (You can, of course, also use some combination of other fields for the salutation, such as Title and LastName, or FirstName.)

| Insert Merge Field ▾ | Insert Word Field ▾ | ᵃᵇ꜀ | ◄ | ◄ | 1 | ► | ►► | |

2 The Mail Merge toolbar appears at the top of the document window under the Formatting toolbar.

Tropical Fish Emporium
1050 Tenth Street
Philadelphia, PA 19119

April 5, 1998

<<FirstName>> <<LastName>>
<<Company>>
<<Address1>>
<<City>>, <<State>> <<PostalCode>>

Dear <<Salutation>>:

We'd like to invite you to an open house on April 20 from 7:30 p.m. to 9:30 p.m. to celebrate our recent expansion into the office next door. Come admire our new 300 gallon tank and take home free guppies for the kids.
There will be plenty of wine and cheese, and as usual, we'll be more than happy to answer all your fish-related questions. Hope to see you there!

Sincerely,

The Staff

3 Type and format the text you want to include above the recipient's address. If you like, you can insert the date automatically with the Insert, Date and Time command.

Insert Merge Field ▾

4 Place the insertion point where you want the first line of the address block to begin, and click the Insert Merge Field button at the left end of the Mail Merge toolbar.

5 Word displays a list of all the fields in the attached data source. Click the first field for the address block (FirstName in this example).

6 Word inserts the field in the main document. Note that Word indicates merge codes by surrounding them with chevron brackets.

How to Run the Mail Merge

In this final step of the merge process, Word merges the main document with the data source. The product of the merge is a document called *Form Letters1* that contains all the merged letters. Before you run the merge, it's a good idea to follow steps 2 through 5 on these pages to confirm that everything is set up properly.

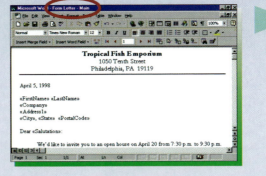

1 Open your completed (and saved) main document on screen.

7 When you're ready, print the form letters using the standard methods for printing a document. Then close the Form Letters document without saving it (you don't normally need to save the merged letters), and close the main document. If Word asks whether you want to save the data source attached to the main document, click the Yes button to save any revisions you've made to the data source.

● If you discover problems in the Form Letters document, close the document without saving it, fix the problem where it originated—in the main document or the data source—and then run the merge again. Fixing problems in the merged letters amounts to treating the symptoms and not the cause.

● To conserve hard disk space, you don't need to save the merged letters. (The Form Letters document could be hundreds of pages long if you have a lot of records in your data source.) Instead, you can keep a record of the date you ran the merge and the names of the main document and data source you used in the merge.

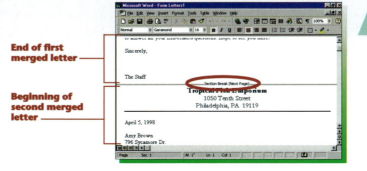

End of first merged letter

Beginning of second merged letter

6 Scroll through the document to view the letters. Word separates the letters with next-page section breaks, so each letter begins on a new page.

2 To check that the merge codes are in the proper places and that the information in the data source is entered correctly, click the View Merged Data button on the Mail Merge toolbar.

Tropical Fish Emporium
1050 Tenth Street
Philadelphia, PA 19119

April 5, 1998

Justin Beard
4467 Waller St
Ardmore, PA 18116

Dear Justin:

We'd like to invi
April 20 from 7:30 p
recent expansion in
admire our new 30
guppies for the ki
There will b
usual, we'll be m
fish-related qu

Sincerely,

The Staff

Tropical Fish Emporium
1050 Tenth Street
Philadelphia, PA 19119

April 5, 1998
Robert Pinkerton
The Croissant Factory
1100 Main St.
West Norriton, PA 16234

Dear Bob:

We'd l

n house on
o celebrate our
or. Come
e home free

ese, and as
r all your
ere!

Tropical Fish Emporium
1050 Tenth Street
Philadelphia, PA 19119

April 5, 1998

Lois Armon
Laser Graphics
8890 Gerard Ave.
Warminster, PA 19225

Dear Ms. Armon:

We'd like to invite you to an open house on April 20 from 7:30 p.m. to 9:30 p.m. to celebrate our recent expansion into the office next door. Come admire our new 300 gallon tank and take home free guppies for the kids.
There will be plenty of wine and cheese, and as usual, we'll be more than happy to answer all your fish-related questions. Hope to see you there!

Sincerely,

The Staff

3 Word displays the data from the first record of your data source in place of the merge codes. Notice that since this record doesn't contain a company name, Word automatically closed up the blank line. Use the red arrows to check the data from a few more records. If you spot a problem, either edit the main document itself or edit the data source.

4 When you're satisfied that everything is set up properly, click the View Merged Data button again to turn it off. Then click the Merge to New Document button on the Mail Merge toolbar. (The Merge to Printer button also runs a merge, but it sends the merged documents directly to the printer, without displaying them on your screen first.)

5 Depending on how many records are in your data source, Word could take anywhere from a few seconds to several minutes to merge the data. When it's finished, it displays the merged letters on your screen in a document named Form Letters1.

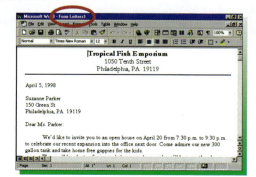

How to Insert a Graphic

The difference between a document that elicits yawns and one that sparkles and demands attention is often the addition of graphics. It only takes a mouse click or two to insert a spiffy graphic. This exercise walks you through inserting the clip art images that come on the Microsoft Office CD.

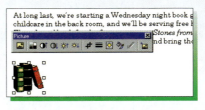

1 Move the insertion point to the approximate position where you want to insert the graphic.

● You can add images to the Microsoft clip gallery. Choose the Import Clips button in the Microsoft Clip Gallery 3.0 dialog box, and in the Add Clip Art to Clip Gallery dialog box, select the desired graphics file and click OK. When Word displays the Clip Properties dialog box, mark the categories in which you want this image displayed, and enter the keywords, separated by spaces, that you want to associate with this image (see steps 5 through 7). Then click OK.

● Most clip art images are stored in more than one category. To change the categories in which an image is stored, click in the image in the Microsoft Clip Gallery 3.0 dialog box, and then click the Clip Properties button. In the Clip Properties dialog box, mark or clear the check boxes under Categories, and click OK.

● If you want to revise the list of categories, click the Edit Categories button. In the Edit Category List dialog box, click the appropriate buttons to create, rename, and delete categories, and click OK when done.

● To insert an image of your own that you haven't imported into the Clip Gallery, use the Insert, Picture, From File command. In the Insert Picture dialog box, click the desired graphics file, and click OK.

8 Word switches to Page Layout view and inserts the image in your document. It also displays the Picture toolbar, which contains buttons for helping you work with images. The white squares surrounding the image (called *sizing handles*) indicate that it's currently selected. You can select a graphic image at any time by clicking on it. If you want to delete an image, select it and press the Delete key.

2 Place the Microsoft Office CD in the drive. (If you installed Word from floppy disks, you need to install the clip art on your hard disk to access it.) Choose Insert, Picture, Clip Art to display the Microsoft Clip Gallery 3.0 dialog box.

Click on different categories to view the images they contain.

3 The Clip Gallery contains tabs for clip art, pictures (photographic images), sounds, and videos. The examples in this chapter use clip art, but you could use similar methods to work with other types of clips as well. In the Clip Art tab, click the various categories to browse the available images. When you click an image (the donkey in this example), the keywords associated with the image appear at the bottom of the dialog box (see steps 5 through 7).

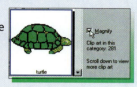

4 To see the images more clearly, mark the Magnify check box. Now when you click an image, it enlarges and its name appears under the clip. If you find an image you want to use, select it and click the Insert button, and then skip to step 8. If you want to search for a particular type of image, continue to the next step.

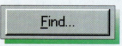

5 If you know what type of image you are looking for, you can search for it by keyword. This is often faster than browsing category by category. Start by clicking on the Find button.

6 In the Find Clip dialog box, type a keyword to describe what you're looking for. In this example, Word will look for images related to books. Keywords aren't related to the actual file names of the images. If you want to search for text contained in the actual file names, use the File Name Containing text box. To restrict the search to graphics of a particular format (WMF, GIF, JPEG, and so on), specify the type in the Clip Type drop-down list. When you've made your choices, click the Find Now button to start the search.

 7 Word searches the CD for images matching the criteria you specified, and then displays the images it finds in a category called Results of Last Find. Click the image you want to use, and click the Insert button.

How to Format a Graphic

Word lets you format graphic images in many different ways (insert an image, display the Drawing and Picture toolbars, and experiment!). You can change the way the text wraps around the image. You can also lighten an image's coloring to turn it into a watermark, and finally, you can even place a graphic image behind your text.

First meeting: Wednesday, August 10 at 7:30 p.m.

Location: The Fernwood Coffeehouse
158 River Road in Pine Grove

1 By default, Word doesn't allow text to wrap around graphic images. In many cases, such as when you're placing a picture in a news article, you need to change this setting to let the text wrap around one or both sides of the image. In this example, the First Meeting and Location text block should wrap around the left side of the image, instead of shifting down below it.

7 If you want to lighten an image's colors so that you can easily read the text placed on top of it, select the image, choose the Image Control button in the Picture toolbar, and click Watermark. In the sample document on this page, the fern image was converted to a watermark after it was sent behind the text.

FYI

● To read descriptions of the various options in the Wrapping tab of the Format Picture dialog box (see step 3), click the small question-mark button in the upper-right corner of the dialog box, and then click the option you are curious about. Word displays a ScreenTip with a concise explanation of the option. (Click again to hide the ScreenTip.)

2 To change the way your text wraps around an image, first select the image, and then choose the Format Picture button from the Picture toolbar (or right-click the graphic and choose Format Picture from the context menu) to display the Format Picture dialog box.

3 Click the Wrapping tab. Under Wrapping Style, click the type of wrapping you want. In this example, the Square option will make the text wrap in a square shape around the image. Under Wrap To, click an option to specify which sides of the image the text should wrap around. Here, choosing Left will allow the text to flow down the left side of the image. Optionally increase or decrease the distance between the text and the image under Distance from Text, and then click OK.

COME JOIN!
THE FERNWOOD COFFEEHOUSE
BOOK GROUP

At long last, we're starting a Wednesday night book group. There will be childcare in the back room, and we'll be serving free house coffee and treats. The selected book for the first meeting is *Stones from the River*, by Ursula Hegi. Please read it before the meeting, and bring thoughts for the discussion and ideas for future books.

First meeting: Wednesday, August 10 at 7:30 p.m.

Location: The Fernwood Coffeehouse
158 River Road in Pine Grove

If you have any questions or would like to help organize future meetings, please call Scott at 746-6645.

First meeting: Wednesday, August 10 at 7:30 p.m.

Location: The Fernwood Coffeehouse
158 River Road in Pine Grove

If you have any questions or would like to help organize future meetings, please call Scott at 746-6645.

4 The text shifts up and wraps to the left of the image.

OME JOIN!
THE FERNWOOD COFFEEHOUSE
BOOK GROUP

5 If you want to place an image on top of your text, first follow steps 2 and 3 and choose a Wrapping style of None. Then simply drag the image over the text.

6 To place an image behind your text, first follow steps 2 and 3 to set the image's wrapping style to None, and then drag the image over the text. Next, right-click the image, and choose Order, Send Behind Text from the context menu. The fern image in the sample document on this page is placed behind the heading.

PART 3

Microsoft Excel 97

EXCEL 97 is Microsoft's powerful spreadsheet application that has a host of new and enhanced features in the Office 97 version.

IN THIS SECTION YOU'LL LEARN ALL OF THE FOLLOWING SKILLS:

- How to Use the Excel Window   72
- How to Enter Data   74
- How to Enter a Formula   76
- How to Sum Numbers   78
- How to Enter Data Automatically   80
- How to Navigate around Worksheets   82
- How to Insert Columns and Rows   84
- How to Delete or Clear Cells   86
- How to Move and Copy Data with Drag and Drop   88
- How to Move and Copy Data with the Clipboard   90
- How to Adjust Column Width   92
- How to Format Numbers in Cells   94
- How to Use Functions   96
- How to Work with Absolute References   98
- How to Name Ranges   100
- How to Search for Data   102
- How to Sort Data   104
- How to Use the ChartWizard   106
- How to Change the Chart Type   108
- How to Work with Chart and Axis Titles   110
- How to Change the Chart Data   112
- How to Draw Shapes on a Chart   114
- How to Use Multiple Worksheets   116

How to Use the Excel Window

When Excel starts, the window is filled with icons and text even before you begin working. The application window that displays has a blank worksheet awaiting your input, along with a great many tools for you to use along the way.

1 Start Excel by choosing Programs from the Start menu, then choosing Microsoft Excel. If you have a shortcut on your Desktop for Excel, double-click the icon for it.

Ready   Sum=6   NUM

8 The status bar at the bottom of the screen shows what's going on in the window. It says "Ready" when Excel is ready for you to enter data. It also lets you know if the Caps Lock or Num Lock key is in use. And, very handy, it shows the sum of any numbers you select.

7 The mouse pointer looks like a plus sign when it's over a cell. It takes on other shapes when you're pointing to different parts of the screen, and those shapes are explained as they occur in the following pages.

● Because you can customize your screen, it may not look exactly like the ones shown here. If your screen seems to be missing an important element, click View on the menu bar. If the Formula Bar or Status Bar entries don't have a checkmark, click that command to display that toolbar. Or click the Toolbars command and make sure the Standard and Formatting toolbars are checked. You'll see a slew of other toolbars listed, and you'll learn about some of them on the following pages.

● When you first open Excel, you only see a portion of the worksheet. An Excel worksheet has 256 columns and 65,536 rows. After column Z, the headings are AA, AB, and so on, through IV. As you use more columns and rows, you have to scroll to see all the data in your worksheet.

A1   ▼   =

6 The formula bar (below the toolbars) displays the contents of the active cell (the left side shows the cell address). The contents of the cell don't look exactly like the characters displayed in the formula bar (you'll learn more about that in the following pages).

2 The title bar displays the title of the workbook file you're using (in addition to the name of the software). Until you save a file and give it a name, Excel calls it Book1.

3 The Excel menu bar is similar to all Windows software menu bars. Click on a menu name to see a list of the commands available for that menu. You can also hold down the Alt key and type the underlined letter in the menu name. To close a menu if you don't want to use a command, click anywhere on the Excel window.

4 The Standard and Formatting toolbars have icons and buttons that give you quick access to many commonly used commands. To see what a button does (if the icon isn't self-explanatory) hold your pointer over it for a few seconds. A *ScreenTip* appears to show you the button's name.

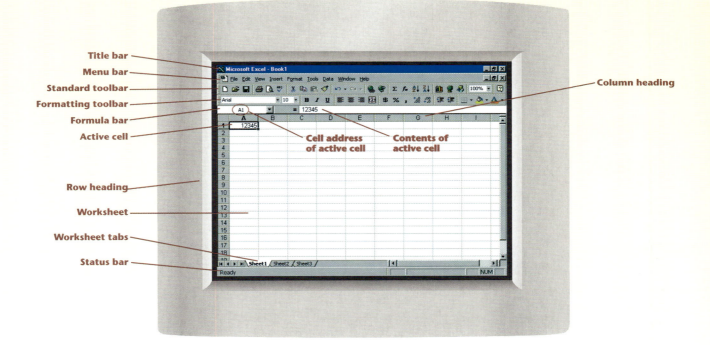

Title bar
Menu bar
Standard toolbar
Formatting toolbar
Formula bar
Active cell

Column heading

Cell address
of active cell

Contents of
active cell

Row heading
Worksheet
Worksheet tabs
Status bar

5 When you're working on a workbook, a highlighted tab at the bottom of the grid tells you which work-sheet you're using (here we're on Sheet 1). Columns are identified with letters, and rows with numbers. The combination of a letter and a number is a *cell address* (cell E7 is at the intersection of column E and row 7). The cell you're currently working in is highlighted with a thick border.

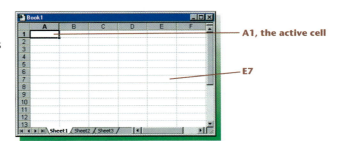

A1, the active cell

E7

How to Enter Data

When you see the word *Ready* in the status bar, you can enter data into your worksheet. As you enter data in a cell, it also displays on the formula bar. If you are entering data that has logical consecutive data after it (days of the week, months of the year, or numbers that have a specific interval), Excel will fill in the data for you automatically.

Click a cell to activate it.

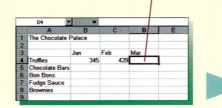

1 Locate the cell in which you want to enter data. If it's not in the window, use the scroll bars to get to it. Click inside the cell to make it the active cell, which is indicated by a dark border. Notice that the column and row headings for this cell look raised so it's easy to determine the cell address.

● After you've entered the data, if you press Enter you will move down one cell (making it easy to enter data in a column). Tab moves you right one cell, and the arrow keys move you one cell in the appropriate direction.

● Excel lets you enter data that is too wide for the cell, and then changes the display so that you see pound signs (#) or scientific notations (1.23E+12). If the adjacent cell is empty, your data will spill over into it; otherwise it is cut off. All the information is there, even if you can't see it. Just widen the column so all your data will be displayed.

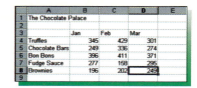

5 Repeat these steps to enter the rest of your data in other cells.

Cancel button **Enter button**

 Type your data into the cell. The characters you type appear in both the cell and the formula bar. The formula bar displays an Enter button and a Cancel button when you start typing. Notice that the status bar displays *Enter* to show you're entering data.

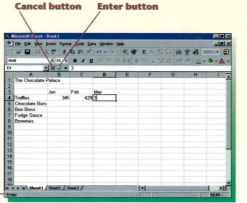

This means you're in the process of entering data.

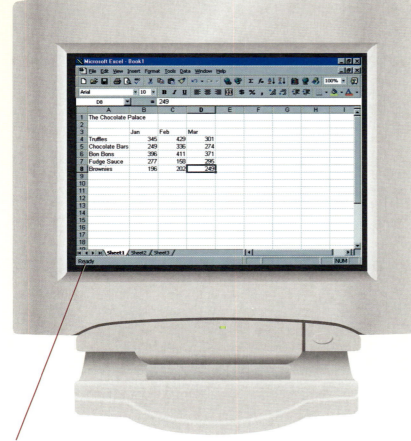

Excel is ready to accept data.

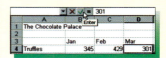

When the data is entered, press the Enter key. You can also click the Enter button on the formula bar, press the Tab key, or one of the arrow keys. For the differences among all those key-stroke choices, check the FYI list.

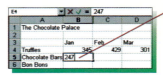

Press Backspace to delete the character to the left of the insertion point.

If you make a typing error, use the Backspace key to delete the wrong character. If you want to erase everything you've typed and start all over again, click the Cancel button or press the Esc key.

How to Enter a Formula

O ne of the magical things about electronic spreadsheets is that cells don't have to contain fixed data. Instead, they can contain formulas—sets of instructions that perform calculations and display the results. The formula can be as simple as =2+2 (all Excel formulas start with an equal sign). And you can use cell references rather than numbers in a formula, which means you can point to a cell address and tell Excel to use the data in that cell in the calculation. If the cell data changes, the calculation changes.

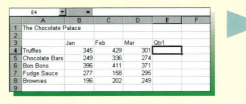

1 Click on the cell where you want to place the formula, which makes the cell active.

SUMIF	▾	X	✓	=	=		
	A	B	C	D	E	F	
1	The Chocolate Palace						
2							
3		Jan	Feb	Mar	Qtr1		
4	Truffles	345	429	301	=		
5	Chocolate Bars	249	336	274			
6	Bon Bons	396	411	371			
7	Fudge Sauce	277	158	295			
8	Brownies	196	202	249			
9							

2 Type an equal sign (=). This tells Excel that you are about to enter a formula. If you don't use the equal sign, Excel will assume that the characters you enter are text.

Jan	Feb	Mar	Qtr1
345	429	301	=B4+C4+D4
249	336	274	
396	411	371	
277	158	295	
196	202	249	

The contents of cell B4 plus the contents of cell C4 plus the contents of cell D4

3 Type your formula. Don't forget you can use cell references instead of numbers. The mathematical operators you can use in formulas include + for addition, - for subtraction, * for multiplication, / for division, and ^ for exponentiation. The formula in this cell adds January, February, and March sales figures to produce a first-quarter total.

X	✓	=	=B4+C4+D4
	B		C

Enter

4 Click the Enter button or press Enter, Tab, or any arrow key to complete the formula entry.

Microsoft Excel - Book1
File Edit View Insert Format Tools Data Window Help

Arial ▾ 10 ▾ B I U

E4 = =B4+C4+D4

	A	B	C	D	E	F	G	H	I
1	The Chocolate Palace								
2									
3		Jan	Feb	Mar	Qtr1				
4	Truffles	345	429	301	1075				
5	Chocolate Bars	249	336	274					
6	Bon Bons	396	411	371					
7	Fudge Sauce	277	158	295					
8	Brownies	196	202	249					
9									

Sheet1 / Sheet2 / Sheet3 /
Ready NUM

The formula itself shows up in the formula bar.

The formula results appear in your worksheet.

E4	▾	=	=B4+C4+D4		
	A	B	C	D	E	F
1	The Chocolate Palace					
2						
3		Jan	Feb	Mar	Qtr1	
4	Truffles	345	429	301	1075	
5	Chocolate Bars	249	336	274		
6	Bon Bons	396	411	371		
7	Fudge Sauce	277	158	295		
8	Brownies	196	202	249		
9						

5 The cell now contains the results of the calculation. Whenever you click the cell to make it active, you'll see the actual formula you entered on the formula bar.

SUMIF	▾	X	✓	=	=B4+C4+D4
		Formula result =1075		OK	Cancel
2					
3		Jan	Feb	Mar	Qtr1
4	Truffles	345	429	301	1+C4+D4

6 You can also enter formulas by first clicking the Edit Formula (=) button on the formula bar. When you use this method, you can see the results of your formula as you go. If you're satisfied you've done it correctly, click OK. If not, click Cancel and begin again.

How to Sum Numbers

In the previous topic you saw how to add numbers by building a formula in which the elements being added together were separated by plus signs. When you have to add many numbers (perhaps 12 monthly totals), this approach can be pretty cumbersome. Luckily, Excel offers the SUM function, a built-in formula that produces the same result with a great deal less effort. The SUM function is useful when you have to add numbers that are in adjacent cells, either along a row or down a column.

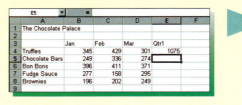

1 Click the cell where you want the sum to appear.

● SUM is just one of hundreds of Excel functions, but you probably will use only a small number of them, depending on the type of work you do. There are functions for statistical, financial, and database calculations.

● A common mistake when using functions is forgetting the equal sign or the opening parenthesis. If you forget the closing parenthesis, Excel will fill it in for you.

6 You can calculate quarterly totals for the remaining items using the same strategy. While this particular SUM function isn't briefer than a formula that uses plus signs, when you have to add a group of ten cells, or 100 cells, the SUM function will make your life much easier.

SUMIF		X √ =	=sum(		
	A	B	C	D	E	F
1	The Chocolate Palace				
2					
3		Jan	Feb	Mar	Qtr1
4	Truffles	345	429	301	1075
5	Chocolate Bars	249	336	274	=sum(
6	Bon Bons	396	411	371	
7	Fudge Sauce	277	158	295	
8	Brownies	196	202	249	
9					

 Type **=sum(**. It doesn't matter if you use lower-case or uppercase, because Excel will convert the letters to uppercase automatically. It's usually easier to use lowercase because you don't have to bother pressing the Caps Lock key.

B5 through D5

SUMIF		X √ =	=sum(b5.d5		
	A	B	C	D	E	F
1	The Chocolate Palace				
2					
3		Jan	Feb	Mar	Qtr1
4	Truffles	345	429	301	1075
5	Chocolate Bars	249	336	274	=sum(b5:d5
6	Bon Bons	396	411	371	
7	Fudge Sauce	277	158	295	
8	Brownies	196	202	249	
9					

3 If you're adding adjacent cells, type the first cell reference, then a colon (:), then the last cell reference. If the cells aren't adjacent, just list the cell references, separated by commas. A rectangular group of cells is called a *range* and is referenced by typing the address of the upper-left cell, a colon, and the address of the lower-right cell. For example, the range B2:C4 includes cells B2, B3, B4, C2, C3, and C4.

SUM function   **Result of SUM function**

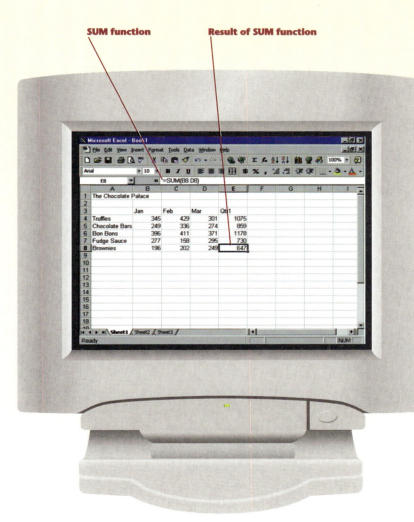

4 Type a closing parenthesis,), and click the Enter button or press the key you usually use to end data entry. The elements of the function enclosed within the parentheses are called the function's *arguments*. Most functions need at least one argument; some need more.

E5		=	=SUM(B5:D5)		
	A	B	C	D	E	F
1	The Chocolate Palace				
2					
3		Jan	Feb	Mar	Qtr1
4	Truffles	345	429	301	1075
5	Chocolate Bars	249	336	274	859
6	Bon Bons	396	411	371	
7	Fudge Sauce	277	158	295	
8	Brownies	196	202	249	
9					

5 The cell now displays the sum of the numbers from the referenced cells and the formula bar displays the SUM function when the cell is active. If you edit the data in any of the cells in the range, Excel immediately recalculates the results.

How to Enter Data Automatically

Excel has some neat tricks for speeding up data entry if the data is part of a series. For example, the days of the week, the months of the year, and numbers that follow a regular interval are all series. The tool Excel offers for this is called a *fill handle,* and you can use it to tell Excel to finish entering a series you've started.

1 Start by entering the initial data. For instance, if you want to enter labels that are the days of the week, enter the name of the day you want to start with (it need not be Monday). You can even use abbreviations (Mon) and Excel will follow your lead. After you've entered the label, make sure the cell is the active cell (notice the fill handle in the lower-right corner).

Fill handle

Because the first two times were one hour apart, Excel generates additional times separated by one hour.

7 Drag the fill handle across the cells you want to fill with data. When you release the mouse button, Excel fills in your data.

When you point to the fill handle, the mouse pointer takes on this shape.

2 Place the mouse pointer over the fill handle, which changes the pointer to a plus sign.

This ScreenTip tells you which value you've reached and helps keep you from undershooting or overshooting your mark.

3 Drag across the cells you want to use for the additional labels in the series. Excel displays a ScreenTip telling you which label will be inserted in the cell you're dragging over.

Excel generated these labels for you.

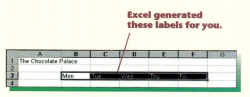

4 When you release the mouse, Excel inserts the labels automatically. You can use this technique for other data, such as Quarter1, Quarter2, and so forth.

5 You can use a similar approach to produce a series of numbers. However, you must start by entering two numbers in the series because Excel needs to see the interval between the numbers. If the first two entries are 1 and 2, Excel will continue with 3, 4, and so on. If you start with 110 and 120, Excel will continue with 130, 140 and keep going.

There's one fill handle for these two selected cells.

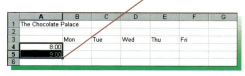

6 Once you've entered the initial two numbers, drag across them to select them as the active cells. You'll see a fill handle in the second cell (either the bottom cell or the right-most cell).

How to Navigate around Worksheets

Most worksheets are too large to fit on the screen all at once. Some Excel worksheets sprawl across dozens of columns and hundreds of rows. For example, a personnel worksheet may contain pay and benefits information for hundreds of employees. A worksheet with a company's financial figures may cover every month in the year. While you can scroll through the worksheet to bring cells into view, there are some faster ways to move around in a large worksheet.

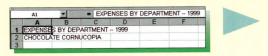

1 To move to cell A1, press Ctrl+Home. This handy keystroke combination moves you straight back to the upper-left corner of your worksheet, no matter which cell you were working in.

● Scrolling changes your view of the worksheet, but it doesn't change the active cell. That means sometimes when you scroll you may lose sight of which cell is the active cell. Check the formula bar, which indicates the current active cell.

● Use Ctrl+G (or F5) to open the Go To dialog box without using the menu bar.

7 A quick way to move up, down, left, or right through columns and rows is to double-click on the appropriate border of the active cell. For instance, if the active cell is within a column of numbers and you click on the bottom border of that cell, Excel activates the last entry in that column. If you double-click on the cell's left border, Excel activates the leftmost cell in that row that contains data.

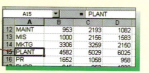

Last cell in active area

Beginning of row

2 Press Ctrl+End to move to the lower right cell in the active area of the worksheet. This cell is the intersection of the last nonblank column and last nonblank row in your worksheet.

3 To move to the beginning of the current row, press Home.

End of row

4 To move to the last nonblank cell in the current row, press End, then press Enter.

Several columns of data are out of view.

Several rows of data are out of view.

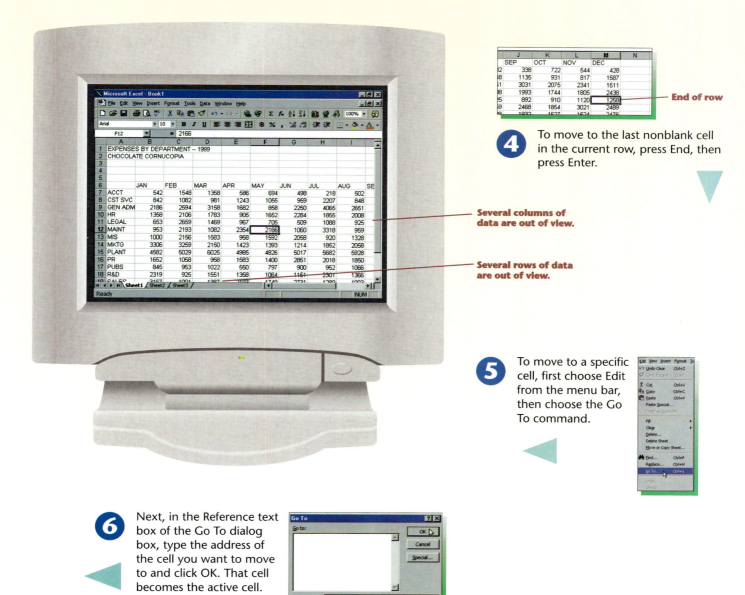

5 To move to a specific cell, first choose Edit from the menu bar, then choose the Go To command.

6 Next, in the Reference text box of the Go To dialog box, type the address of the cell you want to move to and click OK. That cell becomes the active cell.

How to Insert Columns and Rows

To add new data to a worksheet, you almost always have to make room for it. Suppose you have a personnel worksheet on which the rows are arranged in alphabetical order by last name. When a new employee joins the company you can't just stick the name at the bottom of the list. Instead you have to insert the name in the proper alphabetical order. To do this, you have to add a new blank row in the worksheet.

Insert one row above row 6.

	A	B	C	D	E
1	VACATION DAYS ACCRUED AND USED, 1999				
2					
3	LAST	FIRST	1/1 BAL	JAN	FEB
4	Eng	Stephanie	14	-12	1
5	Fuentes	Carla	9	1	-2
6	Lambert	Charles	2	1	1
7	Rothstein	Jay	7	1	1
8	Tashjian	Doris	0	1	1
9					

1 If you want to insert a single row, first activate any cell in the row above the place you want to insert the new row. To insert multiple rows, select a cell in each of the same number of rows. For instance, to insert three rows below row 5, select three cells, one each from rows 5, 6, and 7.

FYI

● When you insert rows or columns and the existing columns and rows are shifted, any formulas that have references to the pre-existing data are updated to reflect the new cell addresses.

● If you add data within the range of an existing formula, the new results are calculated automatically. For example, if your worksheet has the function =SUM(D4:D8) and you add a new row of data above row 6, the function would automatically change to =SUM(D4:D9). However, if you add a row below row 8 or above row 4 and want that row included, you have to go to the cell that has the function and change the data to reflect the new row.

2 Choose Rows from the Insert menu. Excel inserts one or more blank rows, nudging existing data downward as needed. You could also right-click on a row number and choose Insert from the shortcut menu that appears.

	A	B	C	D	E	F	G
1	VACATION DAYS ACCRUED AND USED, 1999						
2							
3	LAST	FIRST	1/1 BAL	JAN	FEB	MAR	BALANCE
4	Eng	Stephanie	14	-12	1	1	4
5	Fuentes	Carla	9	1	-2	1	9
6	Galante	Al	0	0	0	0	0
7	Lambert	Charles	2	1	1	1	5
8	Rothstein	Jay	7	1	1	-5	4
9	Tashjian	Doris	0	1	1	1	3

3 Now you can add data to the new row(s) in the normal fashion.

VACATION

VACATION DAYS ACCRUED AND USED, 1999		EMP #	1/1 BAL	JAN	FEB	MAR	BALANCE
LAST	FIRST					1	4
Eng	Stephanie	3	14	-12	1	1	9
Fuentes	Carla	1	9	1	-2	1	5
Lambert	Charles	5	2	1	1	-5	4
Rothstein	Jay		7	1	1	1	3
Tashjian	Doris	4	0	1			

Please add a new employee AL GALANTE employee #6 vacation balance Ø.

Page 1

	A	B	C
1	VACATION DAYS ACCRUED AI		
2			
3	LAST	FIRST	1/1 BAL
4	Eng	Stephanie	14
5	Fuentes	Carla	9
6	Galante	Al	0
7	Lambert	Charles	2
8	Rothstein	Jay	7
9	Tashjian	Doris	0

Insert one column to the left of column C.

4 If you want to insert one column, first activate any cell in the column to the left of the place you want to insert the column. To insert multiple columns, select a cell in each of the desired number of columns.

5 Choose Columns from the Insert menu. Excel inserts one or more blank columns, shifting any existing data to the right. You could also right-click on a column letter and choose Insert from the shortcut menu.

	A	B	C	D	E
1	VACATION DAYS ACCRUED AND USED, 1999				
2					
3	LAST	FIRST	EMP #	1/1 BAL	JAN
4	Eng	Stephanie	3	14	-12
5	Fuentes	Carla	1	9	1
6	Galante	Al	6	0	0
7	Lambert	Charles	5	2	1
8	Rothstein	Jay	2	7	1
9	Tashjian	Doris	4	0	1

6 You can now add data to the new columns or rows as you normally would.

How to Delete or Clear Cells

There are two ways to erase data from your worksheets. You can *delete* cells, removing them from the worksheet and closing up the vacated space (the cells below or to the right move in to the space). Or you can *clear* cells, which means you delete the contents of the cells, leaving them there (but empty). For example, in a personnel worksheet, you could delete a row for an employee who is no longer with the company. On the other hand, if the employee is still with the company but the information has changed, or was entered incorrectly, you would only clear the cells.

	A	B	C	D	E
1	VACATION DAYS ACCRUED AND USED, 1999				
2					
3	LAST	FIRST	EMP #	1/1 BAL	JAN
4	Eng	Stephanie	3	14	-12
5	Fuentes	Carla	1	9	1
6	Galante	Al	6	0	0
7	Lambert	Charles	5	2	1
8	Rothstein	Jay	2	7	1
9	Tashjian	Doris	4	0	1

1 To delete a single row or column, first activate any cell in the row or column. You can also select at least one cell in each of multiple adjacent rows or columns. To delete specific cells, select them. (Remember, these cells will be deleted, not cleared.)

All
Formats
Contents   Del
Comments

6 If you want to get fancy when clearing cells, choose Clear from the Edit menu to display this submenu. Choosing All clears the contents of the cells in addition to clearing any formatting and special comments. Choosing Formats clears formatting associated with the cells (bold, italic, and so on) but doesn't clear the contents. Choosing Contents clears the contents but keeps the formatting. Choosing Comments clears special comments but leaves everything else intact.

FYI

● When you delete cells, and data shifts to replace them, Excel automatically adjusts any formulas that refer to the shifted data so they continue to produce the correct results.

● When you need to replace data, there's often no point in clearing the cell and then entering the new data. You can simply activate the cell and enter the new data, which automatically replaces the old data. It's often not a good idea to use this method for multiple cells because you may not remember to change all the cells.

Choose Delete from the Edit menu, or right-click on one of the selected cells and choose Delete from the shortcut menu. Don't press the Del key.

In the Delete dialog box, select the Entire Row option button to delete one or more adjacent rows. Select the Entire Column option button to delete one or more adjacent columns. To delete the selected cells without removing the entire column or row, choose Shift Cells Left or Shift Cells Up. Click OK to complete the process.

To delete entire columns or rows without having to use the Delete dialog box, select the column or row (or multiple columns or rows) and choose Delete from the Edit menu or right-click and choose Delete from the shortcut menu.

To clear any number of cells, from a single one to the entire worksheet, just select them and press the Del key.

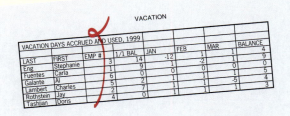

VACATION

VACATION DAYS ACCRUED AND USED, 1999							
LAST	FIRST	EMP #	1/1 BAL	JAN	FEB	MAR	BALANCE
							4
LAST		3	14	-12	1	1	4
Eng	Stephanie	1	9	1	-2	1	9
Fuentes	Carla	6	0	0	0	0	0
Galante	Al	5	2	1	1	1	5
Lambert	Charles	2	7	1	1	-5	4
Rothstein	Jay	4	0	1	1	1	3
Tashjian	Doris						

Page 1

How to Move and Copy Data with Drag and Drop

Drag-and-drop editing is an easy, intuitive operation. This feature lets you move or copy data by dragging it where you want it with your mouse, and then dropping it into place. It's especially effective for moving or copying data to areas that are currently visible on the screen.

Range to move or copy

1 Activate the cell or select the range of cells you want to move or copy.

- When you move cells, formulas that refer to these cells individually are updated. But cell ranges in formulas are updated only if you move the entire range of cells referenced in the formula. Double-check your formulas after you move cells.

- You can drag and drop data between worksheets and between workbooks. To move material to a new workbook, make sure both workbooks are visible and simply drag the data from one to the other. (Use the Ctrl key if you're copying instead of moving.) To move data to a different worksheet within the same workbook, hold down the Alt key while dragging over the desired worksheet tab. (Use both Alt and Ctrl if you're copying data instead of moving it.) Once Excel puts you in the new worksheet, continue dragging until you have the data in the right spot, then release the mouse button.

Cells will be inserted here, pushing the Balance column to the right.

7 To avoid overwriting cells with data in them, hold down the Shift key before releasing the mouse button. The rectangular outline mentioned in step 3 changes to a vertical or horizontal I-beam, indicating where the cells will be inserted. This also indicates whether the existing cells will be pushed to the right (the vertical I-beam) or downward (the horizontal I-beam).

6 If you drop cells you're moving into an occupied area of the worksheet, Excel asks whether you want to overwrite the cells that have data in them. Click OK if you do, or Cancel if you don't. Warning: You will not be alerted if you are copying instead of moving.

2 Point to the border of the cell or range so the mouse pointer changes into an arrow. You can point to any border, but don't point to the fill handle in the lower-right corner.

Mouse pointer for moving or copying

ScreenTip indicating destination range

Destination

3 Hold down the left mouse button and drag the selected cells to the desired spot. A rectangular outline shows you where the cells you are moving or copying will be inserted if you release the mouse button at that point. A ScreenTip also tells you what range the cells will be inserted into.

VACATION

DRAG & DROP

4 To move the cells, simple release the mouse button when the outline is where you want it.

5 To copy the cells, hold down the Ctrl key as you release the mouse button. Be sure you don't release Ctrl before you release the mouse button. Notice that the mouse pointer changes into an arrow with a little plus sign attached.

Pointer with attached plus sign indicating copy operation

How to Move and Copy Data with the Clipboard

As easy as drag and drop seems, there are times when it's a bit difficult. Dragging over long distances can be a slippery proposition. And sometimes when you're dragging large blocks of data, it's hard to maneuver and keep an eye on what you're doing at the same time. In these situations you can take advantage of the Windows Clipboard, which is a temporary storage area where you can stash data. You can paste the data from the Clipboard back into a different area of the same worksheet, into a new worksheet, into a new workbook, or even into certain other Windows programs.

1 Activate the cell or select the range of cells you want to move or copy (same as the drag-and-drop technique).

6 After choosing where to insert the Clipboard data, you can click the Paste toolbar button to insert the data.

● Another convenient shortcut for the Paste command is the Enter key. Just issue the Cut or Copy command (using your preferred method), activate the new location, and press Enter.

● Data you paste from the Clipboard into a worksheet overwrites any data already in the target cell(s). Therefore, be sure to check the target location carefully to make sure it's empty or it has data you planned to replace.

2 Choose Cut or Copy from the Edit menu. The Cut command removes the data from your worksheet as it places it on the Clipboard. A flashing border around the selected cells (called a *marquee*) indicates that the data is on the Clipboard.

3 Select the cell where you want to paste the data. You don't have to select a range the size of the range you cut or copied; the cell you select becomes the upper-left cell of the block of data being pasted.

4 Choose Paste from the Edit menu. If you use Cut, the data is moved to the new location, if you use Copy the data is inserted in the new location and still exists in the original location.

The Cut button

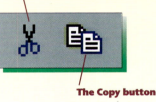

The Copy button

5 If you're fond of mouse shortcuts, you'll like the Cut and Copy toolbar buttons, which you can use to cut or copy the selected data to the CLipboard.

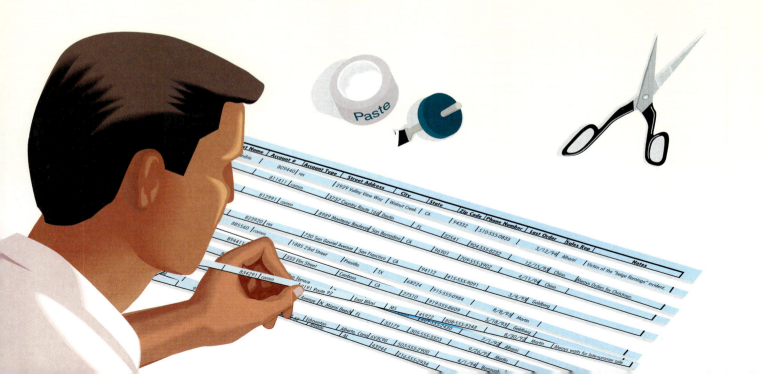

How to Adjust Column Width

Excel's columns often aren't wide enough to accommodate long headings and large numbers. As a result, several things can happen. Text entries spill over into cells to the right if the cells are empty; otherwise the display of text is cut off. Numbers with many decimal places may appear to lose some digits to the right of the decimal point. And large numbers are displayed either in scientific notation or as overflow markers (#####). To display the complete contents of cells, you can widen the column. And, you can narrow columns so they aren't any wider than they need to be in order to display their (shorter) contents.

Mouse pointer indicating that you can drag to change the column's width

1 Point to the line at the right of the column heading you want to change. Notice the mouse pointer changes its shape.

5 If you want to change the width of several columns at the same time, select them (they don't have to be adjacent) and then adjust one. All the selected columns are adjusted to the same width.

● Even if the display of data is truncated, it's all there (Excel keeps track of it). The full data is displayed in the formula bar when the cell is active, and used when the cell is referenced in a formula or function.

● You can adjust row heights in the same way you adjust column widths. Point to the bottom of the row heading and then drag up or down to change the height of the row. You can select several rows and adjust their heights all at once by manipulating any one of them.

Current column width

| A3 | Width: 10.43 | = | LAST NAME |
| A | B | C | D |

1 VACATION DAYS ACCRUED AND USED.
2
3 LAST NAM FIRST NAI EMPLOYE JAN 1. BA
4 Eng Stephanie 3 14
5 Fuentes Carla 1 9
6 Galante Al 6 0
7 Lambert Charles 5 2
8 Rothstein Jay 2 7
9 Tashjian Doris 4 0

Dotted vertical line indicating width of column if you release mouse button now

2 Hold down the left mouse button and drag to the right to widen the column (drag left to make it narrower). A vertical line displays showing you what your changes look like, and a ScreenTip indicates the column's current width as you drag.

3 Release the mouse button and check the new width. Is the data still truncated? Is the column too wide and wasting space?

| A | B | C |
1 VACATION DAYS ACCRUED AND
2
3 LAST NAME FIRST NAI EMPLOYE
4 Eng Stephanie 3
5 Fuentes Carla 1
6 Galante Al 6
7 Lambert Charles 5
8 Rothstein Jay 2
9 Tashjian Doris 4

4 Repeat steps 1 through 3 as needed to make further adjustments to this column, or to adjust another column.

VACATION

VACATION DAYS, 1999							
LAST NAME	FIRST NAME	EMPLOYEE #	JAN. 1 BALANCE	JANUARY	FEBRUARY	MARCH	BALANCE
Eng	Stephanie	3	14	-12	1	1	4
Fuentes	Carla	1	9	1	-2	1	9
Galante	Al	6	0	0	0	0	0
Lambert	Charles	5	2	1	1	1	5
Rothstein	Jay	2	7	1	1	-5	4
Tashjian	Doris	4	0	1	1	1	3

Page 1

How to Format Numbers in Cells

E xcel provides a wide assortment of number formats that let you dress up your numbers with dollar signs, commas for thousands separators, percent symbols, and more. Like font characteristics, number formats apply to cells rather than the specific data contained in the cells.

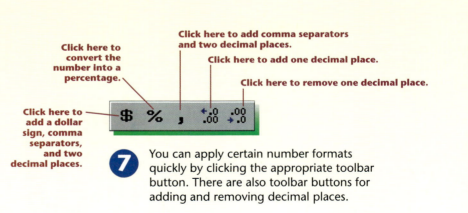

	A	B	C	D	E	F	G	H
1	ADMINISTRATIVE EXPENSES							
2	First Quarter, 1999							
3								
4		January	February	March	Total	Last Year	Difference	
5	Accounting	542	1548	1358	3448	2201	0.5666	
6	General Admin.	2186	2594	3158	7938	7260	0.0934	
7	Maintenance	953	2193	1082	4228	4880	-0.1336	
8	Marketing	3306	3259	2150	8715	5570	0.5646	
9	R&D	3658	4102	3959	11719	7590	0.544	
10	Sales	6258	5277	5960	17495	16299	0.0734	
11	Warehouse	580	885	411	1876	1506	0.2457	
12								
13	Totals	17483	19858	18078	55419	45306	0.2233	
14								

1 Activate the cell for which you want to change the number format or select a range of cells you want to format in the same manner.

Click here to add comma separators and two decimal places.

Click here to convert the number into a percentage.

Click here to add one decimal place.

Click here to remove one decimal place.

Click here to add a dollar sign, comma separators, and two decimal places.

$ % , +.0 .00 .00 +.0

7 You can apply certain number formats quickly by clicking the appropriate toolbar button. There are also toolbar buttons for adding and removing decimal places.

● To remove number formatting, select the cells to be affected, go to the Number portion of the Format Cells dialog box and choose the General format as the category.

● If you type a number that includes commas as thousands separators into a cell that has no number format, Excel assigns the number format automatically. Likewise, if you enter a dollar sign or a percent symbol, Excel assigns the currency or percentage format automatically.

Sample
$542

6 To preview your formatted numbers, look at the display in the Sample section. If it doesn't look quite right, continue tinkering in the dialog box until it is just the way you want it. Then click OK.

2 Choose Cells from the Format menu, or right-click on one of the selected cells and choose Format Cells from the shortcut menu.

3 At the top of the Format Cells dialog box, click on the Number tab if it's not already in the foreground.

LawnBirds, Inc.

ADMINISTRATIVE EXPENSES
First Quarter, 1999

	January	February	March	Total	Last Year	Difference
Accounting	$542	$1,548	$1,358	$3,448	$2,201	56.66%
General Admin.	$2,186	$2,594	$3,158	$7,938	$7,260	9.34%
Maintenance	$953	$2,193	$1,082	$4,228	$4,880	-13.36%
Marketing	$3,306	$3,259	$2,150	$8,715	$5,570	56.46%
R&D	$3,658	$4,102	$3,959	$11,719	$7,590	54.40%
Sales	$6,258	$5,277	$5,960	$17,495	$16,299	7.34%
Warehouse	$580	$885	$411	$1,876	$1,506	24.57%
Totals	$17,483	$19,858	$18,078	$55,419	$45,306	22.32%

4 In the Category list box, choose the type of number you want to display. For example, click on Currency if you are working with dollar figures. If you're not sure what a particular category is for, click on it and read the description at the bottom of the dialog box.

5 Depending on the category you select, you may be able to choose the number of decimal places, a currency symbol, or how you display negative numbers. For example, if you want to display numbers with preceding dollar signs, but no decimal places, select Currency as the category, then enter 0 in the Decimal Places text box and leave the Symbol setting at $. By default, negative numbers are displayed with a minus sign in front of them. You can opt to display them in red text with no minus sign, in black text within parentheses, or in red text within parentheses.

How to Use Functions

These pages present four of Excel's most useful functions: MAX, MIN, AVERAGE, and COUNT. A function is a built-in formula, like the SUM function, which lets you add the contents of numerous cells without having to add each cell separately. Some Excel functions, however, don't merely duplicate standard formulas, but instead perform actions for which you couldn't create a formula.

	A	B	C	D	E	F	G	H	I
1			VACATION DAYS ACCRUED AND USED, 1999						
2									
3	Last Name	First Name	Emp #	1/1 Balance	January	February	March	Balance	
4	Eng	Stephanie	3	14	-12	1	1	4	
5	Fuentes	Carla	1	9	1	-2	1	9	
6	Lambert	Charles	5	2	1	1	1	5	
7	Rothstein	Jay	2	7	1	1	-5	4	
8	Tashjian	Doris	4	0	1	1	1	3	
9									
10							High:		
11							Low:		
12							Avg:		
13									

 1 Activate the cell in which you want the function result to appear.

The equal sign is missing, so Excel doesn't perform the calculation.

High:	MAX(H4:H8)	
Low:	3	
Avg:	5	

 6 Common mistakes when entering functions include misspelling the function name and forgetting the equal sign or the opening parenthesis (Excel will add the closing one if you forget it). If Excel issues an error message or the result looks completely wrong, check for these mistakes, then edit your entry.

● You can type function names in uppercase, lowercase, or a combination of both. Excel automatically converts them to uppercase.

● To include noncontiguous ranges or cells in any function, separate each entry with a comma; for instance =MIN(b4:d8,f4:g8,i10:j10.

2 Enter the function =MAX(range) to display the largest number in the designated range. *Range* is the function's argument, the values on which the function operates. The argument can be a single cell, a range of cells, or several cells separated by commas. Here the range is H4:H8, the balance values for all employees.

March	Balance
1	4
1	9
1	5
-5	4
1	3
High:	=max(H4:H8)
Low:	
Avg:	

High:	9
Low:	=min(H4:H8)
Avg:	

3 Enter the function =MIN(range) to display the smallest number in the designated range.

LawnBirds, Inc.

VACATION DAYS ACCRUED AND USED, 1999

Last Name	First Name	Emp #	1/1 Balance	January	February	March	Balance
Eng	Stephanie	3	14	-12	1	1	4
Fuentes	Carla	1	9	1	-2	1	9
Lambert	Charles	5	2	1	1	1	5
Rothstein	Jay	2	7	1	1	-5	4
Tashjian	Doris	4	0	1	1	1	3

High:	9
Low:	3
Avg:	5

High:	9
Low:	3
Avg:	=average(H4:H8)

4 Enter the function = AVERAGE(range) to display the average of the numbers in the designated range. The AVERAGE function sums the numbers in the range and divides the result by the number of values summed.

5 If you had a lot of employees and wanted to determine exactly how many there were, you could use the COUNT function, as shown here. This function counts any column or row that contains numbers, since its purpose is to determine how many cells in the designated range contain numbers.

High:	9
Low:	3
Avg:	5
Count:	=count(H4:H8)

How to Work with Absolute References

When you use the fill handle to create multiple formulas, the formula cell references change automatically to reflect the correct addresses. These are called *relative references.* But sometimes you don't want cell references to change when you copy formulas. References that don't change are called *absolute references.* In these pages you'll learn how to create absolute references (and why you would want to).

1 First, enter a standard formula and copy it with the fill handle. The formula shown here calculates the correct bonus for Stephanie Eng by multiplying her base pay by the percentage listed in cell B12.

7 If you like, click on one of the cells containing a copied formula to inspect the results. For instance, here the reference to D6 was appropriately changed to D10, but the reference to B12, the cell containing the multiplier, did not change.

- Don't worry when moving a cell that is referenced absolutely somewhere else in the worksheet. For example, you may have the formula =C3*D13, and then move the contents of D13 to D15. The references to the cell adjust automatically to reflect the new location of the cell and they remain absolute, so the formula changes to =C3*D15.

- The reason to reference the cell containing the multiplier instead of including the multiplier in every calculation is that if you want to change the multiplier, you only have to change the cell. You don't have to edit every formula.

6 Again drag the fill handle to copy the formula in E6 down column E. This time you'll get the correct results, to the relief of the employees.

2 Drag the fill handle to copy this formula down column E.

The inaccurate results indicate that these cells contain incorrect formulas.

3 When you release the mouse button, you see these results. What went wrong? Why does Stephanie seem to be the only one in line for a bonus?

LawnBirds, Inc.

	A	B	C	D	E
1		1999 BONUS CALCULATION			
2					
3	Department Heads				
4					
5	Last Name	First Name	Emp #	Base Pay	Bonus
6	Eng	Stephanie	3	$51,935.50	$3,635.49
7	Fuentes	Carla	1	$68,945.03	$4,826.15
8	Lambert	Charles	5	$38,935.49	$2,725.48
9	Rothstein	Jay	2	$42,412.43	$2,968.87
10	Tashjian	Doris	4	$40,095.83	$2,806.71
11					
12	Multiplier:	7%			

E7   =D7*B13

	A	B	C	D	E
1		1999 BONUS CALCULATION			
2					
3	Department Heads				
4					
5	Last Name	First Name	Emp #	Base Pay	Bonus
6	Eng	Stephanie	3	$51,935.50	$3,635.49
7	Fuentes	Carla	1	$68,945.03	$0.00
8	Lambert	James	5	$38,935.49	$0.00
9	Rothstein	Jay	2	$42,412.43	$0.00
10	Tashjian	Doris	4	$40,095.83	$0.00
11					
12	Multiplier:	7%			

4 Highlight one of the cells containing $0.00, and an erroneous formula. For example, here you can see that cell E7 contains the formula =D7*B13. The original reference to D6 was changed to D7, to refer to Carla Fuentes' base pay. That much makes sense. But the reference to the multiplier in cell B12 was also changed to B13, which is an empty cell. Instead, the reference to cell B12 must remain unchanged—it needs to be an absolute reference.

The dollar signs indicate an absolute reference.

5 Double-click on cell E6. Then type dollar signs in front of the column letter and row number in B12 (B12), and press Enter. The reference to B12 is now absolute and it will not change. The reference to D6 will adjust itself to its new surroundings when you manipulate it.

E6   =D6*B12

	A	B	C	D	E
1		1999 BONUS CALCULATION			
2					
3	Department Heads				
4					
5	Last Name	First Name	Emp #	Base Pay	Bonus
6	Eng	Stephanie	3	$51,935.50	$3,635.49

How to Name Ranges

When referring to ranges of cells, so far we've used notation (B6:C7, for example). This is a convenient method, especially when using large ranges. But you could also assign names to cells or ranges, making your formulas easier to enter and easier to read.

	A	B	C
1	ADMINISTRATIVE EXPENSES		
2	Second Quarter, 1999		
3			
4		April	May
5	Accounting	$642	$1,648
6	General Admin.	$2,286	$2,694
7	Maintenance	$1,053	$2,293
8	Marketing	$3,406	$3,359
9	R&D	$3,756	$4,202
10	Sales	$6,358	$5,378
11	Warehouse	$680	$985
12			

1 Select the cell or range of cells you want to name.

Natural language formula

B15	= =April Sales+May Sales		
	A	B	C	D
1	ADMINISTRATIVE EXPENSES			
2	Second Quarter, 1999			
3				
4		April	May	June
5	Accounting	$642	$1,648	$1,458
6	General Admin.	$2,286	$2,694	$3,258
7	Maintenance	$1,053	$2,293	$1,182
8	Marketing	$3,406	$3,359	$2,251
9	R&D	$3,756	$4,202	$4,060
10	Sales	$6,358	$5,378	$6,060
11	Warehouse	$680	$985	$511
12				
13	Totals	$18,181	$20,559	$18,780
14				
15		11,736		

- If you want to delete existing names, just choose Name from the Insert menu and choose Define to display the Define Name dialog box. From there you can delete names by highlighting them and clicking the Delete button.

- If you decide to change a name, choose Name from the Insert menu and then choose Define. Click on the name to be changed. Then click in the Names in Workbook text box, edit the name as desired, and click on Add. Finally, click on the original name (because you'll have two names for the same range) and click the Delete button.

8 Sometimes you can refer to labels without going through the naming rigamarole by using what are called *natural language formulas*. For example, in the worksheet shown here, you could enter =April Sales+May Sales to find the total for those two months, or you could enter =Marketing+Sales in column E to find the quarterly totals for Marketing and Sales. Natural language formulas are not always easier to type than regular formulas, but they are always much easier to read.

The Name box

2 Click on the Name box at the left end of the formula bar. Type a name for the range and press Enter. The name can be up to 255 characters and must begin with a letter or an underscore (it's best to use a short, descriptive name). The name can include letters, numbers, periods and underlines, but cannot include spaces or other special characters (except for the backslash and the question mark).

3 If you want to use existing labels as names, select the range of cells to be named along with the labels.

4 Choose Name from the Insert menu and choose Create from the submenu. One of the best things about this technique is that you can use it to create several names at one time.

5 In the Create Names dialog box, choose Top Row if the labels to be used as names are above the range you're naming. Choose one of the other options if your labels are in a different location. Then click OK.

6 To select a named range, click the down arrow to the right of the Name box. Then click on the name of the desired range in the drop-down list that appears.

7 To use a named cell or range in a formula, enter the formula as usual, but instead of entering the cells or ranges, choose Name from the Insert menu, choose Paste and select the named range from the Paste Name dialog box. If you remember the name, you can type it in directly.

How to Search for Data

S ometimes you want to see only selected portions of your data, especially when your worksheets grow quite large. Excel lets you temporarily "filter" your data, searching for and displaying only the data that meets certain conditions. In these pages you'll learn some of the simple ways to weed excess data out of your worksheet so you can concentrate on the data you need.

Field names

	A	B	C	D	E	F
1	*Projected Salary Increases for 1999*					
2						
3	Department Heads					
4						
5					Projected	Projected
6	Last Name	First Name	Emp. #	1998 Base	% Increase	1999 Base
7	Eng	Stephanie	3	$51,935.50	4%	$54,012.92
8	Savage-Hill	Terry	6	$59,100.00	4%	$61,464.00
9	Martin	Samantha	9	$46,092.83	7%	$49,319.33
10	Bernard	James	8	$36,700.00	7%	$39,269.00
11	Blochner	Hobart	7	$53,082.48	4%	$55,205.78
12	Fuentes	Carla	1	$68,945.03	4%	$71,702.83
13	Lambert	Charles	5	$38,935.49	7%	$41,660.97
14	Rothstein	Jay	2	$42,412.43	7%	$45,381.30
15	Tashjian	Doris	4	$40,095.83	7%	$42,902.54

— Record

— Field

1 If your list is separated from any other data in the worksheet by at least one column and row, select any cell in your list. Otherwise, select the entire list.

Last Name	First Name	Emp.	1998 Ba	Projected % Increa	Projected 1999 Ba
Eng	Stephanie	3	$51,935.50	4%	$54,012.92
Savage-Hill	Terry	6	$59,100.00	4%	$61,464.00
Martin	Samantha	9	$46,092.83	7%	$49,319.33
Blochner	Hobart	7	$53,082.48	4%	$55,205.78
Fuentes	Carla	1	$68,945.03	4%	$71,702.83

9 When you've made the selections you need, click OK to see the filtered version of your list. Notice that rows 10, and 13–15 are hidden here because those employees aren't among the top five money earners.

8 Select the number of values you want to view from the middle spin box. You can also view the bottom of the list (for instance, the lowest-paid employees) by choosing Bottom from the leftmost drop-down list. You can also view a percentage of the top or bottom of the list by choosing Percent (instead of Items) from the rightmost drop-down list.

● AutoFilter does not delete data from your worksheet, it just hides records temporarily.

● When your list is filtered, Excel changes the color of the row numbers to remind you that you aren't viewing the entire list; also notice that row numbers aren't consecutive because data is missing (filtered out).

2 Choose Filter from the Data menu, and then choose AutoFilter from the submenu that appears.

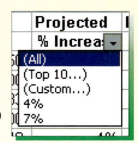

Drop-down arrows

Last Name	First Name	Emp. #	1998 Base	Projected % Increase	Projected 1999 Base
Eng	Stephanie	3	$51,935.50	4%	$54,012.92
Savage-Hill	Terry	6	$59,100.00	4%	$61,464.00
Martin	Samantha	9	$46,092.83	7%	$49,319.33
Bernard	James	8	$36,700.00	7%	$39,269.00
Blochner	Hobart	7	$53,082.48	4%	$55,205.78
Fuentes	Carla	1	$68,945.03	4%	$71,702.83

3 Each field name now has a drop-down arrow associated with it. These arrows let you filter the list by values in particular fields (columns). For example, in this worksheet you could choose to view only the records of employees who are up for a 7 percent raise. There's a value of 7% in the Projected % Increase field for their records.

awnBirds, Inc.

Projected Salary Increases for 1999

Department Heads

Last Name	First Name	Emp. #	1998 Base	Projected % Increase	Projected 1999 Base
Eng	Stephanie	3	$51,935.50	4%	$54,012.92
Savage-Hill	Terry	6	$59,100.00	4%	$61,464.00
Martin	Samantha	9	$46,092.83	7%	$49,319.33
Bernard	James	8	$36,700.00	7%	$39,269.00
Blochner	Hobart	7	$53,082.48	4%	$55,205.78
Fuentes	Carla	1	$68,945.03	4%	$71,702.83
Lambert	Charles	5	$38,935.49	7%	$41,660.97
Rothstein	Jay	2	$42,412.43	7%	$45,381.30
Tashjian	Doris	4	$40,095.83	7%	$42,902.54
		Totals:	$437,299.59		$460,918.67

4 Click on any drop-down arrow. The list that appears shows the contents of each cell in the column, plus some special entries such as (All) and (Custom …).

Lou,
Please run the numbers and see what happens if we give a 7% increase to everyone making under 50,000.
Betty

Last Name	First Name	Emp. #	1998 Base	Projected % Increase	Projected 1999 Base
Martin	Samantha	9	$46,092.83	7%	$49,319.33
Bernard	James	8	$36,700.00	7%	$39,269.00
Lambert	Charles	5	$38,935.49	7%	$41,660.97
Rothstein	Jay	2	$42,412.43	7%	$45,381.30
Tashjian	Doris	4	$40,095.83	7%	$42,902.54

5 When you choose a particular item from the list, Excel filters out all the records that don't match that selected value. For instance, if you choose 7% from the Projected % Increase list, Excel filters out every employee that isn't attached to that value. You can set up several such filters in order to see as many records as you need to.

7 To display the top ten values in a particular field (or the top eight, or top three, and so on), choose the Top 10 item from the appropriate drop-down list. This is a good way to see, for example, the highest paid employees. Ignore the name of this dialog box—it should be named Top Whatever You Want (you can choose to view from 1 to 500 items).

6 If you want to view all the records again, choose (All) from the same drop-down list.

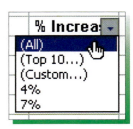

How to Sort Data

Besides filtering out data, you can change or control the way you look at data by sorting it: arranging information in a certain order. When you sort data, you arrange it by the contents of one or more fields (columns). For example, you could sort a list alphabetically by last name. Or you could sort by financial information, looking at data from the highest figure to the lowest. The best thing about sorting data is that you're not stuck with any particular arrangement of your data. If you sort a list one way, then decide to view it from another perspective, it's easy to issue another sort command to rearrange the records again.

 Activate any cell in your list and choose Sort from the Data menu to bring up the Sort dialog box.

 To sort a list quickly in descending order, use the same process as step 7, but use the Sort Descending toolbar button.

 For a quicker way to sort a list in ascending order, select a cell in the column you want to sort, then click the Sort Ascending toolbar button. You can only sort on a single column this way.

● Always save your worksheet immediately before performing a sort. Then, if the sort doesn't work out as planned, you just close the worksheet without saving it and then open it again (in its pre-sorted state).

● Sorting the results of an AutoFilter, and then printing or charting it, is a great way to pull out snippets of data for a presentation or report. For example, you could filter a list of employees with more than five years of service, and then sort the resulting list in descending order by years of service.

Department Summary (Ranked by budget size)				
Department	**Headquarters**	**Dept. Head**	**1999 Budget**	**# Employees**
Manufacturing	Emeryville	Tashjian	$5,465,900	26
R&D	San Francisco	Lambert	$4,958,300	20
Marketing	San Francisco	Eng	$4,109,373	12
Sales	Chapel Hill	Savage-Hill	$3,100,000	16
Shipping	Emeryville	Rothstein	$3,100,000	14
Cust. Service	San Francisco	Martin	$1,894,380	7
Maintenance	Emeryville	Blochner	$1,258,445	10
Genl. Admin.	San Francisco	Fuentes	$1,009,894	8
Accounting	San Francisco	Bernard	$902,435	7

 When you have finished making selections in the Sort dialog box, click OK and Excel begins the sorting process.

Sort from highest to lowest.

2 Under Sort By, click the drop-down arrow to display a list of fields to sort by. Select the field you want to use to sort your list. In this case, the choice is the 1999 Budget field.

3 By default, Excel sorts in ascending order (lowest to highest, A to Z, or earliest to latest dates). If you want to sort in descending order instead, select the Descending option button in the Sort By area.

LawnBirds, Inc.

Department Summary
(Ranked by budget size)

Department	Headquarters	Dept. Head	1999 Budget	# Employees
Manufacturing	Emeryville	Tashjian	$5,465,900	26
R&D	San Francisco	Lambert	$4,958,300	20
Marketing	San Francisco	Eng	$4,109,373	12
Sales	Chapel Hill	Savage-Hill	$3,100,000	16
Shipping	Emeryville	Rothstein	$3,100,000	14
Cust. Service	San Francisco	Martin	$1,894,380	7
Maintenance	Emeryville	Blochner	$1,258,445	10
Genl. Admin.	San Francisco	Fuentes	$1,009,894	8
Accounting	San Francisco	Bernard	$902,435	7

Departments with the same budget are sorted in alphabetical order.

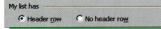

5 By default, the Header Row option button is selected under My List Has. This prevents Excel from using the data in the column headings in the sorting scheme. If you don't use column headings and you do want to include the top row in the sort, select the No Header Row option button.

4 You may want to sort by one or two additional fields (this can be useful for breaking ties); these fields are called *subsorts*. If so, repeat steps 2 and 3 to specify a sort field and sort order. This is a way, for instance, to sort names by last name, then first name, then city.

How to Use the ChartWizard

Excel's ChartWizard guides you step by step through the charting process, asking you which data to chart, which type of chart to create, and which special features (legends, titles, and so on) to add to your chart. There are a lot of options available, and the ChartWizard makes it very easy to design exactly what you need.

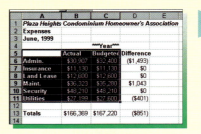

1 Select the data you want to chart. Be sure to include any column and row headings you want to use within the graph. If you forget this step, though, you can always select the data later from within the ChartWizard. Be careful *not* to include totals or you'll skew the chart.

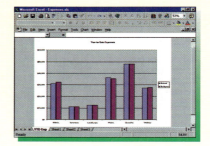

8 If you chose As New Sheet, Excel places your chart in a chart sheet it adds to your workbook. The chart practically fills the sheet.

● **Starting with the second ChartWizard dialog box, you can click the Back button to move backward and change previously made decisions.**

● **You don't have to go through any special procedure to save a chart, because it's saved with the workbook (which you do save, of course). Saving the workbook saves all the charts within it, whether they are on chart sheets of their own or on worksheets that contain data.**

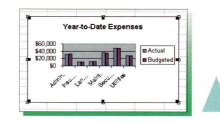

7 If you elected to place your chart in a specific worksheet, the chart may obscure some of the data in the worksheet. Use the Chart toolbar to change the placement and size if you wish.

2 Choose Chart from the Insert menu or click the ChartWizard toolbar button. (Don't be surprised to see the Office Assistant pop up and ask whether you need help with the feature.)

3 In the first ChartWizard dialog box, click on the chart type and subtype you want. And if all of these choices don't seem to be enough, check out what's available on the Custom Types tab of the dialog box. To see a sample of a chart, select it and use the Press and Hold To View Sample button. When you've made a decision, click the Next button.

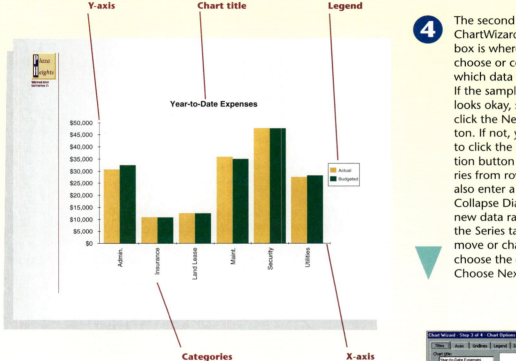

4 The second ChartWizard dialog box is where you choose or confirm which data to graph. If the sample chart looks okay, simply click the Next button. If not, you have to click the Rows option button to tell Excel to take the data series from rows instead of columns. You can also enter a different data range, or click the Collapse Dialog button and then select a new data range by dragging across it. Use the Series tab of the dialog box to add, remove or change the data series, and also to choose the cells to use as X-axis labels. Choose Next when everything is finished.

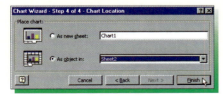

6 In the final ChartWizard dialog box, you can choose to place your chart in an existing worksheet. This is called an *embedded chart*. To do so, select the As Object In option button and choose a worksheet from the drop-down list. To place your chart in a separate chart sheet, select the As New Sheet option button, then you can type an optional sheet name in the text box that's provided. (A chart sheet is a worksheet that contains only a chart, not the data it's based on). Click the Finish button when you've made your selection.

5 The third ChartWizard dialog box lets you choose from a huge assortment of chart features. Among other things, you can enter a chart title and axis titles, turn gridlines on and off, and specify whether to include a legend and where to place it. You should do some exploring here to learn which features are available, although they vary by chart type. Choose Next when you've finished.

How to Change the Chart Type

After you've created a chart, it's not unusual to think that maybe a different type would suit your data better. Relax, it's not too late, nothing you did is etched in cement. Changing the chart type isn't all that difficult. In fact, it's easy enough that you might want to spend some time experimenting with different chart types until you find one that makes you think you've reached the perfect way to display your information.

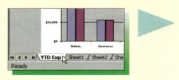

1 To change a chart that's on a chart sheet, activate the sheet that holds the chart.

7 Use the Chart toolbar to make changes quickly, with a click of the mouse. Click the down arrow on the Chart Type button, then select a chart type from the list that appears. If you're working with an embedded chart, you must select it first.

● To remove the Chart toolbar from your window, click the close button (the X in the upper-right corner). Or, if you prefer the long way, choose View, Toolbars, and click Chart to deselect it.

● Excel provides a number of three-dimensional chart subtypes (their descriptions include "3-D"). These charts can look impressive, but they aren't suitable for every purpose. Black and white print-outs of 3-D charts are often hard to interpret. If you choose a 3-D chart, check it carefully to make sure you're displaying all the information you want to in a clear and easy-to-read manner. If not, go back to a two-dimensional chart to ensure clarity.

6 You could also change the chart type with the Chart toolbar, which you can display by choosing View, Toolbars, Chart. Other chart attributes can be altered with this toolbar, too.

2 Choose Chart Type from the Chart menu.

3 You'll see a Chart Type dialog box that's almost identical to the first ChartWizard page you encountered when you created your chart. Choose the new chart type and subtype you want, then click OK.

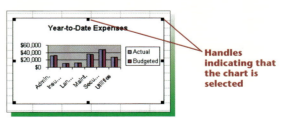

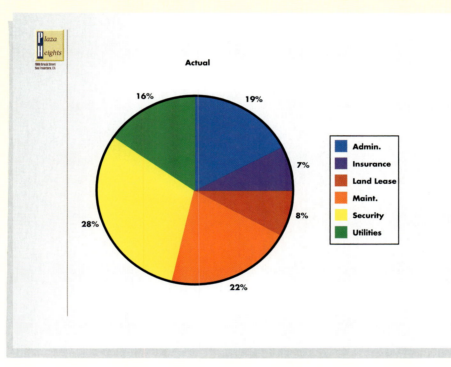

5 As before, choose Chart Type from the Chart menu. Then choose a new chart type and subtype from the Chart Type dialog box.

4 If you want to change an embedded chart (one that's part of a worksheet), click on the chart to select it. You'll see a set of square handles around the chart, and you'll also notice that a Chart menu item appears on your menu bar.

Handles indicating that the chart is selected

How to Work with Chart and Axis Titles

Your charts can include a chart title, an X-axis title, and a Y-axis title. If you didn't specify these elements while you were using the ChartWizard to create your chart, it's easy to add them. If you did include them originally, it's just as easy to change or remove them.

1 Activate the chart sheet or select the embedded chart you want to work with.

● You can change many more options than the titles from within the Chart Options dialog box. For instance, you could add and remove grid-lines, change the position of the legend, and add data labels that show the value or percentage for a particular data point or series. In a pie chart, you might want to add labels showing what percentage of the whole each slice represents.

● You can delete a legend the same way you delete a chart or axis title: Click on the legend (the selection handles appear), and choose Clear from the menu that appears. If you have the Chart toolbar displayed, clicking the Legend button displays a legend if there isn't one, and removes the legend if there is.

6 To delete a title, click on it to select it (the selection handles appear when it's selected) and then press the Del key. You can also right-click on the title and choose Clear from the shortcut menu.

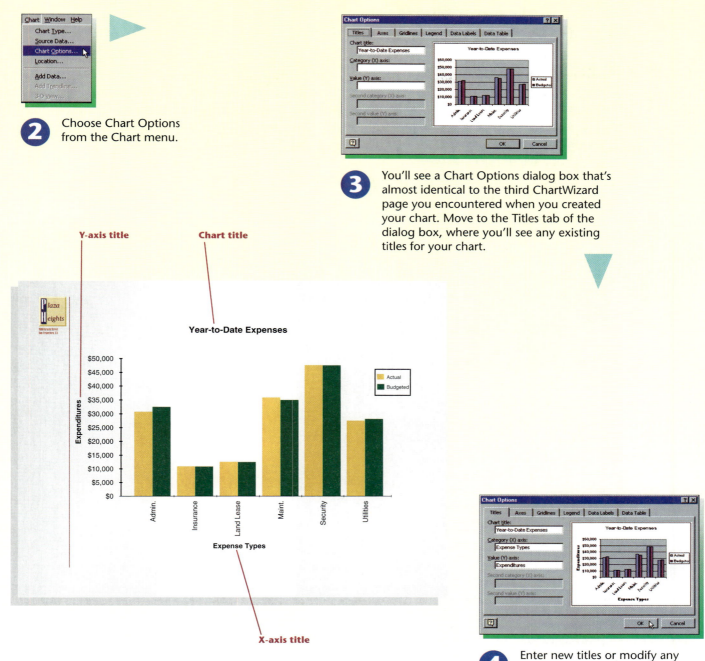

2 Choose Chart Options from the Chart menu.

3 You'll see a Chart Options dialog box that's almost identical to the third ChartWizard page you encountered when you created your chart. Move to the Titles tab of the dialog box, where you'll see any existing titles for your chart.

Y-axis title

Chart title

X-axis title

4 Enter new titles or modify any existing titles. Remember that different chart types have different title choices. Click OK to save your changes.

5 You can also modify an existing title by working directly on the chart. Just click on the title to select it, move your insertion point to the correct spot, and make changes the same way you make changes to text in a word-processing program.

How to Change the Chart Data

Sometimes you create a chart and then realize you didn't include all the data you meant to, or you did include data you didn't mean to. Don't worry, you do not have to re-create your chart; there's a way to reconfigure an existing chart to use exactly the data you need.

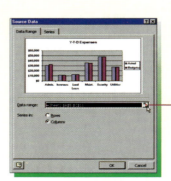

1 Activate the chart sheet or select the embedded chart you want to work with.

● The terms *data series* and *data point* are used frequently to refer to chart data. A data series is just a set of related values that you're charting. A data point is a single value in a data series. For example, the actual expenses for the year is one data series, and budgeted expenses is another. The utilities expenses are a data point. Data series are typically rows or columns of data in a worksheet.

● You can add data to a chart sheet by selecting the data you want to add and copying it to the Clipboard. Activate the appropriate chart sheet and paste the data. Excel automatically integrates the data into the chart.

Click here to reselect the data to be graphed.

7 To add or remove data, you can also choose Source Data from the Chart menu. In the Source Data dialog box, make sure the Data Range tab is selected, then click the Collapse Dialog button. Drag across the new data you want to graph, then press Enter (or click the Collapse Dialog button again). Choose OK.

2 Choose Add Data from the Chart menu.

Chart	Window	Help
Chart Type...		
Source Data...		
Chart Options...		
Location...		
Add Data...		
Add Trendline...		
3-D View...		

Add Data

Select the new data you wish to add to the chart.

Include the cells containing row or column labels if you want those labels to appear on the chart.

Range:

OK

Cancel

Click here to select the data to add to your graph.

3 You'll see the Add Data dialog box shown here. In the Range text box, enter the range of the data you wish to add.

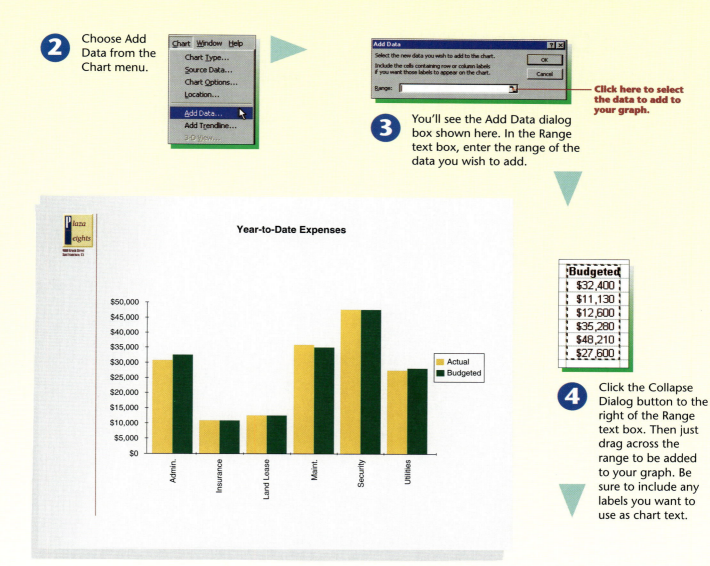

Year-to-Date Expenses

Budgeted
$32,400
$11,130
$12,600
$35,280
$48,210
$27,600

4 Click the Collapse Dialog button to the right of the Range text box. Then just drag across the range to be added to your graph. Be sure to include any labels you want to use as chart text.

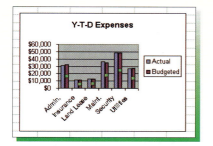

6 To remove data from your chart, click on the appropriate component of the data series (for example, a column of data you don't want to include in this chart). Then press the Del key.

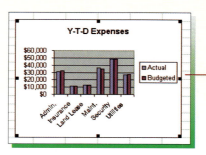

Y-T-D Expenses

The budgeted data has been added to the chart.

5 Press Enter or click the Collapse Dialog button again to return to the Add Data dialog box. Then click OK to return to your chart and inspect it.

How to Draw Shapes on a Chart

Sometimes labels and legends just aren't enough—you want a way to highlight or accentuate information on your chart. You might want to add arrows that point to items on the chart, enclose text in boxes, or use other shapes to clarify or embellish your chart. You can use the tools on the Drawing toolbar to add a wide variety of shapes both to charts and to the worksheet itself.

1 Activate the chart sheet or select the embedded chart you want to work with.

● The AutoShapes option on the Drawing toolbar supplies a vast variety of shapes you can use. Click on AutoShapes, then highlight the desired option in the menu that appears. Click the desired shape and drag across your chart to insert that shape. (If your mouse pointer continues to want to draw after you're finished, double-click to get rid of the problem—some tools behave that way.

● You can add text box borders by drawing a rectangle around a text box. Or, you can select the text box and choose Text Box from the Format menu, then choose the Colors and Lines tab. Pick a color, a line style, and a line weight (thickness).

8 If you want to delete a shape, click the Select Objects toolbar button, click the object to select it, then press Del.

2 If the Drawing toolbar is not visible, display it by clicking the Drawing toolbar button.

3 To draw a rectangle, click the Rectangle button on the Drawing toolbar.

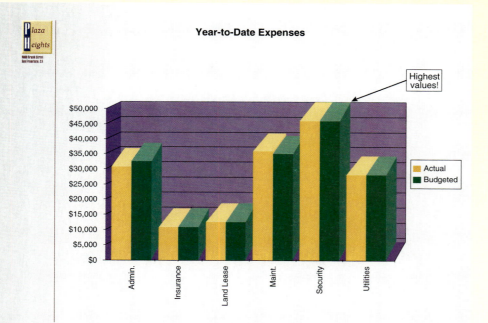

4 Drag over the chart to create a rectangle of the size you want in the spot you want. Release the mouse button to insert it into your chart.

5 If the rectangle obscures text, you have a couple of options: Choose No Fill from the Fill Color Palette (click the down arrow on the Fill Color toolbar button); or choose Draw from the toolbar, then choose Order, Send to Back. The second method actually brings your text to the front and puts the rectangle behind it.

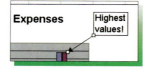

6 To draw an arrow, click the Arrow tool and then drag on the chart to insert the arrow. The arrow head appears at the point where you stop dragging, not where you start.

7 To draw other shapes, repeat the previous steps: Select the appropriate tool and drag across the chart to insert the shape you need.

How to Use Multiple Worksheets

When a workbook contains multiple worksheets, sometimes you'll want to enter data or apply formatting to more than one worksheet at the same time. The data could be column headings; the formatting could be the way you want those headings to appear.

	A	B	C	D	E
1	PET PARADISE PET FOOD AND SUPPLIES				
2	SALES FIGURES -- FIRST QUARTER 1999				
3					
4		January	February	March	Q1
5	Cat Food	2346	3112	2911	8369
6	Dog Food	2199	2635	2783	7617
7	Flea Products	1732	1863	1534	5129
8	Toys	1184	1321	1429	3934
9	Treats	972	842	1299	3113
10					
11					
12					
13					
14					
15					
16					
17					
18					

Quarter1 / Quarter2 / Quarter3 / Quarter4 /

1 Open the workbook containing multiple worksheets that you want to operate on as a group. If you plan on entering data in several worksheets at once, be sure the relevant cells of those worksheets are blank so you don't overwrite any existing data.

7 To work on individual worksheets again, right-click on any of the selected tabs and choose Ungroup Sheets from the shortcut menu. You can also click on any tab outside the group to deselect all worksheets in the group; or, if you've included all the worksheets in your group, just click on an individual worksheet tab to deselect the group.

Ungroup Sheets
Insert...
Delete
Rename
Move or Copy...
Select All Sheets
View Code

FYI

● If you want to remove individual worksheets from a group instead of ungrouping them all, use the Ctrl key while you click on the tab of the worksheet you want to remove from the group.

● Other changes affect all worksheets in a group. Some of them are: insert and delete columns and rows; clear and delete data; and spell-check.

	October	November	December	Q4
Cat Food	2136	4001	3211	9348
Dog Food	2953	2375	2803	8131
Flea Products	1852	1939	1634	5425
Toys	1289	1431	1592	4312
Treats	867	1182	1187	3236
Totals	9097	10928	10427	30452

Calculating the totals on any one worksheet in the group calculates them automatically on all other worksheets.

6 You can even calculate totals on all worksheets in a group, provided that the worksheets are laid out in an identical way. Here, for example, you could calculate totals for all sheets in the group by selecting cells B10:E10 on any sheet and clicking the AutoSum toolbar button.

2 Select a group of adjacent worksheets by clicking on the tab of the first one, then hold down the Shift key and click on the tab of the last one. The selected tabs turn white and the word *Group* appears in the title bar.

This text was entered into the Quarter1 worksheet, but it also shows up in Quarter2, Quarter3, and Quarter4 because the worksheets are grouped together.

3 When you've selected a group of worksheets, you can enter data into every sheet in the group simultaneously by typing the data into any single sheet. For example, if you entered **Totals** in cell A10 of the first sheet (as shown here), it appears in cell A10 of all the worksheets in the group. No matter which worksheet you use to enter the data, all the grouped worksheets receive it.

4 Use the same technique to apply formatting to all the worksheets in the group: Change one of the sheets and all the rest receive the changes. You might want to bold-face a series of column and row headings, for instance.

5 You can apply a wide range of other formatting effects to multiple worksheets. For example, here the column headings of all worksheets have been right-aligned. Again, just perform the necessary steps on one sheet to have all of them receive the formatting.

Even though boldfacing was applied in the Quarter1 worksheet, it affects all worksheets in the group.

P A R T 4

Microsoft Access 97

MICROSOFT ACCESS simplifies the complex world of relational database development to the point where even we mere mortals can create useful, sophisticated databases without having to obtain a college degree first. In this section you will learn the basics of database design and the means to implement your designs with a minimum of effort, and practically no gnashing of teeth.

WHAT YOU'LL FIND HERE

- How to Understand Database Basics 120
- How to Use the Database Wizard 122
- How to Use the Switchboard to Enter Data 124
- How to Plan a Database 126
- How to Create a Table with the Table Wizard 128
- How to Add, Delete, and Change Fields 130
- How to Create a Form with the Form Wizard 132
- How to Modify a Form in the Design View 134
- How to Enter Data in the Database 136
- How to Create a Report with the Report Wizard 138
- How to Modify a Report in the Design View 140
- How to Create a Switchboard Form 142
- How to Dress Up the Switchboard 144
- How to Sort Data 146
- How to Apply Access Filters 148
- How to Use the Simple Query Wizard to Create a Query 150
- How to Import Data 152
- How to Export Data 154
- How to Customize Access 156

How to Understand Database Basics

A database is an organized system for entering, managing, and retrieving information. The basic components of a database are fields, records, tables, forms, and reports.

A database consists of one or more tables, each holding information on a different subject. In an inventory database one table might hold product information, another may contain vendor information, and a third, customer information. The individual pieces of information (name, address, product description, quantity, and so forth) are called *fields*, which are grouped together in *records*. Fields and records together form tables.

Forms are where you enter data. Reports are the organized output of the information contained in your database. A customer list and a telephone directory list are examples of reports.

A simple way to understand the database structure is to take a closer look at a daily planner that contains an appointment book and an address book.

Appointment table   **Address book table**

APPOINTMENTS   CONTACTS

1 The daily planner consists of two tables: the appointment book and the address book. Each contains different types of information.

FYI

● **Another common example of a database is your checkbook register. Each check entry is a record composed of fields (check number, date, description, amount, balance). However, since it contains a single type of information, the checkbook has only one table, and is therefore not a relational database.**

6 Another factor to consider is that both Access and the daily planner are relational databases. This means that the various tables in your database can work together to link related information. This requires a key field present in both tables. In the daily planner the key field would be the contact name. When you make an appointment, you record the individual's name, which you can then use to look up contact information in the address book. Electronic databases frequently use ID codes or numbers (customer number, employee number, and so forth) as key fields.

2 Database tables consist of one or more records. Each complete contact entry or appointment entry in the daily planner is a record.

3 The individual pieces of information (name, address, city, state, and so forth) that make up the record are called *fields*.

4 The page in the daily planner with titles (or hours of the day) and blank spaces for you to add the contact or appointment information is a data entry form.

5 Common reports that you might generate from a daily planner would be a list of appointments for the week or a telephone directory of all the important contacts in the address book.

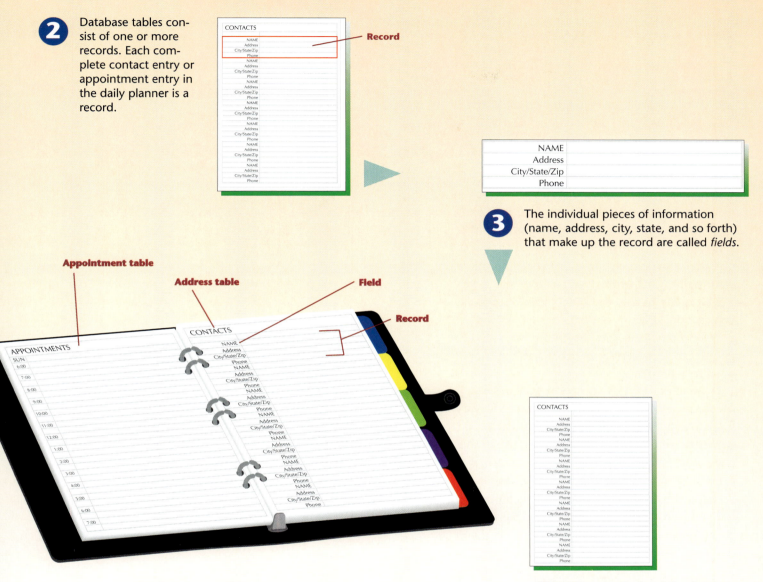

How to Use the Database Wizard

Creating a database used to be a difficult and time consuming process—until the advent of the Database Wizard, that is. The Access Database Wizard comes stocked with pre-formed database shells, called *templates*, for various kinds of databases. Some of the templates available are for inventory control, recipe keeping, expense tracking, asset management, and more. The trick to using a template is to find the one that most closely fits your needs and modify it to perform the task at hand. Once you select the template to use, the Database Wizard walks you through a series of questions which enable Access to build the database according to your needs. For this exercise we'll use the Household Inventory template.

Depending on how you open Access, your means of starting the Database Wizard will vary. If you use the New Office Document option on the Start menu, select the Databases tab in the New Office Document window. If you start the program from the desktop, choose Database Wizard from the Microsoft Access dialog box, then click the Databases tab. If Access is already open, select File, New Database from the menu bar, and then click the Databases tab.

1 From the Database window double-click Household Inventory.mdz to begin the process.

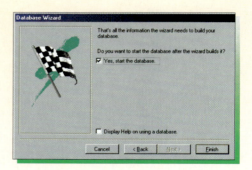

7 Click Next to move to the final Database Wizard screen. Decide whether or not to start the database as soon as it is built and click Finish to create your new database.

6 Click Next to proceed to the Database Wizard title window. Select a title for your database (it can be the same or different from the file name used in step 2), and indicate whether or not to include a picture on all reports.

● If you're new at creating and using databases, you might want to check the Yes, Include Sample Data checkbox found on the second Database Wizard window (step 3). You can see how the sample data is used and enter your information accordingly. When you no longer need the sample data, you can simply delete it.

2 The first thing you have to do is name your new database file. Either accept the name supplied by Access or type your own in the File Name text box. Remember, make it something that will be easily identifiable the next time you want to use the database. When you're through, click Create to move to the next step.

3 The next screen simply tells you that you are creating a database to store household inventory information. Click Next to proceed to the Database Wizard window that contains options for the actual structure of your new database. The left display window (Tables in the database) lists the tables that will be created, while the right display window lists the fields to be included in each table. Choose the table from the left window and select (or deselect) the fields to use in the right.

4 Click Next when you've finished selecting fields to include in your new database. The window that opens offers you several choices of backgrounds for screen displays and forms in the new database. Click each name in the list to display the sample background.

5 Select the background you wish to use and click Next. From the window that opens choose the style for your printed reports.

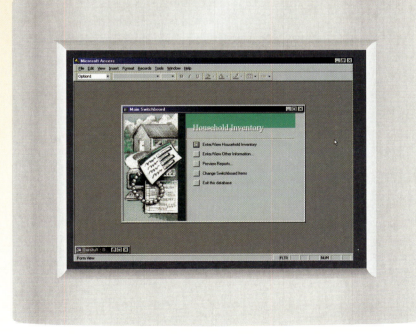

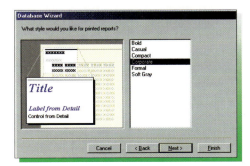

How to Use the Switchboard to Enter Data

One of the nice features of Access 97 is the advent of the switchboard, a handy menu system for entering, viewing, and modifying information in your database.

When you construct a database using the Database Wizard, Access automatically creates a switchboard for you. If you create your own database, you can build a switchboard of your own (see "How to Create a Switchboard Form").

To begin, open the household inventory database you created in the previous exercise. Click the Open Database button on the Database toolbar, then select the file name (you gave it an easy-to-remember name, didn't you?) from the Open dialog box and click Open.

Double-click to open Category form

1 Click Enter/View Household Inventory on the Main Switchboard to open the Household Inventory form. Notice that two of the fields, Category and Room, have drop-down arrows at the right end. This indicates that there is a drop-down list with choices for you to select. However, clicking the Category down arrow reveals that there are no pre-existing categories, which means you must first create your own.

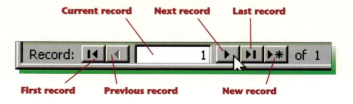

Current record   Next record   Last record

First record   Previous record   New record

7 To enter more records, click the Next Record button on the VCR panel. When you're finished entering records, close the Household Inventory form and return to the Main Switchboard.

FYI

● You can also enter new categories by selecting Enter/View Other Information from the Main Switchboard, and then Enter/View Categories from the Forms Switchboard.

● If you accidentally (or intentionally) close the Main Switchboard, you can reopen it by enlarging the database window (which is minimized upon opening a database containing a switchboard), clicking the Forms tab and selecting Switchboard.

Next record

2 Double-click the Category field to open the Categories form. In the Category Name field, enter a category such as Electronics, Furniture, Antiques, and so forth. Notice that a Category ID number is automatically assigned. When you are through entering categories, click the close button on the Categories window and return to the Household Inventory form.

3 Click the down arrow at the end of the Category field and select one of your newly created categories. Continue to enter information in the other fields until all the desired fields are completed.

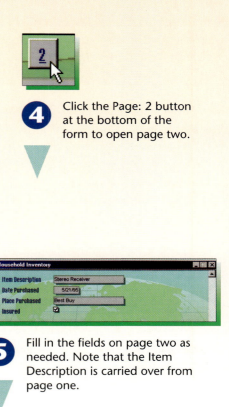

4 Click the Page: 2 button at the bottom of the form to open page two.

5 Fill in the fields on page two as needed. Note that the Item Description is carried over from page one.

6 Click the Preview button to see the Inventory Details sheet. To return to the Household Inventory form, click the close button on the Inventory Details window.

Preview...

How to Plan a Database

Now that you've seen what the Database Wizard can do, you must also be aware of what it can't do. It is unsurpassed at creating small, generalized databases that handle simple tasks. Unfortunately, when it comes to the more exotic or more complex tasks, it just doesn't cut the mustard. In those cases you must design and create your own database.

When creating a database from scratch, the most critical phase is not the actual building, but the planning that goes into it. You certainly wouldn't think of constructing a house or office building without a blueprint. The same goes for putting a database together.

1 Strange though it may seem, the best place to start planning your database is at the end. What categories of information will the finished product contain? What kind of reports do you want to generate? What kind of data will you need access to? It's always a good idea to put guidelines for your database on paper before attempting to build it.

FYI

● Use the Database Wizard to create an Inventory Control database and include the sample data. You can then view the table structure, fields, relationships, forms, and so forth that go into the development of a well constructed database.

● When determining the fields to use, break your information down to its smallest components. Rather than create one field called Name, you will have better control of your data if you create two fields, FirstName and LastName.

6 Enter your data.

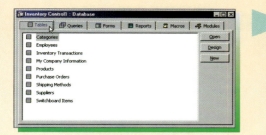

2 Once you've determined what the finished product will contain, you need to determine the tables to include. A separate table should be created for each different type of information (employees, customers, products, vendors, and so forth).

3 The next step is to decide what fields to include in each table. This is usually pretty straightforward, but should be given its due consideration to ensure that you don't end up with extraneous information or insufficient information. While adding and deleting fields is quite simple and can be done at any time, remember that if you add a field after you have a large number of records, you will have to go back and enter all the missing information by hand.

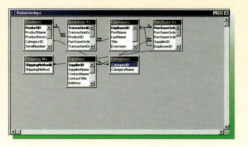

4 The beauty of a relational database (Access) is that all the diverse information that you enter into your database can be combined and used effectively by the development of relationships between common fields of the various tables. For example, using a Customer ID field in both the Customer table and the Order table of an inventory control database allows customer contact information to be filled in automatically on an invoice for that customer.

5 Build and test your design by creating the tables, establishing relationships, and adding a few records. Can you access the data as you initially planned? Produce some simple reports to see if the output is going to meet your needs. Now is the time to make adjustments to your design, before you've entered all your data.

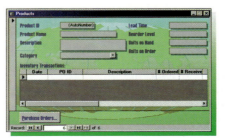

How to Create a Table with the Table Wizard

Once you've designed and refined your database, you can save yourself some time and energy when building your tables by taking advantage of the Table Wizard. You can use the Table Wizard on an existing database or a new database. For this exercise we will create a new database called Test1.

 Click the New Database button on the Database toolbar to open the New window. Select Blank Database and click OK to open the File New Database window.

 Click Next to open the final Table Wizard window. Indicate whether you want to change the table design, enter data directly, or have the Wizard create a data entry form for you, by clicking the appropriate option. After you make your choice, click Finish to create the new table.

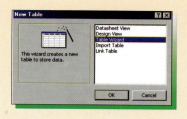

2 Give the new database the name Test1 (type Test1 in the File name text box), and click Create to open the database window.

3 The Tables tab should be selected. If it is not, click it, then click New to open the New Table dialog box.

4 Select Table Wizard and click OK to open the Table Wizard window. Choose Business or Personal to see sample tables for the appropriate category. Then select a sample table from the Sample Tables column to see the available fields. Highlight each field you wish to include and click the right arrow button to add the field to your new table. You can mix and match between personal and business, as well as between the various tables.

5 When you've finished adding fields, click Next to continue. The window that appears asks for a table name and whether or not you want the Wizard to create a primary key for you. Enter **Sample Table** for the table name and let the Wizard determine the primary key.

How to Add, Delete, and Change Fields

Very few things in life remain unchanged for any length of time, including databases. You may find that you have a field that is almost always blank, indicating that it is unnecessary and should be removed. Or you may want to enter information for which you forgot to create a field.

In either case you need to open the appropriate table and make the necessary change. For this exercise we'll use the Household Inventory database that we created earlier. Using the Household Inventory table, we'll add a field called Manufacturer, and remove the ModelNumber field. Begin by opening the Household Inventory (or whatever name you gave it) database.

1 Click the Database Window button on the Database toolbar to open the Household Inventory database window.

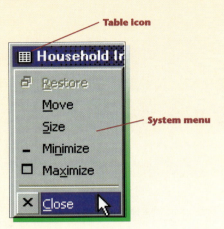

7 Click the table icon to left of the table name in the title bar to open the system menu. Select Close to close the table window and return to the database window. Click Yes in the dialog box that appears asking if you want to save your changes.

FYI

● Although you have changed the fields in the Household Inventory table, the data entry form remains the same and must be manually altered to reflect the changes made to the table.

● Use the field properties sheet in the Table Design View to change things such as the default size of the field, whether or not the field can be left blank when entering data, how many decimal places you want (number fields only), and more.

● You can also delete rows by highlighting them, right clicking, and selecting Delete Rows from the shortcut menu that appears.

6 Click the Delete Rows button on the Database toolbar to remove the highlighted row. Click Yes when asked if you want to permanently delete the selected field.

2 Click the Tables tab, select Household Inventory, and click Design to open the Household Inventory table design view.

3 Place your cursor in the first blank line of the Field Name column and enter the new field name Manufacturer.

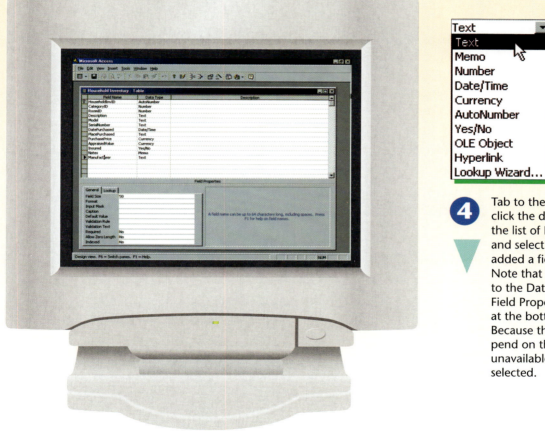

4 Tab to the Data Type column, click the down arrow to view the list of Data Type choices, and select Text. You have now added a field to your database. Note that as soon as you moved to the Data Type column, the Field Properties sheet appeared at the bottom of the window. Because the field properties depend on the data type, they are unavailable until a data type is selected.

5 To remove the ModelNumber field, click the row selector to the left of the field name ModelNumber. This highlights the entire row.

How to Create a Form with the Form Wizard

Access forms come in a variety of flavors—well, three to be exact. There are data entry forms, switchboard forms, and dialog box forms. Data entry forms are self explanatory. Switchboard forms enable you to create a switchboard menu system that makes using your database more intuitive. The third type of form, the dialog box, allows you to provide a vehicle for user input and a follow-up action based on the input.

In this exercise we will focus on the data entry form, the only one of the three that can be produced using the Form Wizard. Like the Table Wizard, the Form Wizard can be used with an existing database or a new database. To begin, open the Test1 database by clicking the Open Database button on the Database toolbar, and double-clicking Test1.mdb.

1 Click the Forms tab of the Test1: Database window if it is not already selected. Notice that at this point there are no forms. The only thing we've created in this database so far is a single table.

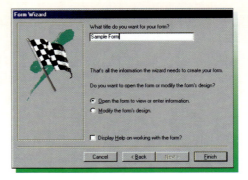

6 The final Form Wizard window opens and asks for a title for the form. Enter **Sample Form** in the text box and click Finish.

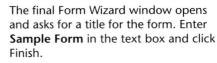

● If you have more than one table in your database, you can select fields from different tables to appear in a single form. During the field selection process, change the table that appears in the Tables/Queries drop-down list and add fields as needed.

Click New to open the New Form dialog box, and select Form Wizard from the list of form options. Click OK to open the Form Wizard window.

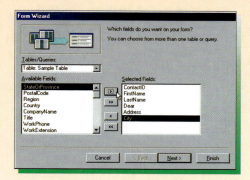

From the Tables/Queries drop-down list select the table that contains the fields you want to include on the form. Then highlight the field you want, and click the right arrow button to add the field to the new form. To add all the fields at once, click the double right arrow button.

When you're finished adding fields, click Next to select your form layout. To see an example of each of the layout options, click the radio button to the left of the option. For this form we'll get a little fancy and select Justified.

 Click Next to open the style selection window. Notice that the style you chose in an earlier exercise has become the default style choice. Select the style and click Next.

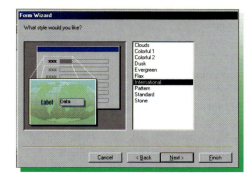

How to Modify a Form in the Design View

The Form Wizard is great for producing a quick form. However, you will frequently find that once you have your quick form, you want to change the layout or the fields that are included. You can easily customize the form to meet your needs by using the Design View.

For this exercise we'll use the Household Inventory database to which we added the Manufacturer field and from which we removed the ModelNumber field in an earlier exercise. We can now redesign the form to accommodate those changes.

If it's not already open, click the Open Database button on the Database toolbar, and double-click Household Inventory.dbd (or whatever you called it).

1 Click the Database Window button on the Database toolbar to open the Household Inventory Database window. On the Forms tab, select Household Inventory and click Design to open the Household Inventory Form in the Design View. The first thing you notice is that the form is divided into Form Header, Detail, and Form Footer (you have to scroll down to see the footer). You place a title or other information to appear at the top of each record in the Form Header section. The actual form appears in the Detail section. Information placed in the Form Footer section appears at the end of each record.

7 Press Ctrl+F4 to exit the Form Design View and click Yes to save your changes.

- When replacing one field with another, you can open the property sheet of the existing field and change the name and control source rather than remove the old field and add the new field.

- Sizing and positioning fields and labels so they match up with their neighbors is a tedious and often frustrating task. It is easier to open the property sheet of an object you want to emulate and simply match the width, height and position (actually you can only use one of the positioning coordinates or else the new object will completely overlay the existing one). In other words if you want the new field to line up vertically you would use the Left position, if you want it to line up horizontally you would use the Top position.

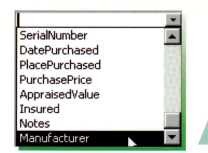

6 Click the Control Source line to open the field drop-down list. Scroll down and select Manufacturer from the list. Press Alt+F4 to close the field property sheet.

2 To modify this form to reflect the changes we made, we'll first remove the ModelNumber field. Note that in addition to the field (the grey text box) there is also a field label. Click the ModelNumber field itself (this highlights both objects at the same time), and press Delete to re-move them.

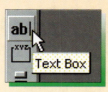

3 Click the Text Box button on the Toolbox toolbar and move the mouse pointer (now a small ab box with a plus sign) to the spot on the form recently occupied by the ModelNumber field. Left click and draw a text box.

4 In addition to the field, a field label has automatically been cre-ated as well. Double-click the field label to open its property sheet and select the All tab. Enter Manufacture Label on the Name line and **Manufacturer** on the Caption line. Press Atl+F4 to close the property sheet. Use the handles on the label box to re-size it appropriately.

5 Double-click the Manufacturer field (Unbound) to open its property sheet. Click the All tab to access all its field properties, and enter **Manufacturer** on the Name line.

How to Enter Data in the Database

While definitely not the most glamorous task in database management, data entry is certainly one of the most important. As a matter of fact, far from being glamorous, data entry is generally tedious and time consuming. It is one of the necessary evils of database management. However, a well designed database will make all that effort worthwhile once you begin accessing the data and receiving meaningful reports.

Data entry can be accomplished in a couple of different ways—either through Form View or the Datasheet View. You can also import data, but that's a subject for another exercise. To begin, open the Test1 database by clicking the Open Database button on the Database toolbar and double-clicking Test1.mdb.

 Click the Forms tab, and select Sample Form.

 Click the Form icon to the left of Sample Form in the title bar to open the system menu. Select Close to exit the Datasheet View and save your changes.

● If you notice that each time you enter data in a form certain fields seem to remain blank, you should consider removing or changing those fields.

● Symbols appearing in the Record Selector (the column of gray buttons at the beginning of each row) in the Datasheet View indicate the status of the record. A right arrow indicates the current record, an asterisk designates a new (blank) record, a pencil reminds you that the record you are editing has not been saved, and a circle with a line through it indicates that the record is locked and cannot be edited.

2 Click Open to bring up the Sample Form. Note that the Contact ID field says (AutoNumber) and refuses to let you enter anything. This field is automatically filled in for you with successive numbers starting at 1. Enter information in each of the fields as needed and use the Tab key to move from field to field. Scroll down to complete the fields hidden from view.

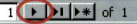

3 When you're through entering information for the first contact, click the right arrow button on the VCR panel to move to the next record.

4 Click the View drop-down button on the Form View toolbar to open the View menu. Select Datasheet View to switch to the Form View.

5 The Datasheet View presents a column and row window which is similar to a spreadsheet window. The field names appear in the column headers. Each row represents a record. Enter the data for each field, using the Tab key to move from field to field.

Contact ID	First Name	Last Name	Dear
1	Ed	Brown	
2	Mary	Samuelson	
3	Fred	Smith	
(AutoNumber)			

How to Create a Report with the Report Wizard

One of the primary reasons for creating a database is to manipulate the information and produce useful reports. With the Report Wizard, the task of creating a meaningful report becomes simple and effortless.

Once again we will use the Test1 Database created earlier. Click the Open Database button on the Database toolbar and double-click Test1.mdb.

1 Click the Reports tab of the Test1: Database window. Then click New to open the New Report window and Select Report Wizard from the list of options.

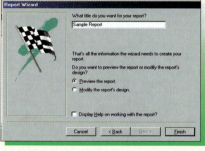

7 Click Next to open the final Report Wizard window. Type **Sample Report** for the report title, and click Finish to create your new report.

● To make your report as effective as possible, do not clutter it up with unnecessary information. Include only those fields that will provide meaningful data to the people who will be viewing the report.

● Because most people respond better to visuals than streams of textual information, it is helpful to include graphics in your reports. Once you've designed a report using the Report Wizard, you can add a chart or other graphic.

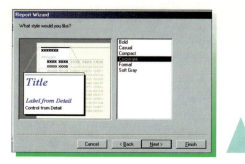

6 Click Next to open the styles window. As with the layout options, you can see examples of the different styles by clicking the options. Choose a style for your report.

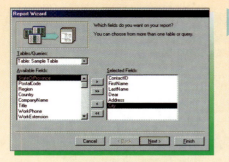

2 Click OK to open the Report Wizard window. From the Tables/Queries drop-down list select the table to use. From the Available Fields display, select the field you want and click the right arrow button to add it to the report. Use the double right arrow button to add all the fields at one time.

3 Click Next to set grouping levels. A report that groups information by relevant categories is much more useful than one that simply lists information alphabetically. From the left display window choose a field to use as a grouping category and click the right arrow button.

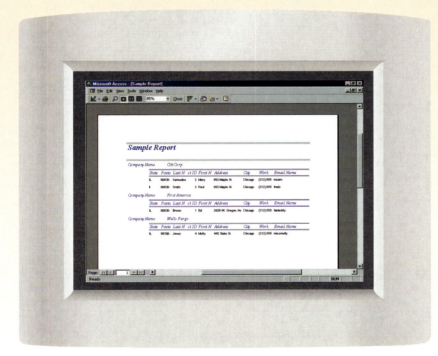

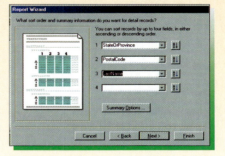

4 Click Next to set the sort order of the report. You can sort by as many as four fields, either in ascending (A-Z) or descending (Z-A) order. A salesman might find it useful to sort his contact list by state first, then by zip code, and then by last name. From the first drop-down list select the field to use for the primary sort and continue until you've chosen as many sort fields as needed. To change the sort order from ascending to descending, click the button to the right of the drop-down list.

5 Click Next to view the layout options. Select a layout option to see an example of how it will look. When you've decided on the layout options, you're ready to move on.

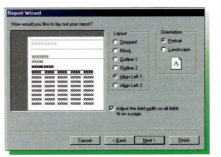

How to Modify a Report in the Design View

As with the other Wizards, the Report Wizard does a great job of creating a quick report, with a minimum of effort on your part. However, to get it just the way you want it you will probably have to do a little customization.

No problem—open the report, switch to the Design View, make your changes, and it's done. Once again we'll use the Test1 database. Open the Test1.mdb database and click the Reports tab to begin.

1 Click Design to open the Sample Report Design View window. Notice that the report is composed of six sections. The Report Header contains information that appears only at the very beginning of the report, the Page Header section contains information that appears at the top of each page of the report, the CompanyName Header contains header information for each page, based on the grouping (CompanyName) selected during the report creation. Detail contains the actual report data, the Page Footer section contains information appearing at the bottom of each page of the report, and Report Footer contains information that appears at the bottom of the last page of the report.

- You can open an object's properties sheet by right-clicking the object and selecting Properties from the shortcut menu that appears.

- To preview your changes before saving the modified report choose View, Layout Preview from the menu bar.

7 To remove any object from a report, including a label, field, or graphic, highlight it and press Delete.

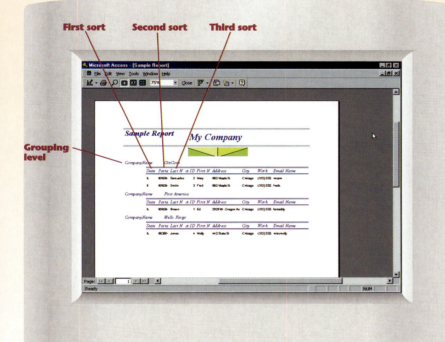

2 To add your company name to the beginning of the report, click the Label button on the Toolbox toolbar. Move the mouse pointer to the Report Header section, click and hold down the left mouse button, and draw a label box. Enter My Company in the label box and press Enter.

3 To change the font size, double click the label box (you may have to deselect it first) to open the properties sheet, scroll down to Font Size and change it to 24. Close the properties sheet to return to the Design View.

4 To enlarge one of the sections, move the mouse pointer to the bottom of the section. When the pointer turns into a cross with the vertical bar appearing as a double ended arrow left, click and drag to change the size of the section.

5 To add a graphic to the top of each page of the report, first enlarge the page Header section as indicated in Step 4, then click the Image button on the Toolbox toolbar. Move the mouse pointer to the Page Header section, hold down the left mouse button an draw an image box.

6 In the Look In drop-down list of the Insert Picture window that appears, select the location of your graphic file (the default location in Office 97 is C:\Program Files\Microsoft Office\Clipart\Popular), and double-click the desired graphic that appears in the display window. The graphic is inserted in your report (you may have to adjust the size of the image box).

How to Create a Switchboard Form

If you've been following the exercises so far, you have already learned to create a database not only by using the Database Wizard, but also from scratch—building first a table, then a data entry form, and finally a report.

The only thing left is to create a Switchboard menu that will make using the new database a breeze. Not so surprisingly, Microsoft has provided a Wizard to make the job of constructing a Switchboard relatively painless. The first thing you need to do is open the Test1 database. By now you know the drill.

1 Select Tools, Add-Ins, Switchboard Manager from the menu bar to start the Switchboard. The first thing you encounter is a dialog box informing you that there is no switchboard for this database.

● When creating a switchboard, it's a good idea to include a command that opens the Switchboard Manager in the event you want to make changes to the current setup. Open the Switchboard Manager, highlight Main Switchboard (default), and click Edit to open the Edit Switchboard Page. Then click New, and enter Edit Switchboard in the Text box. Choose Design Application from the Command drop-down list. Click OK, and Close your way back out of the Switchboard Manager.

6 You should also include an Exit button so that you can close the database from the Switchboard. Click New, type **Exit**, and select Exit Application from the Command drop-down list.

2 Click Yes to indicate that you wish to create one. The Switchboard Manager window appears, with Main Switchboard (Default) listed in its display window. Click Edit to customize the Main Page.

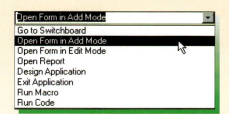

3 Click New in the Edit Switchboard page that appears, to add your first item to the Main Switchboard. Type **Enter/View Sample Information** (the command text should be appropriate for the form) in the Text box.

From the Command drop-down list select Open Form in Add Mode. From the Form drop-down list choose Sample Form. When this command is executed from the completed Switchboard, the Sample Form will open, ready for you to enter data. Click OK to add the command to the Main Switchboard.

4

5 Click New to add another item to the Main Switchboard. Type **Preview Sample Report** in the Text box. From the Command drop-down list select Open Report. From the Report drop-down list choose Sample Report. Click OK to return to the Edit Switchboard Page window, where both new commands are now listed.

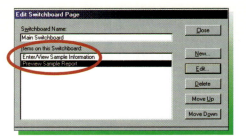

How to Dress Up the Switchboard

In the last exercise you created a fully functional Switchboard. Although it works well, it is rather unattractive. Fortunately, the remedy for that is quite simple.

If the Test1 database is not open, open it now. In the database window select the Forms tab, highlight Switchboard, and click Open.

1 Click the View button on the Form View toolbar to switch to Design View.

7 Click the View button on the Form View toolbar to see how the spruced up form actually looks. Close the form and answer Yes when asked if you want to save your changes.

Label: Label1

Format | Data | Event | Other | All

Name	Label1
Caption	Sample Information
Hyperlink Address	
Hyperlink SubAddress	
Visible	Yes
Display When	Always
Left	2.0521"
Top	0.2917"
Width	3.0625"
Height	0.3125"
Back Style	Transparent
Back Color	16777215
Special Effect	Flat

2 Double-click the Test1 Label box to open its property sheet. Change the caption to Sample Information. Now scroll down to Font Weight and change Normal to Bold. Close the property sheet to return to the Switchboard form.

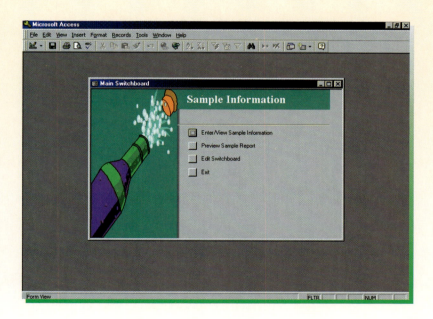

3 Next we'll move the Label box using the drag-and-drop technique. Position your mouse pointer at the edge of the Label box until it turns into a black hand. Hold down the left mouse button and drag the Label box up until it is entirely in the green.

Image: Picture

Format | Data | Event | Other | All

Name	Picture
Picture	(none)
Picture Type	Embedded
Size Mode	Stretch
Picture Alignment	Center
Picture Tiling	No
Hyperlink Address	
Hyperlink SubAddress	
Visible	Yes
Display When	Always
Left	0"
Top	0"
Width	1.8646"

4 To add a graphic, double-click the Image box (large green block) on the left side of the Switchboard form and open its (Image box) property sheet.

5 Click the Picture property line to access the Build button.

6 Click the Build button to open the Insert Picture window. If need be, change the file location for available graphics by using the Look In drop-down menu. Select a graphic and click OK. Close the Properties sheet to return to the form.

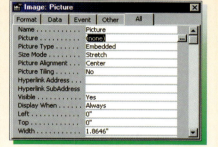

How to Sort Data

If databases just held information only, they wouldn't be worth the time and energy it takes to build and maintain them. Fortunately, information storage is merely the tip of the iceberg. The real value of a database is its ability to manipulate data. One of the most important ways in which a database manipulates data is by sorting it—putting it in a logical order according to criteria you specify.

Open the Test1 database to use for this exercise, and click the Database Window button on the Form View toolbar to open the Test1: Database window.

1 Click the Tables tab and open the Sample Table. Notice that it is currently sorted by Contact ID. Click on a column header, or place your cursor in the column you want to use for the sort.

6 The Datasheet View of the Sample Form not only looks like the Sample Table, it also sorts like it, with one exception: After you select the column to sort by you can use the Sort Ascending or Sort Descending buttons on the Form View toolbar to effect the sort.

2 Select Records, Sort, Sort Ascending from the menu bar to sort the table in ascending (A-Z) order. To sort by descending order (Z-A), select Sort Descending.

3 Close the Sample Table and save the changes. From the Test1: Database window, select the Forms tab and open Sample Form.

4 Place your cursor in the field you want to sort by. From the Form View toolbar click the Sort Ascending (or Sort Descending) button to sort the form by the selected field. Now as you cycle through the forms (using the VCR panel at the bottom of the form) they appear in the new sort order.

5 You can also sort a form in the Datasheet View. Click the drop-down arrow on the View button on the Form View toolbar, and select Datasheet View.

How to Apply Access Filters

In addition to sorting, the ability to filter out specific records based on user input is another miracle of modern database technology. Very often you only want to see information on a certain vendor or group of vendors. Or you may want to find everyone in your address book whose birthday is in the month of May. Whatever the reason, Access enables you to filter out all the records except those you need.

Access provides four methods for applying filters: Filter by Selection, Filter by Form, Filter by Input, and Advanced Filters. Filter by Selection offers the fewest options, while Advanced Filters offers the most. All the filters can be applied in a form, datasheet, or query. In this exercise we will examine the first three methods.

Begin by opening the Test1 database.

1 Open the Sample Form and place the cursor in the field that contains the criteria you want to filter for, and click the Filter By Selection button in the Form View toolbar. Any records that have matching information in the field selected have been retained, while all others have been hidden (filtered out). Filtered) now appears at the end of the VCR panel indicating a filter is on.

● You can also filter out records that contain certain criteria. The regular filter finds records that contain the search criteria and filters out those that don't. The Filter by Excluding Selection returns all records that do *not* contain the search criteria you specify.

● You can Filter by Selection, Filter by Excluding Selection, Filter for Input, and Remove Filters by right-clicking on the appropriate field in a form, and selecting one of the options from the shortcut menu that appears.

6 For a quick search based on input for a certain field, place your cursor in the desired field and right-click. Enter the search criteria in the Filter For: text box on the shortcut menu that appears, and press Enter to apply the filter.

2 To remove the filter, click the Remove Filter button on the Form View toolbar. By the way, when no filter has been applied, the Remove Filter button changes to become the Apply Filter button.

3 Click the Filter by Form button to enter your own criteria for the filter. Notice that all the fields in the form are blank except the one in which the cursor last rested.

Sample Form: Filter by Form

Contact ID	First Name		Last Name		Dear

Address

City		State/Province	Postal Code		Region
Dallas					

Country		Company Name		Title	

Work Phone		Work Extension	Home Phone		Mobile Phone

Fax Number		Email Name		Birthdate	Last Meeting Date

Contact Type ID	Referred By				

Photograph

Look for / Or

4 Type your search criterion in the field of your choice (for example, to search for all contacts who live in Dallas, type Dallas in the City field) and click the Apply Filter in the Form View toolbar. Keep in mind that if you enter data in more than one field, Access will find only records that match both entries.

Look for / Or

5 To search for one thing or another (Access will find records that contain either piece of information), when using the Filter by Form method, click the Or tab at the bottom of the form window. A blank form opens, in which you can enter the new criteria.

How to Use the Simple Query Wizard to Create a Query

Queries are similar to filters in that they extract information based on criteria that you specify. However, Queries are rather more sophisticated and can be used for editing and viewing your data, as well as furnishing the material for forms and reports.

Once again, Microsoft has simplified the process by providing a Wizard to do the work. Open the database of your choice and begin.

1 Select the Queries tab and click New. From the New Query dialog box choose Simple Query Wizard to open the first Simple Query Wizard window.

FYI

● In addition to finding records that contain fields with information you can also use a query to find records that contain blank fields. To search for blank numeric fields use is null for the search criteria. For blank text fields use double quotes ("").

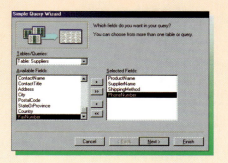

2 Open the Tables/Queries drop-down list and select the first table from which to choose a field. Choose a field and click the right arrow button to add it to your query. Select as many fields from as many different tables as you wish and click Next.

3 If the fields you've selected include any numerical values, you can choose Summary in the window that appears to have those values totaled, averaged, or the minimum and maximum values displayed. To see all fields select Detail.

	Contributor ID	Donor Name	Address	City	State/Province	Postal Code	Country	Hom
▶	1	John Steel	12 Orchestra Te	Walla Walla	WA	99362-	USA	(204)
	2	Helvetius Nagy	722 DaVinci Blv	Kirkland	WA	98034-	USA	(204)
	3	Karl Jablonski	305 - 14th Ave.	Seattle	WA	98128-	USA	(204)
	4	Art Braunschwe	P.O. Box 555	Lander	WY	82520-	USA	(307)
	5	Fran Wilson	89 Chiaroscuro	Portland	OR	97219-	USA	(503)
*	(AutoNumber)							

Record: ⏮ ◀ 1 ▶ ⏭ ▶* of 5

	Contributor ID	Donor Name	Address	City	State/Province	Postal Code	Country	Hom
▶	1	John Steel	12 Orchestra Te	Walla Walla	WA	99362-	USA	(204)
	2	Helvetius Nagy	722 DaVinci Blv	Kirkland	WA	98034-	USA	(204)
	3	Karl Jablonski	305 - 14th Ave.	Seattle	WA	98128-	USA	(204)
	4	Art Braunschwe	P.O. Box 555	Lander	WY	82520-	USA	(307)
	5	Fran Wilson	89 Chiaroscuro	Portland	OR	97219-	USA	(503)
*	(AutoNumber)							

Record: ⏮ ◀ 1 ▶ ⏭ ▶* of 5

4 Click Next to continue. Enter a name for the query in the text box.

	Product Name	Supplier Name	Shipping Method	Phone Number
▶	Aniseed Syrup	New Orleans Cajun Delights	Speedy Express	(100) 555-4822
	Dharamsala Tea	Grandma Kelly's Homestead	Speedy Express	(313) 555-5735
	Tibetan Barley Beer	Grandma Kelly's Homestead	Speedy Express	(313) 555-5735
	Aniseed Syrup	Tokyo Traders	Federal Shipping	(03) 3555-5011
	Chef Anton's Cajun Seasoning	Cooperativa de Quesos 'Las Cabras'	Federal Shipping	(98) 598 76 54

Record: ⏮ ◀ 1 ▶ ⏭ ▶* of 5

5 Click Finish to create your query, which appears in table form.

How to Import Data

Times change and so do the tools that people use. Consequently, there is a need to be able to move information to and from Access as the need arises.

When you bring information into Access from another source, you are *importing*. You might wish to create a contact database and import the existing data from your old contact manager, or you may be switching from another database program, such as FoxPro or Dbase. Perhaps that Excel spreadsheet that you've been using is becoming a little unwieldy and would be better suited as a database.

Whatever the reason, you will eventually find yourself needing to import information into Access. The specifics of the import will vary depending upon the type of information you import, but the basics are similar. For this exercise we will import an Excel spreadsheet.

One last thing: You can only import data into an existing database. So the first thing to do is open the database that will contain the new information.

1 Select File, Get External Data, Import from the menu bar to open the Import window.

7 Give your new table a title and click Finish to import the data. When you get a message that Access is finished importing, click OK. Check out the database window and you'll see your new table (if you created a new table) in the Tables tab.

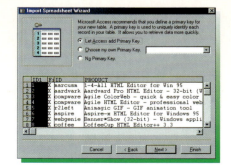

6 Click Next to continue. A primary key is important in creating relationships between the various tables of your database. The window that appears provides options for selecting a primary key (or no primary key). Unless you know what you want, let Access make the selection.

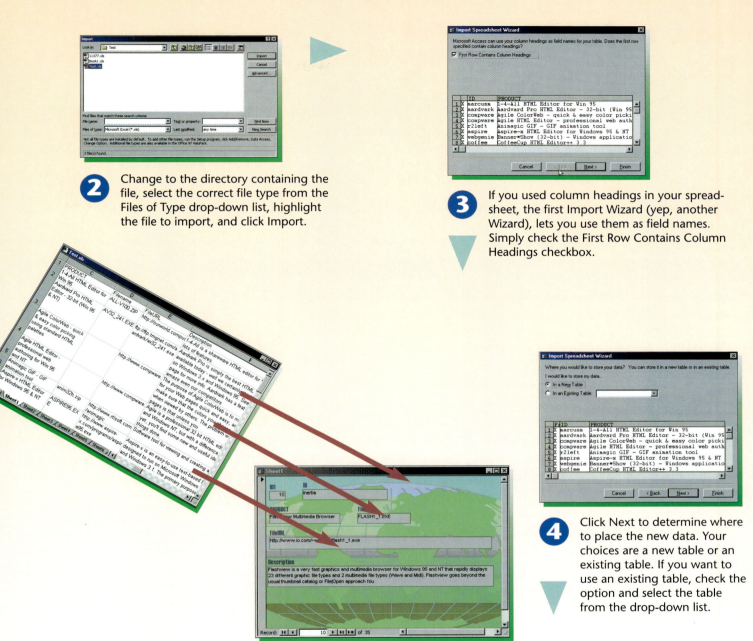

2 Change to the directory containing the file, select the correct file type from the Files of Type drop-down list, highlight the file to import, and click Import.

3 If you used column headings in your spreadsheet, the first Import Wizard (yep, another Wizard), lets you use them as field names. Simply check the First Row Contains Column Headings checkbox.

4 Click Next to determine where to place the new data. Your choices are a new table or an existing table. If you want to use an existing table, check the option and select the table from the drop-down list.

5 Proceed to the field options window by clicking Next. You can change the field names, indicate whether the field is indexed, and even decide to skip the field entirely. Highlight each field (scroll to the right for more fields), and select the appropriate options.

How to Export Data

Sharing data works both ways. The previous exercise covered importing, which allows you to bring information into Access from other sources. There are times, however, when you may want to use your Access data in a different program. At such times you must first *export* your information in a format that can be used by the other application.

You can export to a number of different formats, including Microsoft Excel, Dbase, FoxPro, as well as text and a few others.

All the export procedures start with the same steps. Most are simply a matter of saving the data as a different format. However, exporting to text, which is useful if you want to use the information in a non-standard program such as a contact manager, requires a few more steps.

Therefore, we will cover exporting to text so that you can learn both the basics steps used for exporting any data, and the specifics for exporting to text. To begin, open a database, select the Tables tab, and highlight a table to export.

1 Choose File, Save As/Export from the menu bar to begin the export process and open the Save As dialog box.

● If you are exporting a table with date fields you can use the Advanced button on the final Text Export Wizard window to set the format for those fields. You can set the date order, the character used to separate the month, day, and year, whether or not to use a four-digit year, and more.

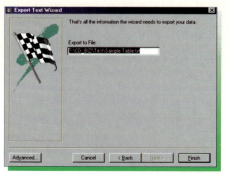

6 Click Next to open the final Export Text Wizard window. Verify the path and title of the export file and click Finish. When the dialog box appears, informing you that the export is complete, click OK.

2 The Save As dialog box offers you the option of exporting the selected table or making a copy that you can also use within Access. Select To an External File or Database to export.

3 Click OK to open the Save Table As window. From the Save As Type drop-down list select the format you want to export to. In this example we'll use Text Files (*.txt; *.csv;*.tab;*.asc). Indicate a location and file name for the exported file.

4 Click Export to continue. For most other formats that would end the process—the table would be exported to the format selected. However, with text there are a few more choices to be made. In the window that appears, indicate the format for exporting the data. For most text files Delimited is the best choice (check with the documentation of the program into which you will import the data from Access).

5 Click Next to select the field delimiter and field names. Although most programs today recognize a variety of delimiters (characters that indicate the beginning and the end of a field), a comma is a good standby when you're unsure. It's a good idea to include field names in the first row of the exported file—it makes it easier to identify the information when you're importing to a new program.

How to Customize Access

Times sure have changed since Henry Ford announced that his customers could have their cars in any color they chose—as long as it was black. There are so many choices today in everything you do it sometimes becomes mind boggling.

Software has kept up with the times by offering users a vast array of options. When it comes to options, Access is no slouch. Access offers a large selection of customization options so you can tailor the program to suit your needs and tastes. Before utilizing the options, open a database.

1 Select Tools, Options from the menu bar to open the Options window.

● If you are using Access in a network environment, changes to options will affect all users who employ the same workgroup information file that you do.

● To reposition a toolbar, place the mouse pointer over the double vertical bar at the left end of the toolbar, click and hold the left mouse button down while dragging the toolbar to a new location. When you've found a new home for the toolbar, let go of the left mouse button to drop the toolbar.

6 Choose Large Icons to increase the size of the object icon. List arranges the icons in a list format, and Details adds additional information about the objects including a description (when available), the date last modified, the date the object was created, and the object type. Note that you cannot combine large icons with the list or detail views.

2 Click each tab to see the available options. There are eight tabs, each with a different set of options. Here you'll find basic options on default field settings, print margins, startup options, and a lot more. When you're through setting options, click OK to return to the database window.

3 To customize a toolbar, right-click the gray area next to any toolbar, and select Customize from the shortcut menu that appears. The Customize window allows you to enable any Access toolbar no matter what view you're in. You can also create your own toolbar by clicking New.

4 Click the Options tab to change the size of toolbar buttons, to hide tooltips, or to show shortcut keys in the tooltips. You can even change the way the menus behave.

5 To customize the information presented in the database window, place the mouse pointer in the database window and right-click. From the shortcut menu select View.

P A R T 5

Microsoft PowerPoint

OFFICE 97 includes a powerful presentation application called PowerPoint. You can use this software to build simple slide shows, self-running presentations, and interactive presentations that you place on your Web page.

THIS SECTION TEACHES YOU THE FOLLOWING POWERPOINT SKILLS

- How to Use the PowerPoint Toolbars — 160
- How to Use the AutoContent Wizard — 162
- How to Use a Template — 164
- How to Edit and Add Text on a Slide — 166
- How to Format and Align Text — 168
- How to Add Text Boxes — 170
- How to Add a Shape — 172
- How to Use Autoshapes — 174
- How to Use Fills, Shadows, and 3-D Effects — 176
- How to Add Clip Art, Pictures, Video, and Sound — 178
- How to Move, Size, and Rotate Objects — 180
- How to Layer Objects — 182
- How to Group and Ungroup Objects — 184
- How to Insert, Delete, and Reorder Slides — 186
- How to Create Speaker Notes — 188
- How to Create Handouts — 190
- How to Set Up a Slide Show — 192
- How to Run a Slide Show — 194
- How to Create a Self-Running Slide Show — 198
- How to Use Pack and Go — 202

How to Use the PowerPoint Toolbars

PowerPoint provides plenty of tools to help you perform tasks quickly. In these pages you'll be introduced to the basic toolbars you'll see when you're working on a presentation.

1 The menu bar is very much like the menu bar for any other Windows software. The Slide Show menu contains commands specific to the work you do with your slide show. Technically the menu bar isn't a toolbar, but it does contain commands, so we're covering it here.

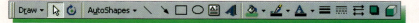

6 Above the Status bar is the Drawing toolbar, which provides quick access to drawing and graphics features.

● There are a number of other toolbars available, and they're handy for certain features as you work in PowerPoint. To add or remove toolbars, right-click on a toolbar to see the list of available toolbars. Click a toolbar that has a checkmark beside it (indicating it's currently on the window) to remove it. Click a toolbar with no checkmark to add it.

● All the toolbars have double bars at their left end. You can click on these and drag the toolbars around if their current position doesn't suit you.

Slide Layout

Apply Design

New Slide

Black and White View

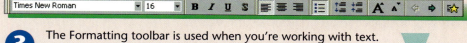

2 The Standard toolbar has icons that give you quick access to many commonly used commands. To see what an icon does (if it isn't self-explanatory), hold your pointer over it for a few seconds. A ScreenTip appears to show you the button's name. Most of the icons are similar throughout all the Office applications, but there are a couple that are unique to PowerPoint.

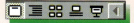

3 The Formatting toolbar is used when you're working with text. You can use the buttons on this toolbar for quick access to commands (instead of using the menu bar, which requires more steps). Check the functions by reading the ScreenTips.

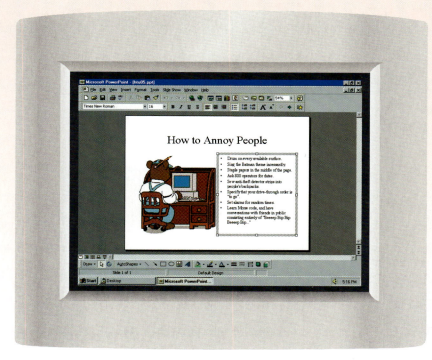

4 Just below the PowerPoint document window, over on the left, are the buttons that change the view of your presentation. You can look at a slide, an outline of the text of your presentation, or run a slide show.

5 The very bottom of the screen has the Status bar, which tells you which view you're currently using and also displays the name of the PowerPoint design for the current presentation.

How to Use the AutoContent Wizard

The PowerPoint AutoContent Wizard provides an easy way to plan and create a presentation. You answer some questions, make some decisions, and the wizard does most of the work. You just have to substitute your own text and artwork for the placeholders created by the wizard.

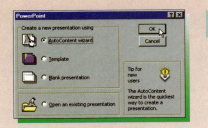

1 Open PowerPoint, and the PowerPoint dialog box offers choices for beginning your session. Select the AutoContent Wizard and choose OK. When the AutoContent Wizard appears, choose Next to get started.

6 In a few seconds, the wizard displays your presentation in Outline view. You can begin to fill in your own words and add your own artwork, using the skills you'll learn in the following pages.

● You cannot open the AutoContent Wizard if you start a new presentation by clicking the New icon on the Standard toolbar. You must use the File, New command.

● If you choose the Kiosk option for presentations, it's assumed you want to create a self-running presentation. This means that all narration, changes of slides, and so on will be programmed into the presentation with the appropriate PowerPoint tools (covered in the following pages).

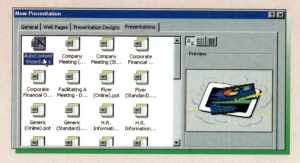

2 If you're already working in PowerPoint, choose File, New and when the New Presentation dialog box opens, move to the Presentations tab. Double-click the icon for the AutoContent wizard. When the AutoContent Wizard appears, choose Next to get started.

3 Choose the type of presentation you want to create and then choose Next. For self-running presentations (instead of slide shows you present yourself), choose Information Kiosk.

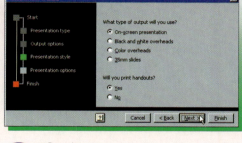

4 Continue to answer questions and make decisions about the style and content of your presentation.

5 Choose Finish when you have answered all the wizard's queries.

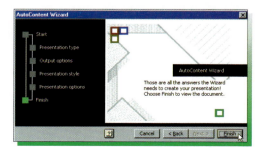

How to Use a Template

PowerPoint comes with pre-designed templates that you can use to give your presentation consistency. Design templates have formats and colors; content templates have formats, colors, and suggested content for specific subjects. On this page, we'll talk about design templates, since using the content templates is very much like using the AutoContent Wizard we discussed on the previous page.

1 Open PowerPoint and choose Templates from the PowerPoint dialog box, then choose OK. Choose the design you like and click OK.

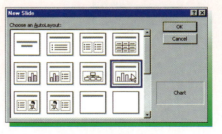

6 Choose a style for this slide, knowing that the color scheme, fonts, and general look of the slide will match the first one. Continue to perform these steps to complete your presentation.

FYI

● **Create your own design template by making changes (color, font, or so on) to an existing template. Then choose File, Save As. In the Save As dialog box, name the new design and select Presentation Templates in the Save As Type box.**

● **If you don't like any of the design templates (including those used by the AutoContent Wizard), start with a blank slide and design your own presentation from scratch.**

2 If you're already working in PowerPoint, choose File, New and when the New Presentation dialog box opens, move to the Presentation Designs tab. Choose the design you like and click OK.

3 Select a slide design for the first slide in your presentation and choose OK.

4 When the slide appears, you can begin to put your own text and artwork into the placeholder boxes on the slide.

5 Add the next slide by clicking the New Slide tool on the Standard toolbar. (You could also choose Insert, New Slide from the menu bar or press Ctrl+M.)

How to Edit and Add Text on a Slide

Whether you've used the AutoContent Wizard, adopted an existing design template, or created your slides from scratch, eventually you have to put meaningful text on your slides. This means you'll be editing placeholder text or adding new text, or both.

You can add text in Outline View or directly on a slide, depending on which method you feel more comfortable with.

1 To open your presentation, click the Open icon on the Standard toolbar (or choose File, Open from the menu bar, or press Ctrl+O). When the Open dialog box appears, select the presentation you want to work on.

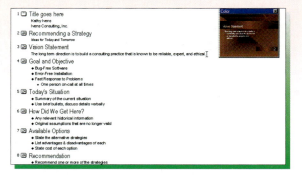

6 Enter the additional text directly on the slide, or on the outline.

● Notice that as you enter text in Outline View, the text wraps on the slide to fit the text box. Having the slide miniature available in Outline View is handy.

● If you're going to add a lot of text, it's best to work directly on the slide so you can have a better sense of when the slide is getting too cluttered to be effective.

2 In Outline View, select the text you want to edit by dragging the mouse across it. Then enter the replacement text.

3 In Slide View, click on the text to select the text box, then select the specific text you want to edit. Change whatever text needs to be altered.

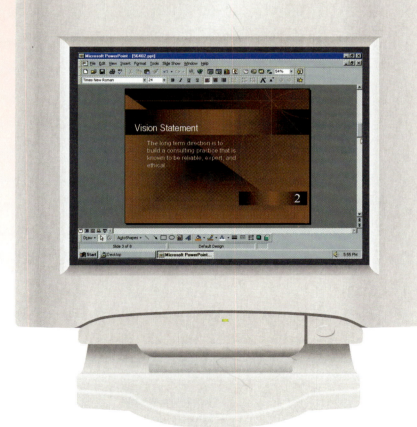

4 Press Enter while you're in a bullet list to add another bullet item. If you want to make it a sub-item, press Tab.

5 To add regular text instead of a bullet list item, deselect the Bullets tool on the formatting toolbar. (If you are editing existing text, select the text first.)

How to Format and Align Text

You can format your text to make it stand out, or just to make it look more attractive. Formatting means changing the way the text looks by adding attributes (such as bold or italic), or changing the font or size.

Text alignment is the way text lines up against the margins (in the case of a slide, that means the margins of the text box).

 To work on text, click on it to select the text box.

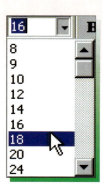

 Click the arrow on the Font Size box to choose a different size for the selected text.

- If dragging the mouse across a small amount of text is awkward, place your insertion point at the beginning of the text and hold down Ctrl+Shift while you press the right arrow key. Each time you press the right arrow key another word is selected.

- If you have a text box next to a graphic (such as a picture), try aligning the text along the margin that's closest to the picture.

2 Select the text you want to format by dragging the mouse across it.

Bold Italic Underline Shadow

3 Click the appropriate icon on the formatting toolbar to change the attribute of this text (in this case, I'm making it bold).

Align on left margin   Align on center   Align on right margin

4 To change the alignment, select the text and use one of the alignment tools on the formatting toolbar.

Take Your Daughter To Work

Next week, don't forget about Take Your Daughter to Work day. Many businesses are supporting this special day.

It's a way to show daughters what the working world is like and to reinforce the notion that all the jobs they see are open to them

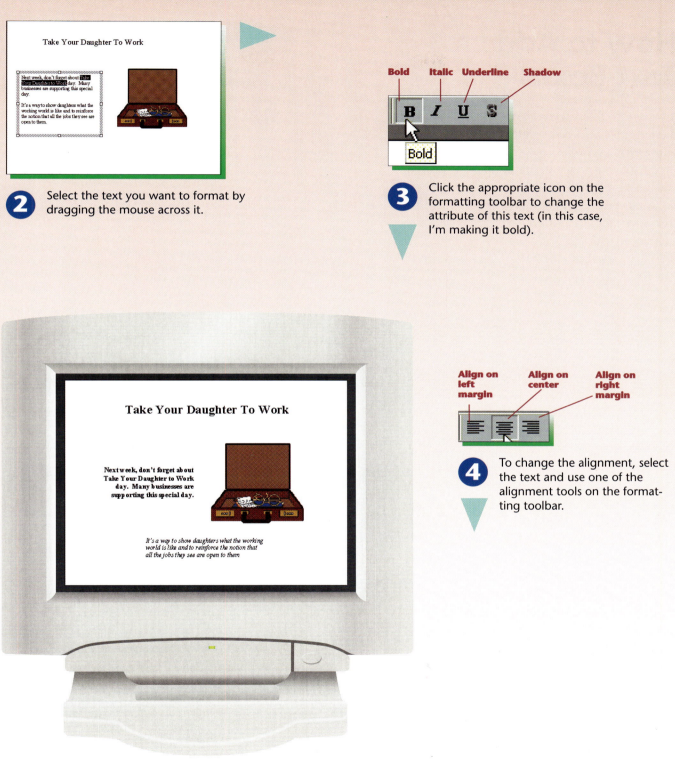

5 Click the arrow on the Font list box to see the choices when you want to change the font for selected text.

How to Add Text Boxes

I f you are creating your own slide from scratch (starting with a blank slide), you have to add your own text boxes.

However, even if you are using a design that was created by the AutoContent Wizard, there are occasions when you need some additional text on a slide. In that case, you must add a text box in order to add the text.

1 Click the Text Box tool on the Drawing toolbar.

The History of the Computer

Be sure to check the library for more books on t

5 If the text box isn't large enough to hold all the characters you want to type, don't worry—it expands as you continue to type. Text boxes grow with your words.

● Most of the time when you drag a text box to a certain size, it ends up a smaller size. PowerPoint doesn't pay much attention to your efforts. As you enter text, the text box will expand.

● Be careful not to place text boxes too close to the edges of the slide. A good-sized margin ensures readability.

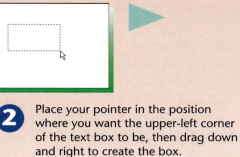

2 Place your pointer in the position where you want the upper-left corner of the text box to be, then drag down and right to create the box.

3 Release the mouse, and the text box is on the slide, with your insertion point waiting for you to begin entering text.

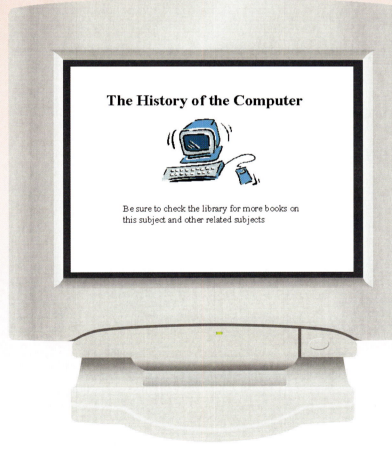

The History of the Computer

Be sure to check the library for more books on this subject and other related subjects

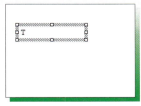

4 Begin typing immediately, even if it's only one letter. Unless you do, clicking anywhere else on the slide or on the PowerPoint window makes the text box disappear.

How to Add a Shape

Graphic shapes, placed and used correctly, can add a lot of pizzazz to a slide. You can use shapes to emphasize text, draw the eye to a specific spot on the slide, or even to hold text instead of using a text box.

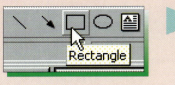

1 Click the appropriate tool on the Drawing toolbar.

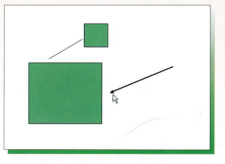

5 Drag an arrow and release the mouse to complete it. The arrow head appears on the end where you released the mouse.

● If you click instead of drag a rectangle or oval, you get a perfect square or circle.

● Click on a shape and begin typing to add text to the shape.

2 Place your pointer in the position where you want the upper-left corner of the shape to be and click.

3 To control the size of the shape, instead of clicking, drag your mouse down and right until the shape is exactly the way you want it. Release the mouse to end the process.

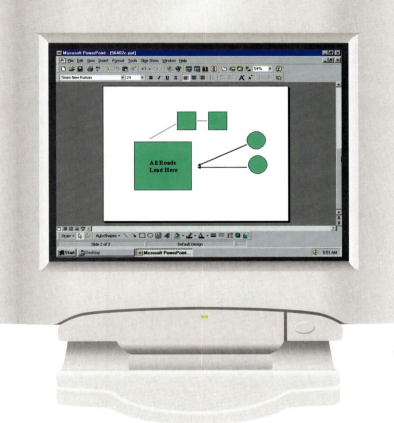

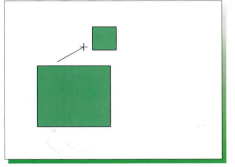

4 To draw a line, you must drag the mouse—clicking on the slide doesn't work. Release the mouse to complete the line.

How to Use AutoShapes

PowerPoint provides a slew of interesting and useful shapes you can use to create some pretty dynamic graphics. Some of them work well as stand-alone graphics, others are designed to create a special effect (for example, there are lots of arrows you can use to point to other elements on your slide).

1 Click the arrow on the AutoShapes button to see the menu of available choices.

6 When you release the mouse, the Action Settings dialog box appears so you can configure the action for this Action Button AutoShape.

● When you drag an AutoShape to insert it, you can create interesting effects by changing the basic shape. If you want to maintain the AutoShape while dragging, hold down the Shift key.

● Double-click on an AutoShape on your slide to bring up the Format AutoShape dialog box, where you can change the color, size, or position of the AutoShape.

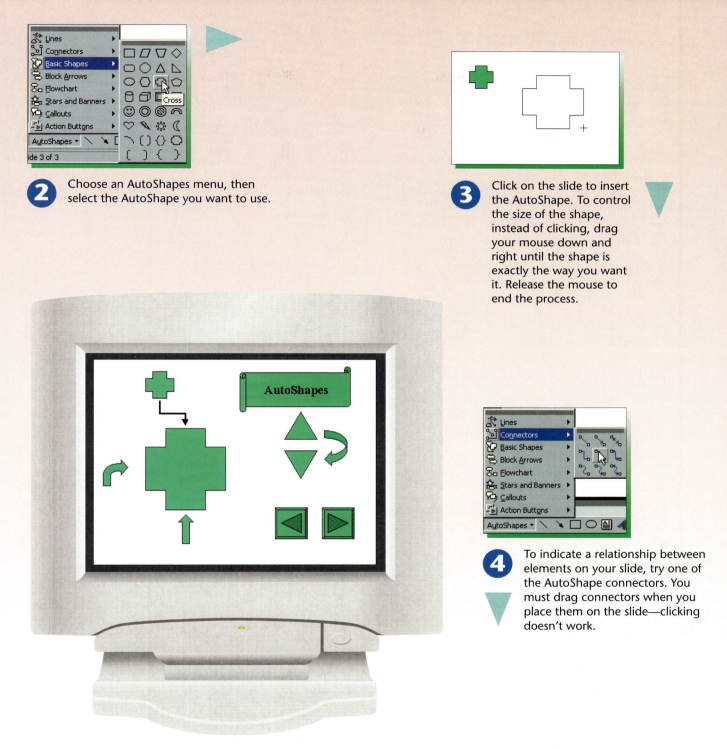

2 Choose an AutoShapes menu, then select the AutoShape you want to use.

3 Click on the slide to insert the AutoShape. To control the size of the shape, instead of clicking, drag your mouse down and right until the shape is exactly the way you want it. Release the mouse to end the process.

4 To indicate a relationship between elements on your slide, try one of the AutoShape connectors. You must drag connectors when you place them on the slide—clicking doesn't work.

5 Use Action Buttons on your slides to insert hyperlinks or other actions.

How to Use Fills, Shadows, and 3-D Effects

To add interest to your graphics, you can decorate them with fills, shadows, and 3-D effects.

Fills are solid colors or textured patterns that are applied to graphic shapes. Shadows are drop shadows that give the illusion that the sun is shining from a specific direction and creating a shadow on the opposite side of the shape. Of course, 3-D effects give the illusion of adding depth to a shape.

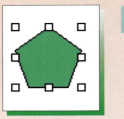

1 To apply an effect to a shape, first select the shape. Sizing handles will appear to indicate the shape is selected.

6 Select a shape and choose the 3-D tool from the Drawing toolbar. Then choose the 3-D effect you want to use for the shape.

● **If you use an AutoShape that is already a three-dimensional shape, the choices on the 3-D Tool are not accessible.**

● **Some of the 3-D effects are quite exaggerated and stretch your shape, so you may have to move the shape to make sure you're within the margins you want to establish for your slide.**

2 Click the arrow on the Fill Color tool on the Drawing toolbar to see the Fill dialog box.

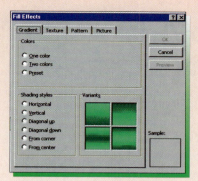

3 Click a color to change the color of the selected shape. Choose Fill Effects to choose special fill patterns from the Fill Effects dialog box. If you want a gradient fill pattern, configure it from the Gradient tab.

Text Box

4 For different types of fill patterns, choose a fill from the Texture tab or the Pattern tab.

5 Select a shape and choose the Shadow tool from the Drawing toolbar. Then choose the shadow you want to use for this shape.

How to Add Clip Art, Pictures, Video, and Sound

PowerPoint provides an enormous collection of clip art (drawings) and pictures you can use in your presentation. If you're going to present your slide show on a computer (or over the Internet), you can add video and sound clips to entertain your audience and elucidate your material.

Click to add title

Click to add text

Double click to add clip art

1 If you created your presentation with the AutoContent wizard, there are placeholders for your clip art. Double-click on a clip art placeholder.

● Most of the clip art and other objects in the Clip Gallery remain on your Office 97 CD and are not transferred to your hard drive during installation. Be sure the CD is in the CD-ROM drive when you're choosing objects from the Clip Gallery.

● When you place an object from the Clip Gallery into your presentation, it is embedded and you don't need to have the original file available. However, the size of your presentation file grows considerably.

 Choose an animated video from the Video tab and choose Play to watch it.

2 If you're working on a blank slide, choose Insert, Picture, Clip Art from the menu bar.

3 The Microsoft Clip Gallery displays with the Clip Art tab in the foreground. Choose a category, select an image, and choose Insert (or double-click on the image).

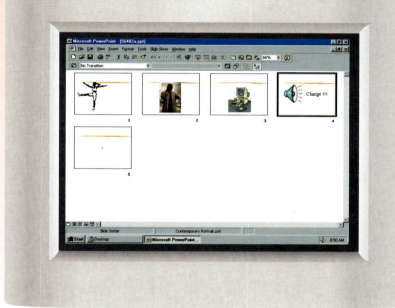

4 Use the Pictures tab to insert a picture that looks like a photograph.

5 Choose a sound from the Sounds tab. You can click the Play button to hear the sounds as you make your decision.

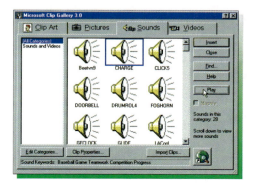

How to Move, Size, and Rotate Objects

G raphics add a great deal to your slide show, and tweaking them to make them just perfect enhances their effect.

If you add text directly on a graphic (instead of using a text box), you can manipulate the text at the same time you manipulate the graphic object.

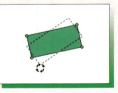

1 Select the object you want to manipulate. Sizing handles appear around the object to indicate that it's been selected.

6 Choose Free Rotate to control the rotation yourself. The mouse pointer turns into a rotation symbol, and you can rotate the object with any corner sizing handle.

FYI

● You can also use the Free Rotate tool on the Drawing toolbar to rotate objects.

● If you select clip art and the rotation choices are inaccessible (greyed out), it means the clip art is a group of objects. Ungroup them, then re-group them to rotate the clip art. More information about grouping and ungrouping is found later in this section.

2 When your mouse pointer is shaped like a four-headed arrow, you can move the object by dragging the mouse to the new position. For text boxes, you must move your pointer to the hatch-mark border in order to change the mouse pointer to the moving pointer.

3 Use the sizing handles to resize the object. Place your pointer over a sizing handle (the pointer changes to a double-headed arrow). Drag the side or top handles to widen or lengthen the object; use the corner handles to resize the height and width of the adjacent sides at the same time.

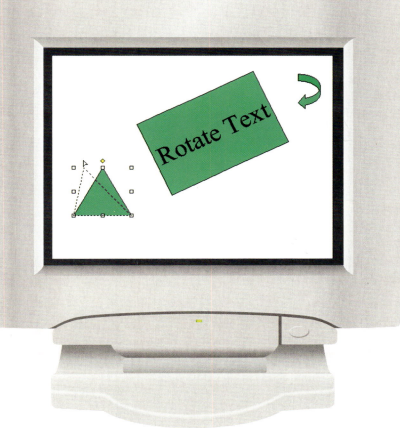

4 If the object has a yellow diamond near a sizing handle, you can drag the diamond to rotate the object.

5 You can rotate any object by selecting it and choosing Draw, Rotate or Flip from the Drawing toolbar. Then choose the rotation type you want to perform. The Right and Left Rotate options are for 90 degrees.

How to Layer Objects

You can stack objects on top of each other or overlay two objects for an interesting effect. All it takes is to drag one object over another one.

When you layer objects, however, you sometimes have some surprises: an object you want to place on top of another object refuses to go there—instead it wants to hide behind the other object. This happens as a side effect of the natural layering order of objects. Luckily, you can interfere with the natural layering order and configure it for your own uses.

 Create and insert objects as needed on a slide.

● Each time you select Bring Forward or Send Backward, you move one layer up or down. If you have many layers, it's sometimes easier to choose Bring to Front, then choose Send Backward once or twice.

● After you have a group of objects layered correctly, you may need to move them to another position on the slide. Drag your mouse in a rectangle that encloses all the objects, and when you release your mouse, you've created a group. Drag the group to another part of the slide, and the layers keep their places. Click anywhere outside the group to ungroup the objects.

5 When you move a text box over another object, the text disappears unless it is in the foreground. It's always a good idea to put a text box in the front (as opposed to merely moving it forward).

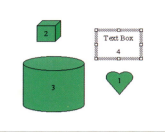

2 Objects are layered from the bottom up, in the order in which they are inserted on the slide.

3 When you attempt to place an object on top of another object and it doesn't work, it means the layering order is wrong.

4 Right-click either object and change the layer by choosing Order from the shortcut menu and then selecting the appropriate action.

How to Group and Ungroup Objects

Grouping objects means uniting them so that whatever you do to one, you do to all. The objects travel as a group when you move them, or rotate as a group when you spin them. This is a very handy feature. You can group objects temporarily or permanently—usually a temporary group is formed for the purpose of manipulating all of the elements in the group at one time.

Some objects in PowerPoint are already grouped when you choose them (there are many clip art objects that are groups). Knowing how to ungroup means you can make changes to the individual elements of a grouped object.

1 You can create a group out of objects that are stacked, overlapped, or not touching at all. The definition of a group is merely that the objects have some relationship that you want to keep intact.

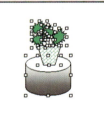

7 Right-click on a group and choose Grouping, Ungroup from the shortcut menu when you want to change an individual element of a group. After you make changes, use the shortcut menu (Grouping, Regroup) to put the group back together.

6 A permanent group has one set of sizing handles and will behave as a single object forever (unless you ungroup it).

2 To group objects, place your mouse pointer in a position that is outside the furthest side of any element in the group, then drag a rectangle that includes all the elements of the group.

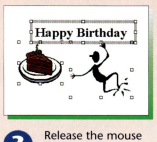

3 Release the mouse and you see the sizing handles for every element in the group.

4 Move, rotate, or resize the group (dragging a resizing handle for any object in the group resizes all objects to the same degree). Click outside the group to un-group the objects (this means you created a temporary group).

5 To create a permanent group, right-click in the temporary group and choose Grouping, Group from the shortcut menu.

How to Insert, Delete, and Reorder Slides

As you work on your presentation, you'll find you frequently need to add slides (perhaps even in the middle of your slide show), get rid of slides that don't really work well, and change the order in which slides appear.

Performing these tasks is not onerous; the biggest problem is deciding how you want to accomplish these chores because PowerPoint offers several choices.

1 I find it easiest to move to Slide Sorter view when I'm making decisions about slides. Click the Slide Sorter tool to get there.

6 To delete a slide in Slide view, choose Edit, Delete Slide.

● If you insert a slide while you are working in Slide View, the new slide comes after the slide currently in the PowerPoint window.

● You can only reorder slides in Slide Sorter view.

2 To insert a slide, select the slide that will immediately precede the new slide, then click the New Slide tool on the Standard toolbar.

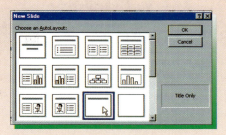

3 The New Slide dialog box appears so you can choose a layout. Click OK when you have picked the slide style you need. The new slide is inserted immediately after the slide you've selected.

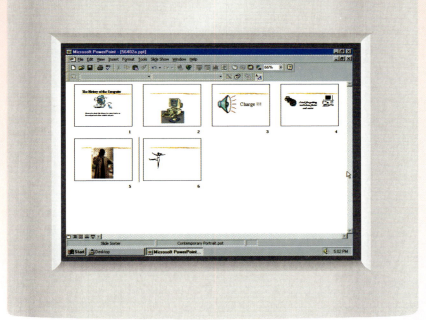

4 To delete a slide, select it and press the Del key. Poof! It's gone! PowerPoint does not ask you to confirm the deletion. If you delete a slide by mistake, immediately click the Undo icon, don't do anything else first.

5 To change the order of a slide, drag it to the new location. Release the mouse to place it in the new spot.

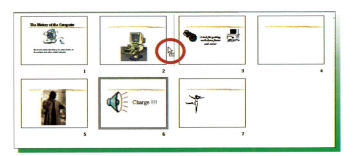

How to Create Speaker Notes

When you present your slide show, it's a good idea to have notes that you can use to guide you through your presentation. PowerPoint provides two ways to create notes.

You can enter your Speaker Notes in a dialog box or you can enter them directly on a notes page that is attached to each slide.

1 To enter notes, select a slide in Slide Sorter view, Outline view, or bring a slide into the PowerPoint window. Choose View, Speaker Notes from the menu bar.

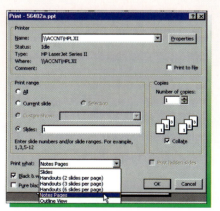

6 To print your notes, choose File, Print, then choose Notes Pages from the Print What text box list. The printed document contains the slide on the top of the page and your notes below it.

- To view slides in the PowerPoint window without the notes, choose View, Slide.

- You can use the Notes Page for additional information for the audience and print the notes as handouts.

2 A Speaker Notes dialog box appears, with the number of the selected slide displayed. Enter your notes. Choose Close when you have finished. As you work on additional slides, continue this process.

3 To use the notes space attached to the slide, select a slide from any view (or put the appropriate slide into the PowerPoint window) and choose View Notes Page from the menu bar.

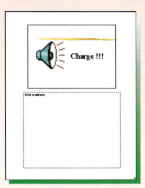

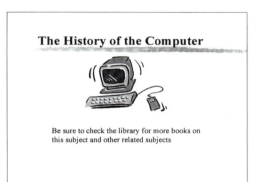

4 The slide, along with its Notes Page, is placed in the PowerPoint window. The top of the Notes Page says *Click to add text*. You may want to use View, Zoom to zoom in on the Notes Page.

5 Click on the text and the Notes Page turns into a text box. If you already made notes for this slide with the dialog box, those notes appear on the Notes Page. Click anywhere in the box to add more notes.

How to Create Handouts

Many presentations include audience handouts. These are hard copies of the information presented in the slide show, sometimes distributed before the show, and sometimes afterward. Handouts differ from notes in that only the slides are part of the handouts.

You can design handouts to meet whatever criteria you need. The whole point of handouts is to help the audience absorb and remember the important points of your presentation.

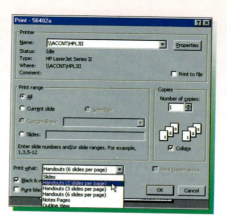

1 To create a master design, choose View, Master, Handout Master. (Even though a handout is a printed copy of the slide, you probably want some additional information on the handout in order to jog the memory of the recipient.)

6 To print your handouts, return to one of the PowerPoint views. Then choose File, Print, and select the appropriate Handouts option from the Print What text box list.

● You can use the same techniques for customization on the Speaker Notes pages as discussed here. Choose View, Master, Notes Master to get to the master page for notes.

● Remember that the more slides on a Handout page, the smaller each slide. If your slides have a lot of text, you might want to avoid the six-slides-per-page option (which is shown on these pages).

2 A Master configuration document displays, and the Handout Master toolbar is in your PowerPoint window.

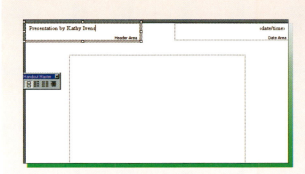

3 Use the Handout Master toolbar to look at the layout options. You can choose two, three, or six slides to a page (the default, initial view is six). It's a good idea to drag the toolbar off to the side so you can work more easily in the document (click on the blue title area and drag the toolbar away).

Presentation by Kathy Ivens

The History of the Computer

Be sure to check the library for more books on this subject and other related subjects

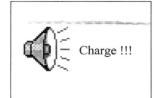

Charge !!!

A tool for getting work done faster and easier

4 Click the Header Area or the Footer Area (or both) to select the text box that is preconfigured. Then use View, Zoom to move in on the area. Enter the text you want to appear on every page (delete the placeholder text). Enter information in the Date Area if you want to print the date. (The page number prints automatically unless you delete it.)

5 You can drag any of the text areas to another part of the page.

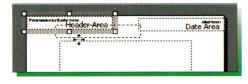

How to Set Up a Slide Show

Before you present your slide show, you have to do some work to set it up, in addition to creating each slide.

The setup procedures vary, depending upon how your show is going to be run. If you're going to be presenting the show yourself, the pre-show work is different from the work you need to do if the presentation is self-running.

1 Choose Slide Show, Set Up Show to tell PowerPoint how your show is going to be presented.

6 To adjust the timing for a slide, select the slide and choose Slide Show, Slide Transition, then change the timing.

● If you select **On Mouse Click** in addition to selecting automatic timing in the **Slide Transition** dialog box, you can override the automatic timing by clicking when you present your slide show.

● In the **Set Up Show** dialog box, if you select **Browsed at a Kiosk**, the slide show is automatically set up to loop continuously.

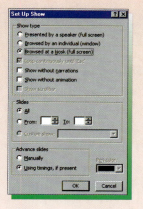

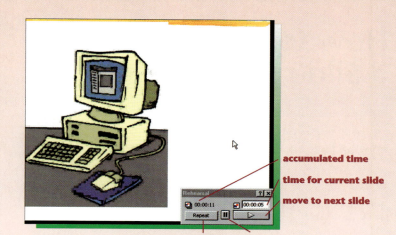

accumulated time
time for current slide
move to next slide

restart timing for current slide   **pause**

2 Choose the option(s) you need from the Set Up Show dialog box.

3 To set up the timing for each slide so you don't have to click the screen to change slides during your presentation, choose Slide Show, Rehearse Timings. The slide show begins playing back the way it will when you present it. Rehearse your narration out loud and click each time you're ready for the next slide. PowerPoint keeps a record of the timing for each slide change.

4 If you're happy with the timings, tell PowerPoint to record them.

5 The Slide Sorter view shows the timing for each slide.

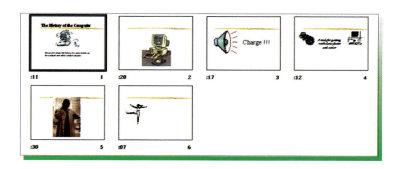

How to Run a Slide Show

The most common (and easiest) way to run your presentation from your computer is to hook up to a projection device and run the show.

You can open PowerPoint and start the show, or you can configure the presentation to run without opening PowerPoint.

These pages discuss running your presentation from within PowerPoint. The next pages explain how to set up your presentation so you can run it without opening PowerPoint.

1 To run your presentation from within PowerPoint, click the Slide Show icon.

6 If you configured an animated entry for any element of the slide (such as flying text in from above the slide), clicking the mouse starts the animated entry instead of advancing to the next slide.

(Continued on next page)

● If you have automated timings for each slide, and you want to override them with your mouse during the show, be sure to establish that configuration in the Slide Transition dialog box. Select both transition options, On Mouse Click and Automatically, to have this choice available during the show.

● When you are using the pen, clicking the mouse does not advance the slides—you must switch back to the arrow.

2 If you have not set timings for the slides, click the mouse each time you want to display the next slide.

3 To make notes on the screen, right-click and choose Pen from the shortcut menu.

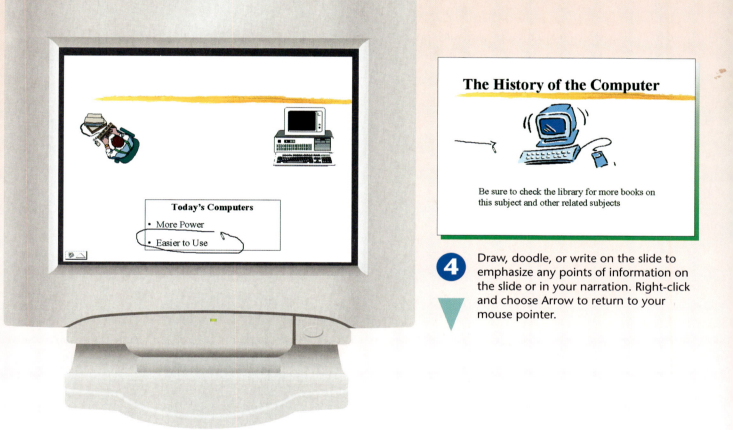

4 Draw, doodle, or write on the slide to emphasize any points of information on the slide or in your narration. Right-click and choose Arrow to return to your mouse pointer.

5 To start a video or audio effect, click the icon. Then click outside the icon to move to the next slide (or click the icon again to repeat the effect).

How to Run a Slide Show (Continued)

You can design and configure your slide show so that you don't have to open PowerPoint in order to run the presentation. Instead, you open an icon from your desktop.

This method of presenting your show is a bit slicker because your audience doesn't have to watch you open the PowerPoint software, go through the opening screens to select a presentation file, and so on.

 7 Open PowerPoint and choose the presentation you want to configure.

 12 The shortcut to the show is on your desktop. Double-click it when you want to start the presentation. When the presentation ends, you are returned to the desktop.

● **You can create a folder on your desktop for presentations and move each show shortcut into it. This makes the desktop less cluttered and makes it easier to find your presentations.**

● **To edit the title under the shortcut, right-click and choose Rename. Enter a new (better) title and press Enter.**

8 Choose File, Save As from the menu bar.

9 In the Save as Type field of the Save As dialog box, choose PowerPoint Show. Then choose Save.

10 Close PowerPoint and open Explorer. Open the folder in which your PowerPoint files are kept and find the PowerPoint Show file, which has a file extension of .pps.

11 Right-drag the file icon to your desktop. When you release the mouse button, a menu appears. Choose Create Shortcut(s) Here.

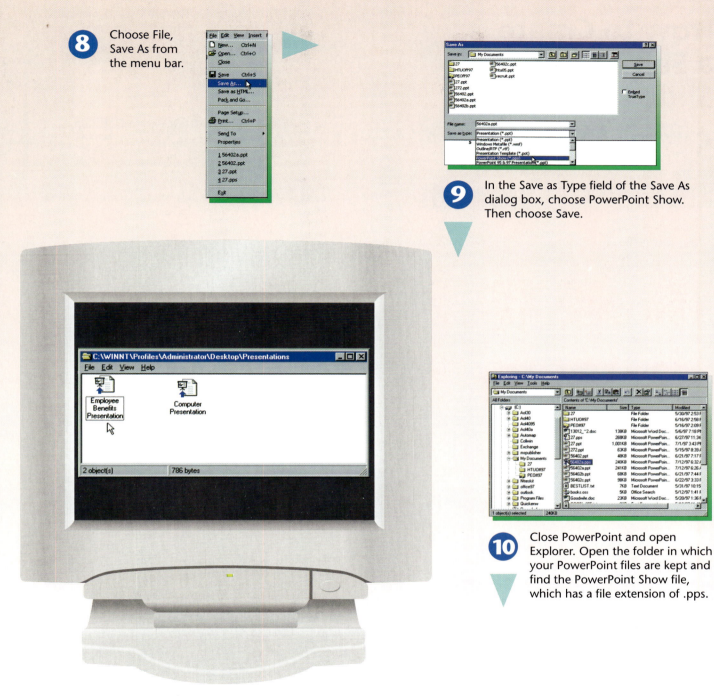

How to Create a Self-Running Slide Show

S elf-running presentations are for information that you want to present to the public without the need to be in front of your computer narrating. Convention exhibit areas, kiosks, and other large public venues are the ideal spots for these shows.

You must set up your show so that everything (animation effects and slide changes) is automatic. This requires more setup, but none of the configuration work is terribly onerous.

1 Open PowerPoint and choose the presentation you want to configure as a self-running show.

6 Choose Slide Show, Set Up Show, and select Browsed at a Kiosk. This automatically configures the show as a continuous loop.

(Continued on next page)

FYI

● Run your slide show to test it, then adjust timings, transitions, animation, and any other effect that didn't work properly. You'll probably have to do this several times.

● In the Set Up Show dialog box, make sure you selected Using Timings for the Advance Slides option.

2 Establish timings for each slide in your presentation.

3 For movies and video, right-click the icon and choose Custom Animation. Then select automatic animation.

4 On the Play Settings tab of the Custom Animation dialog box, choose the options you want for pausing or continuing the slide show, and when to stop playing the file (this choice is for audio clips).

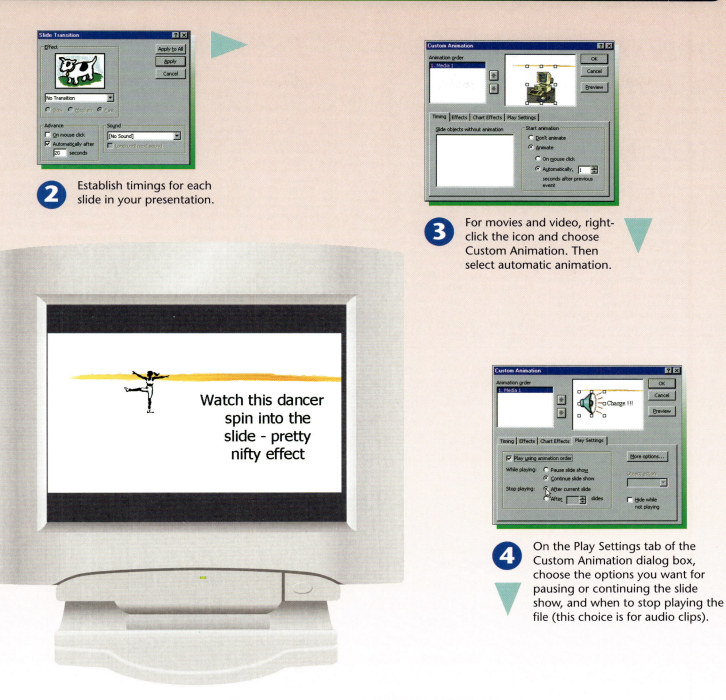

5 Make sure that entry effects such as flying text are configured for automatic transition.

How to Create a Self-Running Slide Show (Continued)

You can also establish a self-running slide show in a way that lets the viewer control the show.

You can let the viewer advance the slides, or even skip to a specific slide using a hyperlink.

Once you've configured your self-running show as described on the previous pages, you can add the necessary options.

7 To create a button that a viewer can click to make something happen (such as advancing to the next slide), choose Slide Show, Action Buttons. Select the button you want to use. (The slide to which you are attaching this button must be in the PowerPoint window.)

12 On the target slide for a hyperlink, choose an action button to create a button to return to the slide that has the hyperlink.

● When you add action buttons, you cannot test them without running the slide show. Clicking them in the normal PowerPoint window means you want to edit the graphic.

● To label action buttons ("Go to next slide", "Return to last slide"), create a text box under the button.

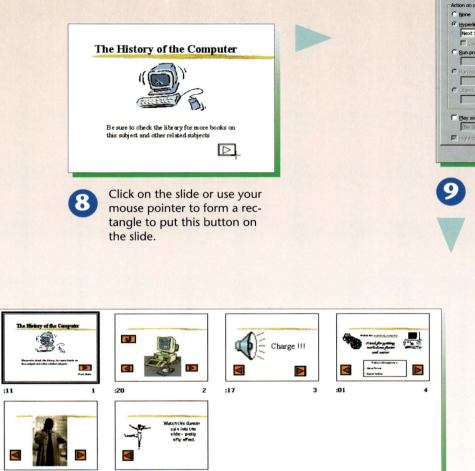

8 Click on the slide or use your mouse pointer to form a rectangle to put this button on the slide.

9 When you release your mouse button, the Action Settings dialog box appears. Specify the action that will take place when the viewer clicks this button.

10 To insert a hyperlink to another slide, select the text you want to use for the hyperlink, then right-click and choose Action Settings from the shortcut menu. When the Action Settings dialog box appears, select Hyperlink To, then click the arrow to choose the target slide.

11 If you select Slide as the target, the Hyperlink to Slide dialog box appears so you can select the appropriate slide (a picture appears so you know when you've chosen the right slide). Notice that the text changes color to indicate that it's a hyperlink.

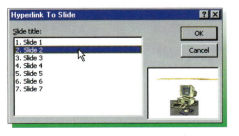

How to Use Pack and Go

If you need to travel with your presentation and you don't want to drag your computer with you, you can show the presentation on any computer if you pack it up for traveling.

PowerPoint has a traveling presentation feature called Pack and Go, and you can use it to make your slide show portable. In fact, all you have to carry with you is a floppy disk.

1 Open the presentation you want to travel with, and then choose File, Pack and Go from the menu bar.

7 The Wizard copies linked files and your presentation file and performs all its wizardry to pack up your presentation.

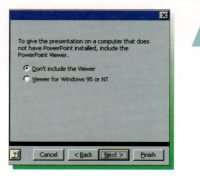

6 If the computer you are going to use has PowerPoint installed, you don't need to include the PowerPoint Viewer. Click Finish, since this is the last question the Wizard has.

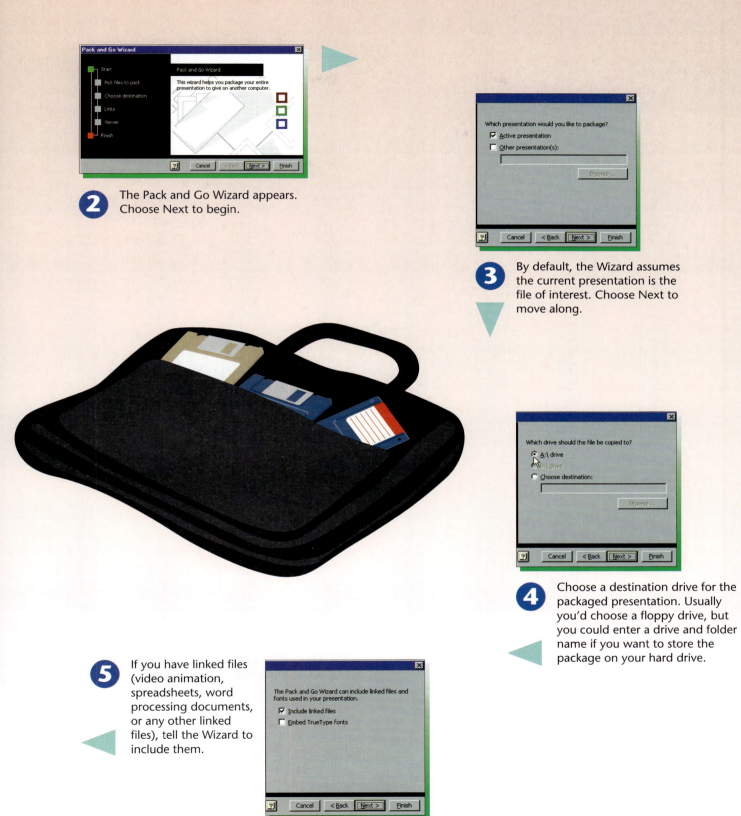

2 The Pack and Go Wizard appears. Choose Next to begin.

3 By default, the Wizard assumes the current presentation is the file of interest. Choose Next to move along.

4 Choose a destination drive for the packaged presentation. Usually you'd choose a floppy drive, but you could enter a drive and folder name if you want to store the package on your hard drive.

5 If you have linked files (video animation, spreadsheets, word processing documents, or any other linked files), tell the Wizard to include them.

PART 6

Outlook 97

IF YOU'RE TIRED of looking for matchbook covers and cocktail napkins with phone numbers on them, Outlook 97 is for you. If you want all of your appointments in one place, with a calendar and to-do list right at your finger tips, Outlook 97 is for you. If you want to organize all your personal information so that e-mail, contact information, schedules, notes, documents and more are available whenever you need it, Outlook 97 is for you.

This section gives you crash course in getting organized with Outlook 97.

WHAT YOU'LL FIND HERE IS

- **The Opening Window**   206
- **How to Use the Personal Address Book**   208
- **How to Compose and Send E-Mail**   210
- **How to Attach a File to a Message**   212
- **How to Open and Read E-Mail**   214
- **How to Reply To and Forward Messages**   216
- **How to Manage Received Attachments**   218
- **How to Create an Appointment**   220
- **How to Create a Recurring Appointment**   222
- **How to Create Tasks Quickly**   224
- **How to Create Contacts**   226
- **How to Send E-Mail to a Contact**   228
- **How to Autodial Contacts**   230
- **How to Autorecord Journal Entries**   232
- **How to Record Manual Journal Entries**   234
- **How to Use AutoArchive**   236

The Opening Window

Your first view of Outlook can be somewhat confusing unless you understand the basic elements. Although not as complex as the cockpit of a 747 jumbo jet, the opening window does pack quite a few features in a small space.

In addition to the standard menu and toolbar system, the Outlook window also contains a wide vertical bar, on the left side, that displays icons. The Outlook bar, as it is so aptly named, is the Outlook control center. Each of the icons located in the Outlook bar is a shortcut to an Outlook feature or an Outlook folder.

The Outlook bar has several parts, or groups, each with its own icons. The main group contains shortcuts to each of the primary Outlook folders, the Mail group provides access to the mail features, and the Other group allows you to utilize non-Outlook features from within Outlook.

1 To open a primary Outlook folder, click the icon in the Outlook bar. For example, clicking the Calendar icon takes you to the Outlook Calendar window.

● If you frequently use a folder that does not have an icon on the Outlook bar, you can add one yourself. Open the folder list, right-click the folder you want to add, and select Add to Outlook bar. An even easier way is to simply drag the folder from the folder list and drop it on the Outlook bar where you want it to appear.

● Clicking on the folder name (Inbox, Contacts, Sent Items, and so forth) that appears above the Information Viewer (the large Outlook window that displays the contents of the selected folder) opens the folder list, enabling you to view a directory tree structure of all the folders available in Outlook.

6 Click the Other button (tab) in the Outlook bar to display the group of shortcuts that provide access to features outside of Outlook. The shortcuts that appear are My Computer, My Documents, and Favorites.

2 Click the Mail button (tab) in the Outlook bar to slide the Outlook bar up, revealing the e-mail–related icons.

3 Unless you've changed the default e-mail options, Outlook automatically saves a copy of each message you send in the Sent Items folder. To review e-mail that's been sent, click the Sent Items shortcut.

Menu bar
Toolbar
Outlook bar

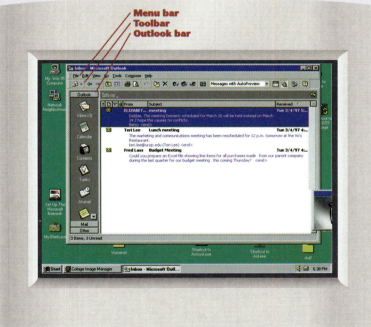

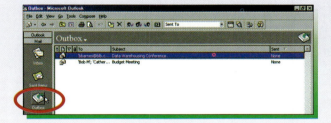

4 Unless you're on a network with a direct connection to an e-mail post office, mail that you send is stored in the Outbox until you make your modem connection and actually send it. To see your outgoing mail, click the Outbox shortcut in the Outlook bar.

5 To view any items that you've deleted, click the Deleted Items icon, which appears in both the main Outlook Bar group and the Mail group.

How to Use the Personal Address Book

One of the Outlook features you'll learn to rely on is your Personal Address Book. This is a personal database of all the e-mail addresses you use to send messages. If you aren't working on a network with a mail system, this is your primary list of mail recipients.

The first thing you have to do is open your Personal Address Book (PAB). Then you have to begin entering data into it. If you're connected to a network Exchange Server mail system, you can copy addresses from the Global Address Book (GAB) instead of entering them from the keyboard. There are a couple of rules about entering addresses, and there are lots of optional entries.

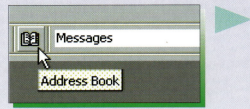

1 The easiest way to open your PAB is to click its icon on the toolbar. If you opened any Information Viewer from the Mail group in the Outlook bar (Inbox, Sent Items, Outbox, or Deleted Items), the icon is there. Otherwise, choose Tools, Address Book from the menu bar (or press Ctrl+Shift+B).

- The Add to Personal Address Book icon on the PAB toolbar may be inaccessible to you. This is used when the Global Address Book is displayed and you want to copy a name from it into your PAB. If you're not on a network mail system, it's never available. If you are on a network mail system, it's only available when you select the GAB in the box labeled Show Names From The.

- If you get e-mail from someone who is not in your address book, right-click on the sender's name when the message is open (it's the From field). Then choose Add to Address Book from the menu that displays.

- If you're adding an entry for someone on AOL or CompuServe, that's an Internet Address. For AOL, use the screen name followed by @aol.com. For a CompuServe address that is a number (for example, 74222,4120), substitute a period for the comma in the identification, then add @compuserve.com.

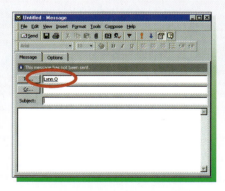

6 Most of the time you'll use the PAB when you are composing a new message—you start a new message, then call up the PAB to select a recipient. However, you can perform those steps in the other way, calling up a new message form from the PAB. Select the listing in your PAB you want to send a message to, then click the New Message icon on the toolbar. A message form appears, the recipient's name is filled in, and your cursor is waiting in the Subject field.

New Entry

Find

Properties

Delete

Add to PAB

New Message

Help

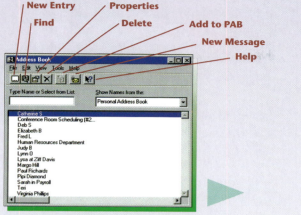

2 The PAB opens, and it looks like a mini-software window. It has a menu bar, a toolbar, and entry boxes.

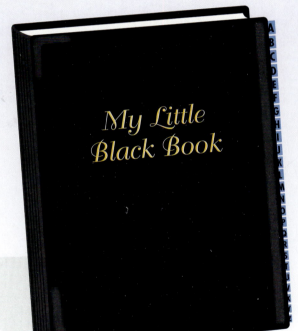

My Little Black Book

3 To add an entry to the PAB, click the New Entry icon on the toolbar (or, if you like doing things the long way, choose File, New Entry from the menu bar). The New Entry dialog box appears. The first step is to indicate the address type for this entry. Your choices may look different from this illustration, and may include entry types such as cc:Mail, Microsoft Mail, or X.400, depending upon the setup of the network you're connected to. Most of the time, since this is a personal entry instead of a company entry, you should select Internet Mail. Click OK when you have selected the address type.

4 Enter a display name for this entry. This is the name or phrase that appears in your PAB. There's nothing official or technical about it—it's your own way of referring to this person. You can use "Mom" or "Aunt Tessie" or "the good looking guy in accounting." However, when you send this person e-mail, this display name appears in the To box of the message, so don't use anything you wouldn't want the recipient to see. In the Email Address box, enter the official, technical e-mail address for this recipient. The checkbox about Rich Text Format is available so that if you know that this recipient has a mail system that can handle RTF, you can format message text with fancy attributes. If it can't handle RTF, your formatted message could arrive as unreadable garbage. When you have filled out the dialog box, click OK.

5 When you return to your PAB window, the new entry is on the list. You can scroll through the list to find it, but if you have a long list, that can be inefficient or even annoying. A quick way to get to a name on your list is to enter characters in the Type Name or Select from List text box. As you type each character, you move to the entry that matches the characters you're entering.

How to Compose and Send E-Mail

E-mail is the heart of your Outlook system. It's where you'll probably spend most of your time, it's the easiest part of Outlook, and it's fun. The ability to send and receive messages electronically is one of the most important developments in communications, and you'll wonder how you ever lived without it.

Sending e-mail is easy; there are only three basic steps: fill out the header, write the message, click Send. Outlook takes care of the rest.

1 Choose File, New, Mail Message from the menu bar to open a blank message form. Since the To field is required (you can't send it if it has nowhere to go), click the To button and select a name from your address book. Note that you can select multiple recipients from the address book by holding down the Ctrl Key and clicking on the names to add.

FYI

● If you enter an e-mail address directly into a recipient field, you can right-click it and choose Add to Address Book if it isn't in there already.

● If you click the To button on the message form in order to use the Select Names dialog box to enter the recipient name, you can enter the Cc and Bcc names at the same time. Just click an entry to highlight it, then click Cc or Bcc to place that entry into the right part of the Message Recipients pane. This eliminates all the steps involved in returning to the message, and then entering the recipients for the Cc field and the Bcc field.

● You can enter names directly, including partial names, in the fields for copies, the same way you do for the To field.

6 Press Tab to move to the message text section (or click anywhere in the text box). Type the body of your message. When you're through, click the Send button to send the e-mail (if you're on a network), or place it in the Outbox (if you use a modem connection for e-mail).

2 You don't have to press To and use the address book, you can enter a name into the To field directly. Outlook checks the address book, and if it finds the name, it underlines it. You can even enter a name that isn't in your address book, but you can't use a display name, you must enter a valid e-mail address. Outlook checks the address book and if it doesn't find the name, it then checks your typing to make sure you entered a valid e-mail address format. If so, it underlines it. (Of course that doesn't mean you have the address right, it just means you typed it in a valid format.) If you enter multiple names directly, put a semicolon between them.

3 If you want to send a copy of the message to another recipient, or multiple recipients, you have to enter the name in the Cc field. Click on the Cc button to bring up the Select Names dialog box, then double-click on the entry you want. Because you clicked the Cc button, double-clicking automatically places the name in the Cc portion of the Message Recipients pane. Click OK to return to the message. The names in the Cc field are visible to the recipient of the message.

4 If you want to send a copy to someone and you want it to be a secret, that's called a blind carbon copy. The recipient will not see any indication of this copy on the message. You can add a name to the Bcc field by clicking either the To or Cc button in order to bring up the Select Names dialog box (there is no Bcc button on the message form until you use the Bcc feature). Select the person that you want to send a blind copy to, then click Bcc. The display name for that person is placed in the Bcc section of the Message Recipients pane.

5 Move to the Subject box, either by pressing Tab or clicking in the Subject box. Enter a short phrase that describes what this message is about. Remember that when the recipient looks at his or her received messages, it may be only the header that's seen, so this phrase becomes a clue that helps determine whether the message gets read now or sits in the Inbox until the recipient gets around to reading it. Many Internet recipients use software that cannot reveal any of the message, so the text in the Subject box is the only clue to the message contents.

How to Attach a File to a Message

When you want to attach or insert something, most of the time you'll find that it's an existing file that was created in a software application you use. For example, you may have created a letter or report in a word processor. Or perhaps you created a presentation in PowerPoint or Microsoft Publisher. When you need to share the information in those files with others, you can send them an e-mail message with the appropriate file attached to the message.

In order to view or open the file, the recipient has to have the software associated with the file. Don't send a Word 97 document to a Word 2.0 user.

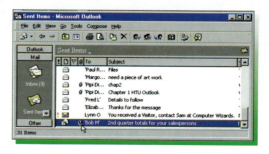

1 Start by writing an e-mail message as you usually do. That means you fill out a header, subject, and message text. It's polite to tell the recipient what file it is you're sending, and why.

● Although Outlook offers a variety of fancy ways to include the contents of a file in the body of your message as text, the easiest way is to just cut and paste. You can select exactly which information to include and you won't end up with a bunch of weird formatting characters (which frequently happens when you use the Insert File dialog box with the Insert As Text option turned on).

● You can also drag a file onto an open message form.

● You can select multiple files and drag them to the Inbox icon or an open message form.

6 After the file is sent, when you see its listing in the Sent Items folder, a paper clip icon appears in the listing to remind you that you attached a file to this message.

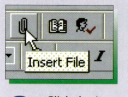

2 Click the Insert File icon on the message toolbar.

3 The Insert File dialog box opens. By default, Outlook searches the folder named My Documents. If the file you need isn't in this folder (or its subfolders), use the Up One Level icon to begin navigating around your hard drive so you can locate the file.

4 When you find the file you need, select it and choose OK (or double-click it).

5 The dialog box closes and an icon representing the file is in the message. Click Send to ship the message, together with the file, to the recipient.

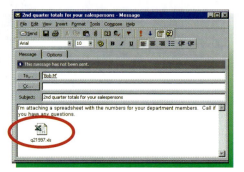

How to Open and Read E-Mail

Okay, the mail carrier has been here or you've dialed out to get your mail from a remote mailbox. Now it's time to open and read the messages. There's nothing difficult about opening and reading messages, you could probably figure it out without my help. But I'm assuming you get tons of messages, that all those interoffice memos, all those questions from other employees, all those directives and assignments from the bosses, whew...they pile up every day.

You have other things to do, deadlines to meet, places to go, people to see, you have a life—so sometimes there just isn't time to read and take care of all your e-mail right away. This section covers the ways to figure out what to read, and what to do about messages that require follow-up.

1 Before you start opening and reading messages, you should decide which messages to read first. There are a couple of clues in the Inbox listing that help you make this decision. The text in the Subject column is always a big clue (or should be, but some people don't know how to write good Subject phrases). In addition, senders can mark messages to draw attention to special features about them. A red exclamation point means important; a blue down arrow means not important; a red flag means the message requires some follow-up action by you; and a paper clip indicates there's a file attached to the message.

7 To close the file, click the Close button on the message window, or press Alt+F4, or choose File, Close from the menu bar. The message closes and its listing changes so that it is no longer bold. If your Inbox listing is set up for AutoPreview (some of the message text displays), no text displays for this message because AutoPreview only acts on unread messages.

6 If you have no reason to keep this message, delete it by clicking the Delete icon on the toolbar.

2 After you decide which messages require your immediate attention, open them and read them. To open a message, double-click its listing. The message opens and there's lots of stuff on the top part of the message, but the important part is the text in the message box. Read it. If you're following along with messages in your own Inbox, I'll wait...Okay, ready to move on?

3 If this message requires some follow-up action by you, give yourself a reminder by flagging it so a red flag is next to its listing when you look at the Inbox. Click the Flag icon on the toolbar of the message window to display the Flag Message dialog box. Click the arrow to the right of the Flag box and choose a Flag message from the drop-down list, or enter your own reminder message. If appropriate, click the arrow to the right of the By text box, and click a date on the calendar that displays to set a deadline for yourself. Click OK to close the dialog box.

Tasks in Progress

New Tasks

4 If you want to print the message, click the Print icon on the toolbar. The message prints immediately. If you have to set up a printer, or pick a printer, or need the Print dialog box for any reason, press Ctrl+P (or choose File, Print from the menu bar).

5 If you want to save the message as a file, choose File, Save As from the menu bar. The subject of the message becomes the file name, but you can change that if you wish. By default, Outlook saves the message as a Rich Text Format file 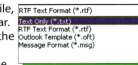 (some word processors, including MS Word, can handle RTF files), but you can press the arrow to the right of the Save as Type box and choose another file type. You can also change the folder in which you save the message.

How to Reply To and Forward Messages

Replying to a message means sending a message back to the person who sent you an e-mail message. Forwarding a message is sending that message to a different person, because you believe there's some reason that third party has an interest in the message contents.

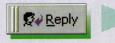

1 When you open a message, the message window contains all the tools you need to make responding to the sender quick and easy. To reply to the sender, click the Reply button on the toolbar.

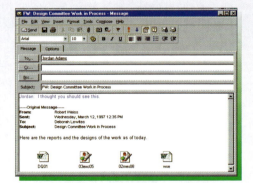

6 Enter the name of the recipient and add any comments of your own above the message text (usually something like "I thought this would be of interest to you"). If there are attachments on the original message, they are forwarded also. If you don't want to forward any or all of the attachments, delete them by selecting them and pressing Del. Click Send to forward the message, then close the original message.

- If you don't want to include the original header or message (or either) in your reply, select the text and delete it.

- When you are replying (either to the recipient or to all recipients), you can add any additional recipients you wish. The new recipients can be direct recipients (in the To field) or copied recipients (in either the Cc or Bcc field).

- If you choose to reply to all recipients, you can subsequently delete any of the multiple recipients you wish to.

2 A message form opens with a lot of information filled in automatically. The recipient is there, and of course, it's the sender (that's why we call it a reply). The subject is the same as the original subject, except it has RE: before the subject text. The original message header and message text are in the message area, and your insertion point is waiting just above that. All you have to do is enter your response.

3 Notice that when you enter your response, the characters on the screen are blue. (If you are using Outlook in Exchange Server, and the recipient is on your Exchange Server system, the recipient will see your entry in blue.) You can also enter comments directly in the original message. To draw attention to the fact that you're entering text inside an existing message, each time you enter text, Outlook inserts your name. Click Send when you are finished writing your reply. Then close the original message.

4 If you receive a message that displays a number of additional recipients in the Cc box, you can choose to reply to every recipient. Click Reply to All and then proceed as described in the previous steps.

5 Sometimes you'll receive a message you think would be of interest to another person. You don't have to write that person a note detailing the information in the message you received, you can simply forward the message. To do so, click Forward on the toolbar. A new message form opens with the subject filled in, preceded by *FW:* to indicate that this is a forwarded message.

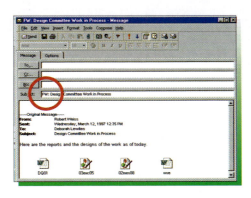

How to Manage Received Attachments

If someone wants to send you all the important information in a report, it's easier to send the entire report than it is to type in all the text of the report. For that and many other reasons, people attach documents to e-mail messages. These attachments are handled separately from the message, since you can't see the contents of the attachment when you open the message.

You know before you open a message that it contains an attachment because a paper clip icon appears in the attachment column to the left of the message listing in your Inbox. You have several options for handling attachments and this section covers them.

1 Some attachments can be viewed quickly without opening them or otherwise manipulating them by using the Windows Quick View program. This is a software application that is installed with your Windows operating system, and it has the ability to display the contents of certain kinds of files (the specific file types are dependent upon the way Quick View was installed). Right-click the attachment's icon and choose Quick View to open the Quick View window. The contents will display, but you won't see any formatting or other special effects. If there is no Quick View viewer for the file type, an error message will inform you of that fact.

6 For a really quick look, using Quick View, you don't even have to open the message. Right-click the listing in the Inbox and choose View Attachments. If there are multiple attachments, they're listed in a submenu and you can click the one you want to view.

- If you open an attachment and make changes and save the file, when you close the associated software and return to the message the attachment icon represents the new, changed file.

- If you select an attachment icon and click the Print icon on the message toolbar, the message prints, not the attachment. You must use the right-click menu to print the attachment without opening it.

- If you don't have the appropriate software to open an attachment, copy it to a floppy disk. Then take the disk to a computer that does have the right software.

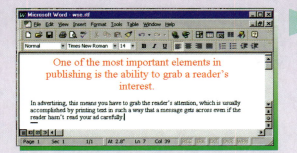

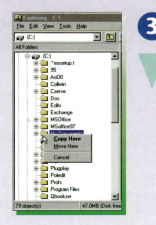

3 You can move or copy the attachment to a folder for later attention. Open Explorer or My Computer, then drag the attachment to the appropriate folder. If you right-drag, a menu is offered when you release the mouse button so you can choose to move or copy the file. If you left-drag, the attachment is copied.

2 You can open the attached file by double-clicking it. *Open* means that the software application that can handle this file (usually the same application that created it) opens, and the attached file is then opened in the software window. If you don't have the associated software, the file won't open (unless your software application has a file conversion utility). Once the software is open and the attachment is loaded in the software window, you can use all the tools the software offers to manipulate the file. That means, for example, you can edit it, save it, print it, and so on. When you exit the software, you return to the message.

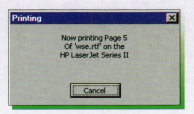

4 You can print the document by right-clicking it and choosing Print. The associated software opens, loads the file in its software window, prints the file, and then closes.

5 You can choose Cut or Copy from the right-click menu, then paste the attachment into a folder or even into a message you're sending to someone else.

How to Create an Appointment

Whether you're using a date book, a wall calendar, or post-it notes to keep track of your appointments (you are keeping track of them, aren't you?), you have to record certain basic information, like who, what, when, and where. In that respect Outlook is no different from a manual tracking method.

1 In the Calendar window click the New Appointment icon on the toolbar to open a blank appointment form.

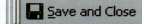

6 Click the Save and Close icon to save the new appointment and return to the Calendar window.

Subject: | Meet with John J. to discuss marketing for new product

2 Complete the Subject field with a brief description that explains the reason for this appointment (one that will jog your memory). Then fill in the Location field so you know where to go.

Start time: | Fri 3/7/97 | 8:30 AM
End time: | Fri 3/7/97 | 9:30 AM

3 Press Tab to move to the Start Time field and enter the date and time for this appointment. You can use the drop-down list (click the down arrow at the right of the field) or type the information directly into the field.

☑ Reminder: | 15 minutes | ◁⑂

4 Press Tab to move to the Reminder field and click the Reminder checkbox to enable a reminder for this appointment. From the Reminder Time drop-down list select the amount of advance warning you want the reminder to give you. By default Outlook plays a chime sound when the reminder displays. To change the sound that plays, click the speaker icon next to the reminder time and select a different file (sounds are really files).

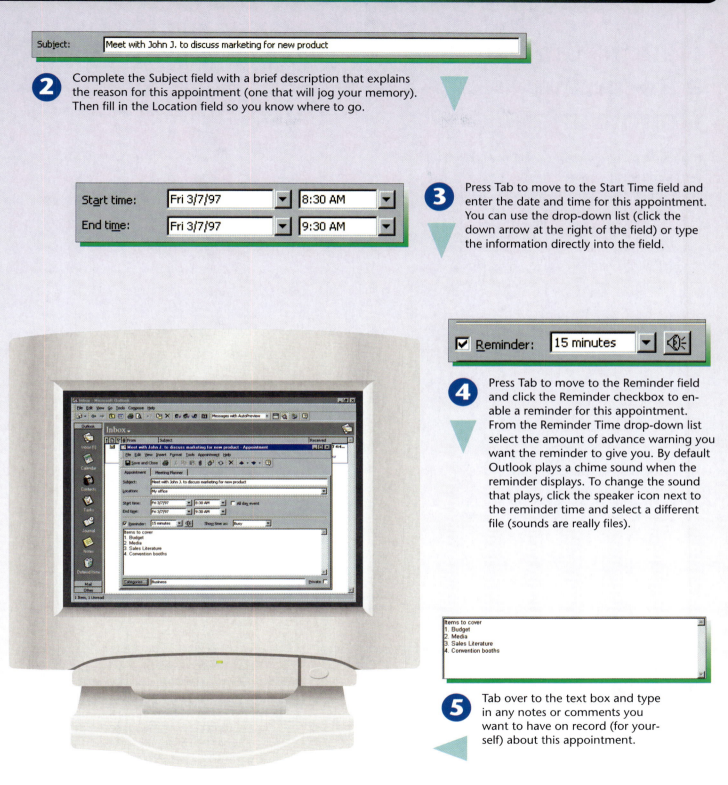

Items to cover
1. Budget
2. Media
3. Sales Literature
4. Convention booths

5 Tab over to the text box and type in any notes or comments you want to have on record (for yourself) about this appointment.

How to Create a Recurring Appointment

Recurring appointments are those appointments that just don't seem to go away. You know the ones I mean, the weekly strategy meeting, the monthly sales meeting, and the daily session with your therapist. Rather than create a separate appointment for each occurrence, Outlook allows you to create one appointment that automatically occurs at regular intervals.

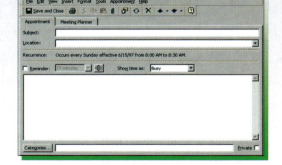

1 To create a recurring appointment, choose Calendar (make sure you're in the Calendar window first), New Recurring Appointment from the menu bar.

6 Click OK to go to the new appointment form for this recurring appointment. The steps for filling out the Recurring Appointment form are the same as those for creating a non-recurring appointment, except that the dates and times are already set for the recurring appointment. When you have filled out the Subject, Location, and other fields, click Save and Close.

FYI

● As with a non-recurring appointment, you can select a date from the Date Navigator and double-click the appropriate time slot to open a new Recurring Appointment form.

● Right-clicking on the daily calendar in any of the time slots activates a pop-up menu which offers a number of choices, including a New Recurring Appointment form.

2 The Appointment Recurrence dialog box that displays provides three sets of options. You can set the appointment time, the recurrence pattern, and the range of recurrence.

3 Enter the start time for the appointment. Notice that the end time is automatically set depending on the duration setting. You can reset the end time or the duration time by clicking the arrow at the right of each field and making your selection from the drop-down list.

4 Select the frequency with which you want the appointment to occur from the Recurrence Pattern options. Depending on the selection of daily, weekly, monthly, or yearly, the other Recurrence Pattern options vary. Choose the number of recurrences per time period and the specific day for each occurrence.

 5 Choose the start date and the end date from the Range of Recurrence options. You can elect to set no end date, limit the appointment to a specific number of occurrences, or set a fixed end date.

How to Create Tasks Quickly

Depending on the type of To Do list you require, you can make an Outlook task as simple or complex as you like. Outlook provides several ways to create a task. Since we're looking for the quickest way to create a task, let's start with the electronic equivalent of scribbling a quick entry on a lined notepad.

With that in mind, switch to the Tasks folder by clicking the Tasks icon in the Outlook bar.

Tasks ▾		
Subject		Due Date
Click here to add a new Task		
Write proposal for a Standards Committee		None
Sam's birthday		Thu 4/10/97
Call Dr. for Checkup Appointment		None
Get signed contracts for Axelrod project		Fri 5/30/97
Change Budget Spread Sheet Column Headings		None
Prepare Presentation for the board meeting		Thu 5/29/97

1 The default view in the Tasks information viewer is the Simple List. It doesn't get much simpler than a subject and a due date. Enter a brief description of the task in the text box where you see *Click here to add a new Task.*

2 Click the Due Date text box to activate the down arrow at the end of the field. Click the down arrow and select a due date from the drop-down calendar that appears.

3 Another handy task feature appears in the Calendar window. If you happen to be working in the calendar and need to add something to your To Do list, you're in luck. Click the Calendar icon in the Outlook toolbar to switch to the Calendar folder. Outlook conveniently provides a scaled-down version of the Tasks list in the form of the TaskPad.

4 As in the Simple List of the Tasks folder, you can jot down a quick description of your new task in the textbox at the top of the TaskPad and press Enter to add it to the list.

5 Now return to the Tasks folder by clicking the Tasks icon in the Outlook bar. You can see that the new task you created in the TaskPad now appears on the Simple List. From here you can add a due date if you so choose.

How to Create Contacts

At its most basic level, contact management is the storage and retrieval of information you need in order to get in touch with another individual. The minimum requirements are a name to identify the contact, and either a postal address, phone number, e-mail address, or even a ham radio frequency by means of which to transmit information to the individual.

Of course, you can and should include all the information you have for each contact.

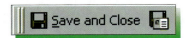

1 Click the New Contact icon on the Outlook toolbar to open a blank Contact form.

6 Click Save and Close to save the new contact and return to the Contacts window.

2 Fill out the Contact form with as little or as much information as you wish. Remember, the purpose of the contact database is to provide you with the information you need, not necessarily every piece of information you possess. However, in some cases they may be the same thing.

3 You can enter additional name information, such as a title or suffix, by clicking the Full Name button and opening the Check Full Name dialog box. Type the information and click OK to return to the Contact form.

4 The default address is a business address. To include a home or other address, click the down arrow on the right side of the Address Type field, select the type of address to enter, and enter the new address in the Address field. This does not replace the business address, but rather attaches a second address.

5 To include more detailed personal information, click the Details tab on the Contact form to open the Details information sheet. Add any pertinent data and click the General tab to return to the Contact form.

How to Send E-Mail to a Contact

Sending e-mail to a contact is a simple matter of opening the Inbox and composing a message. But what if you happen to be in the Contacts window? Do you have to return to the Inbox to send an e-mail message to a contact? The job of an information manager is to simplify your life; therefore, the answer is no.

Outlook allows you to perform a number of contact-related actions from within the Contacts window, including sending e-mail.

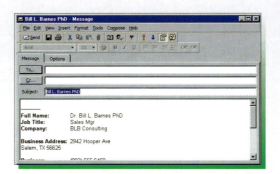

1 To send an e-mail message to someone listed in your contact database, highlight the contact's name and click the New Message to Contact icon in the Contacts window toolbar.

● You can also use drag and drop to create an e-mail message to a contact. Simply drag the contact by holding down the left mouse button, and drop it on the Inbox icon in the Outlook bar. A new Message form appears with the contact's e-mail address inserted in the To field.

● The drag-and-drop method can also be used to quickly address a single e-mail message to more than one contact. Highlight the contacts to use by holding down the Ctrl key and clicking each contact. Then drag (using the left mouse button) any one of the highlighted contacts to the Outlook bar and drop it on the Inbox icon. A new Message form pops up with the selected contact's e-mail address in the To field.

6 Select Copy Here as Message with Text to open a new Message form. Notice that the contact name is inserted in the Subject field, and the contact data is included in the message body. This is great for quickly passing along contact information to third parties. Complete the Message form and click Send.

2 A new message form opens with the contact's e-mail address inserted in the To field. Complete the header as necessary, compose your message, and click Send to dispatch your e-mail.

3 Occasionally you may enter a contact without an e-mail address. If you attempt to send a message to the contact from within the Contacts window, a dialog box appears informing you that the contact has no e-mail address and you must therefore enter it manually. Click OK to proceed.

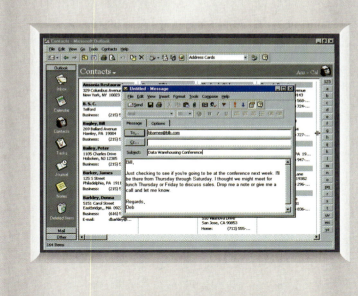

4 As soon as you click OK, a new message form opens with the contact's name inserted in the To field. Move to the To field and type the correct e-mail address for the contact. Then complete the message and click Send to transmit the message.

5 Another handy e-mail feature available in the Contacts window is the ability to create an e-mail message with a contact as the subject, and include the contact's data in the message. Use the right mouse button to drag and drop the contact onto the Inbox icon in the Outlook bar. A pop-up menu offers a number of choices.

How to Autodial Contacts

If you have a modem connected to your PC, you can use the Outlook AutoDial feature to make calls to contacts with valid phone numbers.

If your modem is already connected to your computer, the dialing properties were probably set during the modem installation. However, you might want to check them just to be on the safe side. Once the dialing properties are set, you're ready to begin using the AutoDial feature.

1 Highlight the contact you wish to call, then click the AutoDialer icon in the Contacts window toolbar to open a New Call dialog box. The name and business phone number of the contact are filled in.

6 To view the phone call journal entry, double-click the contact to open the Contact form and click the Journal tab. In the display window you will see the newly recorded journal entry, which you can open to view or edit by double-clicking.

- You can also activate the AutoDialer by right-clicking the contact and selecting AutoDialer from the pop-up menu.

- Press Ctrl+Shift+D to start a new call and manually enter the name and phone number.

2 Click the Dialing Properties button to open the Dialing Properties dialog box. Make sure that the area code field reflects your correct area code. In the How I Dial from This Location section, add any prefix numbers that you need to get an outside line. Do not include the number 1 in the long-distance field. Outlook automatically dials a 1 before making a long-distance call. Click OK to return to the New Call dialog box.

3 If you want to take notes and log the call, click the Create New Journal Entry When Starting New Call option. Click Start Call to dial the number.

4 Several things happen simultaneously. The modem dials the phone number, a Journal Entry form is opened, and a dialog box pops up informing you that you should lift the receiver and click Talk to talk, or click Hang Up to disconnect.

5 When you click Talk, the timer in the Phone Call Journal Entry form begins tracking the time. Note that the contact name as well as the date and time of the call are recorded. You can take notes on the conversation in the text window. When you finish the conversation, click Save and Close to save the journal entry and return to the New Call dialog box. Click End Call to disconnect the modem. Then click Close to return to the Contacts window.

How to Autorecord Journal Entries

The Outlook AutoJournal feature automatically records e-mail messages you send to selected contacts. If you are on an Exchange Server network, it also records meeting and task requests that have been sent to contacts on the same network.

The first thing you must do to ensure that the automatic journal entries are properly recorded is set the global Journal options.

1 Since global options apply to the entire Outlook program, you can access them from any Outlook window. Choose Tools, Options from the menu bar to open the Options dialog box.

FYI

● If you change the global options for recording Microsoft Office documents in the journal, you must reboot your computer before the new option setting takes effect. Merely exiting and logging off of Outlook does not reset the option. A rather poor way to enable options, it adds insult to injury by not even advising you that you must reboot.

● The automatic journal recording option can be turned on and off for each contact by accessing the Journal tab in the Contact form, and clicking the Automatically Record Journal Entries for this contact. A checkmark enables automatic recording, no checkmark disables the option. Note that changing this option resets the global Journal option for this contact.

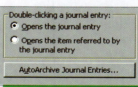

6 Depending on your choice in the Double-Clicking a Journal Entry option box, either the journal entry itself or the item (e-mail message or letter) to which it refers will open when you double-click a journal entry. Journal entries that contain notes only, and no files, e-mail messages, or documents, have no associated items to open. Consequently, the journal entry itself opens regardless of the settings of this option.

2 Click the Journal tab to access the Journal options. You can see that it contains four sections of options: items to automatically record, contacts for whom you want the items automatically recorded, Microsoft Office programs from which you want all files automatically recorded, and double-clicking options for journal entries.

3 In the Automatically Record These Items display box, click each of the items you want automatically recorded. Remember that unless both you and the contact are on the same Exchange Server network, only the e-mail feature works. Automatically recorded e-mail messages and other journal entries appear on the Journal tab of the contact form as well as in the Journal window.

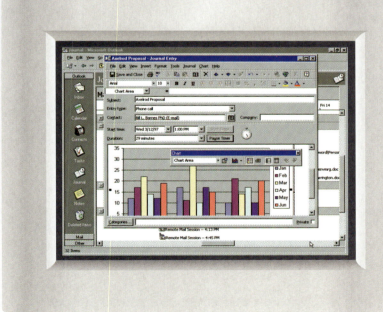

4 The next step is to decide which contacts to apply the Auto-Journal feature to. From the For These Contacts list select the contacts you wish to include. If you have casual contacts with whom you rarely exchange important data, there's probably no reason to add them to the list. Place a checkmark next to the contacts you want to include by clicking the appropriate names.

5 A Journal feature that you'll either love or hate is the automatic logging of all Microsoft Office documents you create. This can be rather overwhelming if you do a lot of work in Office. If you decide you can't take it anymore, just turn it off. To eliminate the automatic recording of Office documents, deselect (remove the checkmark from) the desired Office programs in the Also Record Files From box.

How to Record Manual Journal Entries

AutoJournal works fine for e-mail (and meetings and tasks if you're on Exchange Server), but that leaves quite a few other types of information unrecorded. No problem—you can record just about anything in Outlook as a journal entry. You just have to do a little more of the work yourself.

While you can create a journal entry anywhere in Outlook by pressing Ctrl+Shift+J, this exercise begins in the Journal window. So before proceeding, click the Journal icon in the Outlook bar to open the Journal window.

1 To open a blank Journal Entry form in the journal, click the New Journal icon in the toolbar. You can also press Ctrl+N to open a blank Journal Entry form in the Journal window.

● You can quickly create a manual journal entry by dragging (with the left mouse button) a contact onto the Journal icon in the Outlook bar. As soon as you drop the contact on the Journal icon, a new Journal Entry form opens for the selected contact. Fill in the necessary information and save the journal entry.

● Manual journal entries are perfect for recording phone conversations with contacts. Open the contact in the Contacts window and use the AutoDial feature (if you have a modem connected) to place the call, then move to the Journal tab and click New Journal Entry to enter a manual journal entry for the call.

6 Associating the manual journal entry with a specific contact results in the entry being logged into the Journal sheet of the individual's Contact form. Open the Contacts window by clicking the Contacts icon in the Outlook bar. Double-click the contact you associated with the new journal entry to open the Contact form, and click the Journal tab to see the new entry.

2 The blank Journal Entry form allows you to enter a subject, the type of journal entry it is, the contact with whom it is associated, and additional information to create an electronic "paper" trail for tracking a contact or project. Begin by filling in the Subject field with a brief description of the journal entry.

3 The default entry type is a phone call. Since it is already inserted, it's easy to pass right by and leave it as a phone call even when it is something else. For it to be truly useful, it's important to properly identify the entry type. Click the down arrow at the end of the Entry Type field and select the correct entry type from the drop-down list.

4 Associating a journal entry with a contact saves a lot time and aggravation by allowing you to refer directly to a specific phone call or e-mail message to resolve a question or find a piece of important information. To associate the journal entry with one or more contacts, click the Address Book icon at the end of the Contact field and select the contact(s) from the Select Names dialog box that appears. Click the Add button to include them, then click OK to return to the Journal Entry form.

5 Complete the remainder of the form with appropriate information. The timer is great for phone calls or meetings that take place in real time. Adding notes may not seem necessary at the moment, but you'll be glad you did later on when the event is no longer fresh in your mind. When you're through, click Save and Close to save the new entry and return to the Journal window.

How to Use AutoArchive

The Outlook AutoArchive feature automatically creates an archive, and periodically copies the Outlook items you specify into the archive. Since Outlook cannot read your mind, you have to tell it when and how to perform these periodic archives. You accomplish this by setting the AutoArchive options.

Setting AutoArchive options requires two separate operations. The first is setting the global options, the second is setting the individual folder AutoArchive options. Note, however, that all folder specific AutoArchive options take precedence over the global autoarchive options. For example, if you specify archive.pst as the default archive file in the global options, but set it to inbox.pst in the Inbox properties, all Inbox archiving is done using inbox.pst.

All original Outlook folders, with the exception of Contacts, can be AutoArchived. AutoArchiving rules are based on the creation or edit dates of items. Since contacts are more or less permanent entries, they are not considered candidates for AutoArchiving.

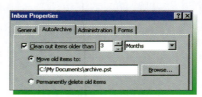

1 You can set global AutoArchive options from any folder. Choose Tools, Options from the menu bar to open the Options dialog box.

6 If the AutoArchive option is turned off, click Clean Out Items Older Than to place a checkmark in the box to the left and enable Auto-Archiving for the folder. Then set the age condition. Be careful when making your selection on the final option. Choosing Permanently Delete Old Items results in the irretrievable loss of any items meeting the criteria you specified when an AutoArchive is performed.

- The default AutoArchive settings for the Deleted Items folder is Clean Out Items Older Than 2 Months, with Permanently Delete Old Items selected. Since you deleted the items in the first place, there is probably no reason to change this setting, but you should be aware of it just in case.

2 Click the AutoArchive tab to access the AutoArchive options. The first of five available options is to enable or disable AutoArchiving. If you disable AutoArchiving, no other options are available. If you enable it, the remaining options are the frequency of AutoArchiving, whether or not to display a prompt before AutoArchiving, an option to delete expired e-mail, and the default archive file.

3 Enabling the prompt before AutoArchiving causes a dialog box to display each time Outlook is about to autoarchive, informing you of its intentions, and asking for your confirmation. This provides you with an opportunity to stop the process in the event you need access to an item that is about to be removed to the archive file.

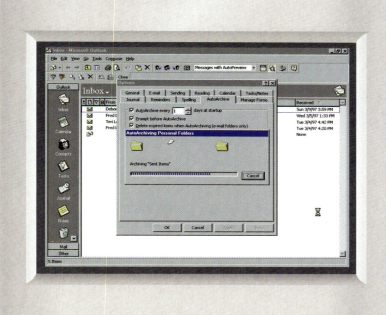

4 To set folder-specific AutoArchiving options, open the properties sheet for the folder you wish to set up. Right-click the folder icon in the Outlook bar and choose Properties from the pop-up menu that appears.

5 Click the AutoArchive tab to open the AutoArchive properties sheet. The global options turn on AutoArchiving and determine the frequency, but if the individual folder called AutoArchiving Options is not enabled, nothing will happen at the specified time intervals. It's like setting a timer for a coffee maker that's not turned on. The timer makes the electricity available to the coffee maker at the appropriate time, but you don't get your morning coffee because the coffee maker is switched off.

P A R T 7

Working with the Internet

THE INTERNET IS HOT, and everyone knows it, including Microsoft. Which is why they've incorporated a variety of Internet features into Office 97. With Microsoft Office 97, taking advantage of the Internet is as easy as falling off a diet. Microsoft has provided easy access to the World Wide Web by integrating its Web browser, Internet Explorer, with Office 97. This section gets you started using the Internet features found in Office 97 (remember you must also have a modem and an Internet service provider account to access the Internet).

WHAT YOU'LL FIND IN THIS SECTION

- How to Search the Web   240
- How to Find Files on the Web   242
- How to Download Files   244
- How to Get Online Support   246
- How to Make the Web Part of Your Office Document   248

How to Search the Web

It's ironic that one of the Internet's principal attractions sometimes proves to be one of its major sources of frustration. The tremendous volume of information available on the Web means that there's hardly a subject that is not covered. Unfortunately, it also means that to find a single piece of data that you need, you usually must sort through a mountain of stuff you probably never knew existed. This is where a good search engine and the ability to use it are invaluable.

The following examples were created using the Excite search engine. Most search engines work in a similar fashion and provide many of the same features. However, since each search engine has its own design, the specifics may vary somewhat.

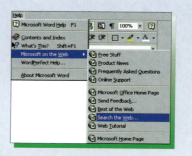

1 To search the Web from within any Office 97 application, select Help, Microsoft on the Web, Search the Web.

● Many Web sites send "cookies" that are stored on your computer without your knowledge. Although these cookies are not harmful, they do contain information that allows a Web site to identify you and see where you've been. Unfortunately, avoiding cookies is practically impossible since you must accept them blindly, or reject them one at a time as they are sent (only if you turn on the Windows 95 Internet Cookies Alert option). There is a way, however, to outsmart the marketing geniuses behind the "cookie conspiracy." If you're using Netscape Navigator, search your hard drive after each Internet session for the file called cookies.txt, and delete it. If you're using Internet Explorer, open the file c:\windows\cookies and delete all the files except the .dat files (Internet Explorer won't work without them). For more information on cookies visit The Magic Cookie site at http://www.in-dranet.com/cookie.html.

6 In addition to tips, most search engines also provide search options to improve your chances of success. Click the Search Options link to view the available options. Many search engines allow you to search newsgroups as well as Web sites.

2 Office immediately launches your Web browser, and whisks you away to the Microsoft Find It Fast Web page. This page contains several major Internet search engines as well as direct links to a number of sites listed by category.

3 Enter a word or phrase in the text query box and click Search to begin scouring the Web for the desired information. As the search engine encounters Web pages containing that word or phrase, it returns a listing with the page title and a brief summary of the page contents. Each item on the list is referred to as a "hit." The broader the topic, the more hits. Don't be shocked if your first search results in thousands or even millions of hits.

95% HOT Salsa [More Like This]
URL: http://hotx.com/hotsalsa/
Summary: HINT: If you're not from Texas or just new to this stuff, remember, it's easier to add a little more heat to your brew than it is to cool it down. Drinking milk will help cool off your firey tongue better than water or beer.

4 Scroll through the listing until you find a hit that is relevant to your search. To view the entire Web page, click the title (title text is usually underlined and of a different color than the rest of the text).

5 Most search engines provide helpful tips on finding your particular needle in the electronic haystack that is the Internet. Click the Search Tips link to get detailed assistance on formulating your search query to ensure that you get the best results with the least amount of hassle.

How to Find Files on the Web

Information is not the only thing you'll find in abundance on the Internet. It's also knee deep in software, sound, video, graphics, and text files. Since files are more easily categorized and organized, finding them is generally much simpler than locating relevant information sources.

1 From any Office 97 application menu bar select Help, Microsoft on the Web, Best of the Web. This takes you to Microsoft's selection of the best sites on the Web. Click computers & technology in the Best of the Web column.

● If you know the Internet address (by the way, the technical term is *URL*, which stands for Universal Resource Locator) of a Web site, you can type it in the Location text box of your browser, and press Enter to contact the site. Although all Web site addresses begin with http:// you can type the address beginning with www (i.e. www.microsoft.com) and your browser will include the http:// part for you.

● Many companies use their name followed by .com as their Web site address. To speed up your search for a company, try this first. In your browser's Location text box type www.company-name.com (substitute the company's real name for *companyname*).

6 In addition to the specific Web pages cited above, you can always click the Search (Net Search) button in your browser and use the associated search engine(s) to locate different files. Try clip art collections for graphics files, sound collections for sound files, and so on.

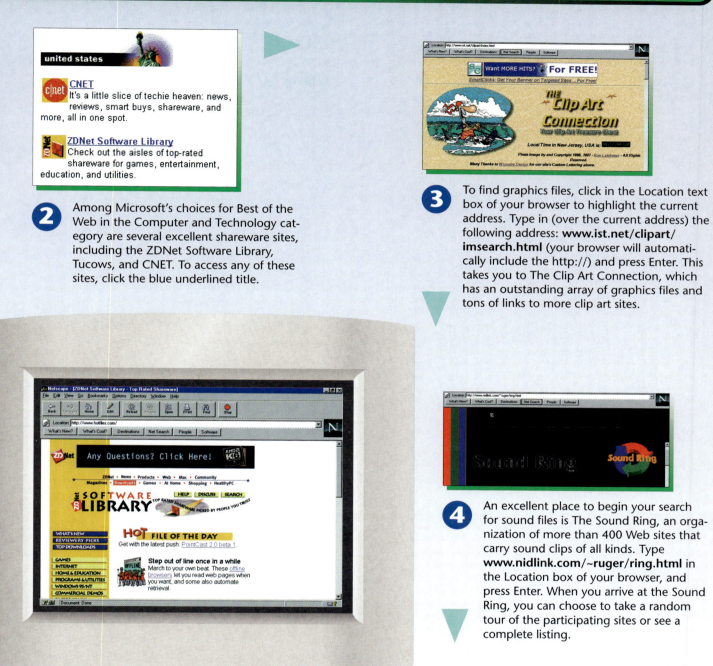

2 Among Microsoft's choices for Best of the Web in the Computer and Technology category are several excellent shareware sites, including the ZDNet Software Library, Tucows, and CNET. To access any of these sites, click the blue underlined title.

3 To find graphics files, click in the Location text box of your browser to highlight the current address. Type in (over the current address) the following address: **www.ist.net/clipart/ imsearch.html** (your browser will automatically include the http://) and press Enter. This takes you to The Clip Art Connection, which has an outstanding array of graphics files and tons of links to more clip art sites.

4 An excellent place to begin your search for sound files is The Sound Ring, an organization of more than 400 Web sites that carry sound clips of all kinds. Type **www.nidlink.com/~ruger/ring.html** in the Location box of your browser, and press Enter. When you arrive at the Sound Ring, you can choose to take a random tour of the participating sites or see a complete listing.

5 One of the most important, but often overlooked, benefits of finding files on the Internet is the ability to download software updates, patches (bug fixes), and drivers. One site which contains a nice selection of patches and drivers is Windows95.com. Type **www.windows95.com** in the Location box of your browser and press Enter. Click the desired category icon to locate the appropriate files.

How to Download Files

Once you find that perfect shareware program, or just the right clip art picture for your newsletter, the next step is to transfer a copy from the Internet site on which it resides to your computer. This is known as "downloading." (File transfer is called "downloading" when you receive the file and "uploading" when you send the file.)

The process is relatively simple, but requires a little forethought to ensure a trouble-free download. Be sure that you have enough room on your hard drive to accommodate the file. Also keep in mind the time it takes to download. While small files (less than 100kb) can take as little as a minute or two, large files (5-10+ megabytes) can take hours, even with a 28.8 modem. Remember, it's not only the speed of your modem, but the speed of your connection and how many other people are downloading from the same Web site that affect actual download times.

Netsite: http://www.usr.com/home/online/upgrades.htm

1 Locate the Web page containing the desired file(s), either by typing the address in the Location box or by performing a search using a search engine.

FYI

● You should be aware that any file you obtain from the Internet, or any source for that matter, can contain a computer virus. To keep your computer virus free (as much as possible), consider purchasing an anti-virus program. Some anti-virus applications such as Norton's specifically check for viruses while you are downloading from the Internet to ensure that a tainted file does not reach your computer.

● If you have to download large files, try to do it during a time when most other users will not be using the Internet. If you're on the East Coast, download early in the morning before the rest of the country has had a chance to wake up. If you're on the West Coast, download late at night when everybody else is asleep.

2 Files, like links, are usually of a different color than the rest of the text and underlined. In addition, passing your mouse pointer over one turns the pointer into a hand with an extended index finger. Click the file name to begin the download process.

3 The Save As dialog box appears, providing you with the opportunity to specify the location on your hard drive for saving the file.

4 If you wish to change the save location, click the down arrow to the right of the Save In text box to open the Save In drop-down list. Click on the correct drive to display a list of all the folders contained on the drive. Select the folder for the new file and click the Save button.

5 Once the download begins, the Saving Location dialog box opens, providing you with detailed information on the file as well as the progress of the download.

How to Get Online Support

O ne of the many advantages of being connected to the Internet is the availability of
online help. From the vast number of technical
support calls that Microsoft receives, their support department has developed a large database
of knowledge, tips, common questions (and,
thankfully, answers), as well as up-to-the-minute
update information and files.

To avail yourself of this wealth of information,
take a minute to check out the online support
available from within any Office 97 application.

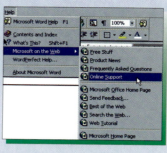

1 Select Help, Microsoft on
the Web, Online Support
from the main menu.

● Many of the computer periodicals regularly report on tips and tricks for various software applications including, of course, the Office 97 suite.
Check ZDNet, CNET, and other sites to see what
hot little tidbits their writers have uncovered
recently.

● It's a good idea to stop at the Microsoft Office
Help Files, Service Packs & Other Files page on
occasion, to see what updates, patches, add-ons,
and utilities are available for Office 97. You can
reach this page by selecting Support from the
menu bar across any Microsoft Web page.
Choose Office for Windows from the drop-down
query box list and click the Go button. In the
Support Highlights window, click Help Files,
Service Packs, & Other Files from the blue menu
at the left.

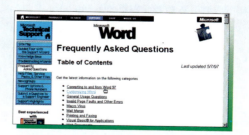

6 Select the version of the Microsoft application you're using to open the FAQ
Table of Contents. Click the topic you
want information on, then select the appropriate question.

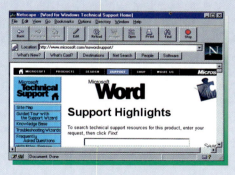

2 Your Web browser transports you to the Microsoft Support page for the Office 97 application from which you launched your online excursion.

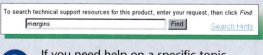

3 If you need help on a specific topic, use the search feature. Type in a word or phrase to search for, and click the Find button.

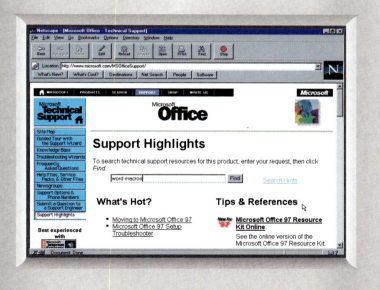

4 The Microsoft Support search performs just like an Internet search engine and returns a listing of articles that contain the search word(s). Click on the title that most closely matches the topic you need help on.

5 Another place to find solutions is in the Frequently Asked Questions (FAQ) area. On the Microsoft Technical Support menu located on the left side of the Web page, click the Frequently Asked Questions button.

How to Make the Web Part of Your Office Document

Including pages and pages of Internet information within a letter, memo, or some other document you create and distribute is impractical at best. However, there are times when the information contained in a Web site is precisely what you need to make a point, or strengthen an argument, or just pass on because of its inherent value.

Inserting a live Internet address (URL) in your Office 97 document accomplishes the same thing with practically no bother. Clicking a live URL included in a document launches the users' browsers and takes them to that site.

Connect to the Internet using your browser and go to the Web page you wish to include in your document. Click the address in the Location box to highlight it. Then press Ctrl+C to copy the address to the Windows Clipboard.

 Once you've arrived at the desired page, return to the Office document, and the URL is automatically inserted in the Link to File or URL field of the Insert Hyperlink dialog box. Click OK to insert the address at the location of your cursor.

FYI

● You can also use the Insert Hyperlink feature to place a link within your document to another document or file that resides on your hard drive or even on the company intranet (if you have one).

In order to stay ahead of the competition it is imperative that every member of this team keep abreast of what's happening in the industry. To this end I strongly suggest that you sign up for Ziff Davis' (free) Personal News service.

You can find information about, and register for the service at the following Internet address:

http://community.zdnet.com/pview/login.cgi

2 Return to the Office document in which you want to include the Internet address. Move the cursor to the insertion point for the address, and press Ctrl+V to paste the address in your document. Add a space or a hard return (press the Enter key) to complete the insertion.

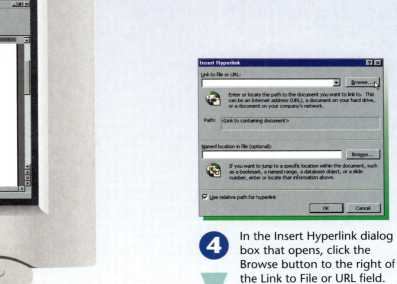

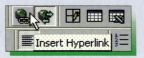

3 If you don't know the Internet address or want to find a new address to include in a document, you can use the Office 97 hyperlink feature. Click the Insert Hyperlink button on the standard toolbar.

4 In the Insert Hyperlink dialog box that opens, click the Browse button to the right of the Link to File or URL field.

5 Click the Search the Web button in the Link to File dialog box that opens. This launches your Web browser and brings you to the default start page. Go to the Web page you wish to include in your document.

PART 8

Office 97 Small Business Edition

THE Small Business Financial Manager and AutoMap Streets Plus are included in the Small Business Edition of Office 97. If you've purchased that edition, this section is an overview of those applications, including these topics:

- How to Install the SBE Applications — 252
- How to Create Income Statements — 254
- How to Create Balance Sheets — 256
- How to Create a Trial Balance — 258
- How to Create a Cash Flow Report — 260
- How to Create a What-If Scenario — 262
- How to Find and Mark Locations in AutoMap — 264
- How to Highlight a Travel Route in AutoMap — 266

How to Install the SBE Applications

Installing the Small Business Edition of Office 97 is a bit different from installing most software suites. The SBE is a group of individual applications, and you pick and choose the software you want to install. To begin, you need the SBE CD and the serial number for the CD.

For this section, we'll install the Small Business Financial Manager (SBFM), which isn't a self-contained software application—it's an add-in for Excel. (You must install Excel before you begin the installation of the SBFM.)

1 Place the CD in your CD-ROM drive and in few seconds you'll see your mouse pointer turn into an hourglass. This indicates the AutoRun program on the CD is working. (If AutoRun doesn't work, read the FYI section on this page for an alternative procedure.)

FYI

● **If AutoRun doesn't work and the CD opening menu isn't presented, open My Computer and double-click the CD-ROM drive. Then double-click AutoRun.Exe.**

● **After you install the first software package, the opening window of the CD should display on your monitor so you can pick the next package. If it doesn't, use the instructions above to run AutoRun manually.**

6 When the installation is finished, open Microsoft Excel. You should see a new menu item called Accounting on the menu bar.

Install Financial Manager 97

2 Click the icon for the application you want to install. Start with Excel, then return to the CD and choose Install Financial Manager 97.

3 The Setup dialog box appears to warn you to close any applications that are currently running. Click Continue to begin the installation. Answer the questions or fill out information as needed.

4 Click the Custom icon to begin the installation of the files.

5 Deselect the accounting software converters you don't need and click Continue. Then answer the question about the country version you want to install (the choices are United States and Canada).

How to Create Income Statements

O nce you've imported all your accounting data into the SBFM, you can begin to build reports that are customized exactly the way you need them.

Your accounting software, of course, can produce an income statement, but the way it groups, subtotals, and totals the accounts may not match the design you'd use if it were up to you. With the SBFM, there are many pre-configured choices so that you can get the income statement you want.

 Choose Accounting, Report Wizard to begin this process.

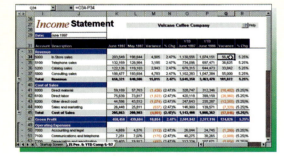

 The report displays in the Excel window. You can select any cell to see the formula in the Excel formula bar that appears just above the income statement.

● Your accounting software may call an income statement a profit and loss report. It's the same thing, just different terminology.

● You can save this report as an Excel worksheet by using the standard Excel Save techniques.

● You can change the formulas for this report if you want to show different data.

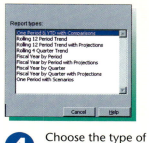

2 When the SBFM window appears, choose Report.

3 Select Income Statement as the report, and make sure your company name is selected in the Company Name text box. (The sample company that SBFM installs is also listed, and in fact we'll use that sample company throughout these pages.) Choose Next when you have made the selections.

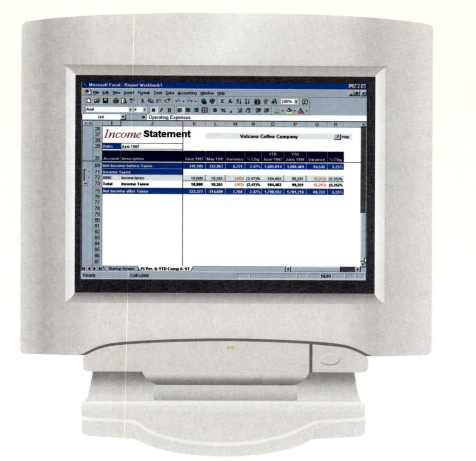

4 Choose the type of income statement you want to see. Then choose Next.

5 Select an end date for the report. If you chose a report that includes the current period in addition to the year-to-date figures, the end date specifies the month you will see as the current period. Click Finish.

How to Create Balance Sheets

A balance sheet is the essence of your financial health, it's your assets, liabilities, and the value of your equity.

Your accounting software produces a balance sheet, but you probably don't have much in the way of choice about what it shows. Most balance sheets give you a choice between the current period and YTD, or just YTD. Not much of a selection.

1 Choose Accounting, Report Wizard to start.

6 The report displays in the Excel window. You can select any cell to see the formula in the Excel formula bar.

● You can also choose a balance sheet with a what-if scenario built in. See the discussions on scenarios throughout this section.

● You can save this report as an Excel worksheet by using the standard Excel Save techniques.

2 When the SBFM window appears, choose Report.

3 Select Balance Sheet as the report, and make sure your company name is selected in the Company Name text box.

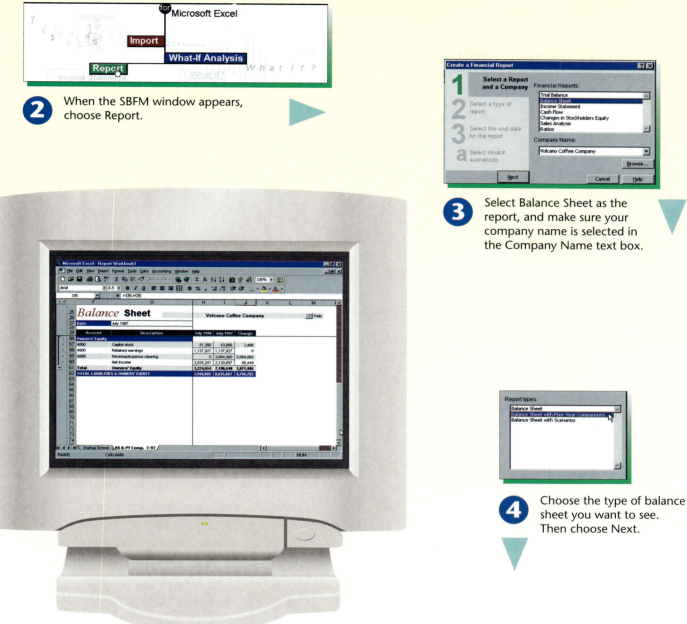

4 Choose the type of balance sheet you want to see. Then choose Next.

5 Select an end date for the report, then click Finish.

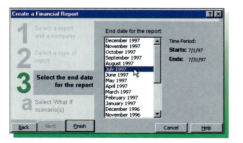

How to Create a Trial Balance

The best use of a trial balance is to track where you are with specific items. Sometimes you just want to see how much you're spending, other times you want to see what the earnings are for specific items or services. And sometimes you need to see if the trial balance is in balance. (Unfortunately, with some accounting software applications, it's possible to go out of balance without a murmur from the software—or a way to fix it.)

The trial balance report can be used as a basis for a balance sheet or an income statement; the figures are all there, and you just have to do the math.

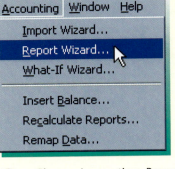

1 Choose Accounting, Report Wizard to start.

6 A complete audit report of the general ledger totals and changes displays in the Excel window.

● You can also choose a trial balance with a what-if scenario built in. See the discussions on scenarios throughout this section.

● You can save this report as an Excel worksheet by using the standard Excel Save techniques.

2 When the SBFM window appears, choose Report.

3 Select Trial Balance as the report, and make sure your company name is selected in the Company Name text box.

4 Choose the type of trial balance you want to see. Then choose Next.

 5 Select an end date for the report, then click Finish.

How to Create a Cash Flow Report

O ne of the more difficult reports to get from accounting software is a good cash flow report. Accountants charge a great deal of money to do these, and they take a long time to prepare.

SBFM has a number of preconfigured formulas that produce cash flow reports with excellent detail.

1 Choose Accounting, Report Wizard to start.

6 A detailed statement of money in and out displays. You can use this to analyze the flow of cash (and other assets).

- For this example, we chose a simple cash flow report, without projections. This is the easiest way to analyze your cash flow. Cash flow with projections, however, is another common report that accountants are asked to do (especially if you're looking for a line of credit).

- You can save this report as an Excel worksheet by using the standard Excel Save techniques.

2 When the SBFM window appears, choose Report.

3 Select Cash Flow as the report, and make sure your company name is selected in the Company Name text box.

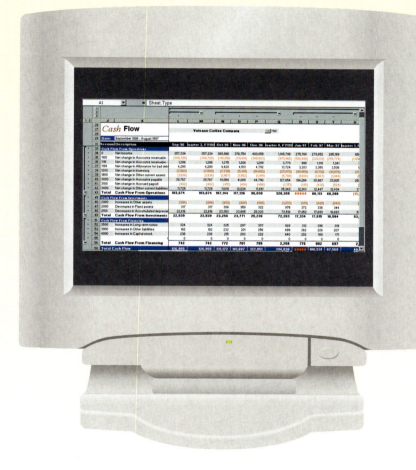

Report types:

One Period & YTD with Comparisons
Rolling 12 Period Trend
Rolling 12 Period Trend with Projections
One Period with Scenarios
YTD with Scenarios

4 Choose the type of cash flow report you want to see. Then choose Next.

5 Select an end date for the report, then click Finish.

End date for the report:

December 1997
November 1997
October 1997
September 1997
August 1997
July 1997
June 1997
May 1997
April 1997
March 1997
February 1997
January 1997
December 1996
November 1996

Time Period:

Starts: 8/1/97
Ends: 8/31/97

How to Create a What-If Scenario

What-If is a highly educational game. You play it by looking at financial reports, then changing the numbers to match your what-if question. What if the cost of a raw material were to go up by 2%? What if all the employees got 3% raises?

SBFM has a number of preconfigured what-if scenario formulas you can use to plug in the numbers that match your questions. Then you can see the answers.

1 Choose Accounting, What-If Wizard to start.

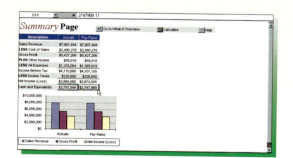

6 Use the buttons in the top rows to change the view. Choose Compare What-If Scenarios to see a summary.

● The cells in a what-if scenario are protected so you cannot change them; you must use the arrows to change amounts or percentages.

● Use the Save button on the top row of the worksheet to save the details of the scenario. Use the Excel Save button to save the worksheet.

● Use the SBFM Help system to learn about all the different analysis topics available.

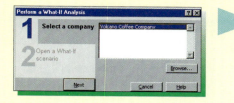

2 When the Wizard appears, pick the company you want to examine and choose Next.

3 If this is a new scenario, enter a name, then specify a beginning and end date for the time period you want to cover. You could also select any scenarios you'd previously created. Choose Finish. A Save dialog box appears so you can save the workbook.

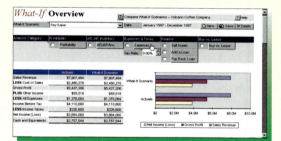

4 When the worksheet appears, pick a category from the middle section to change.

5 Locate the specific category and use the arrows to raise or lower the amount planned for this category (by dollars or percentage). Keep an eye on your totals as you make changes.

How to Find and Mark Locations in AutoMap

AutoMap is a comprehensive and easy-to-use mapping program that covers the United States thoroughly, and shows major cities of neighboring countries. It contains street maps of almost every city, town, and village in America, and even lets you pinpoint exact street addresses with a surprising degree of accuracy.

It comes with plenty of national, regional, and local sites already in its vast database of locations, and lets you add your own favorite places. When you've decided where to go, highlight a travel route, print it, and you're on your way.

Installation is a snap — throw the CD in your CD-ROM drive, confirm that you really do want to install it, what your name is, tell it where to install, what program group to place the AutoMap icons in, and you're done. As a matter of fact, if you accept the defaults, four mouse clicks is all it takes.

1 You can choose to run AutoMap as soon as the install is complete. Remember, the CD must be in the CD-ROM drive in order to run AutoMap. The opening screen contains a number of options ranging from viewing the entire map to finding a specific street address.

● When you locate a place or a street address, AutoMap creates a description text box and a pushpin on the site for you automatically. To close the text box, click the x in the upper right corner. To view the site's description text box after you close it (from any zoom level), double-click the pushpin. To zoom in on the site quickly, or to see nearby points of local interest, click the pushpin and make a selection from the menu that appears.

6 Type the name of the place in the Find dialog box that appears, and click Locate. AutoMap then displays a list of possible matches. As with the Find an Address feature, select a location and double-click to zoom in on the site.

2 Click Find an Address to view the map and open the Find an Address dialog box. Enter the exact street address, city, state, and zip code if you have it. The more information you provide, the higher your rate of success.

3 When you've finished entering the information, click OK to locate the street address. AutoMap presents you with a list of possible addresses, beginning with the one that most closely matches the information you supplied.

4 Double-click the address that you wish to view. AutoMap zooms in and pinpoints the exact location and attaches a balloon text box with the address information. You can add your own text for future reference.

5 Select Find, Places from the main menu bar to find site locations by name. Cities, national parks and monuments, museums, and even hotels and restaurants are included in the extensive AutoMap database.

How to Highlight a Travel Route in AutoMap

Traveling can be an extremely enjoyable experience or your worst nightmare, depending on how you handle it. A little planning can go a long way in transforming your ordeal into an unforgettable pleasure trip.

AutoMap can assist by letting you plot the sights you want to see, pick the routes you'll take to get to them, map the whole trip out, and then print a detailed map to guide you.

1 Start by zooming out to get a view of the entire United States. Right-click anywhere on the map, and select Zoom, U.S. (48 States) to get a perfect picture of the continental United States.

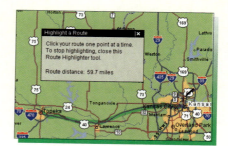

● If you make a mistake while highlighting your route, simply click the undo (left arrow) button on the main menu bar to remove the last point you placed. To delete the entire route and start over, select Route, Clear Route.

● You can also use a series of shortcut keys to perform some of the AutoMap operations discussed here. To activate the Measuring Tool, press Ctrl+E. To use the Highlight a Route feature, press Ctrl+H.

6 Once you've determine the route you want to take, select Route, Highlight a Route from the menu bar to activate the route highlighter and turn your cursor into crosshairs and a pen. Place the crosshairs over your starting point, click and hold the left mouse button and drag the cursor along your route. To lay down points, click at each bend in the road. After laying down the last point (at your destination), click the x in the upper right corner of the Highlight a Route information box to end the highlighting.

Click the area selector button (it's the rectangle with an arrow) located on the toolbar at the bottom of the

screen. Position your mouse pointer at a place on the map near your starting point. Press and hold the left mouse button and move the cursor to create a rectangle encompassing both your starting point and your destination. Release the mouse button, move your cursor inside the newly created box, and click to zoom in on your selection.

To get an approximate distance of your route, use the AutoMap Measuring Tool. Select Tools, Measuring Tool from the main menu to activate this handy feature. The cursor becomes a crosshair and ruler combination. Place the crosshairs on the starting point and left-click to begin measuring. Drag the cursor to the destination point and click to get a rough estimate. (For a more accurate figure follow the route closely, clicking at each curve to lay down a point.)

If your trip is going to require spending one or more nights enroute, you can use the Points of Interest feature to locate motels or hotels along the way. Place your mouse pointer over a spot where you plan to stop for the night and click. From the menu that appears, choose Points of Interest to activate the listing of Nearby (to the spot you clicked) Points of Interest. Click the checkbox next to Lodging to see the hotels and motels in the area.

 Double-click a listing to see more detailed information about the desired stopping place. To zoom in on the place, click the Locate button. If you have an Internet connection, you can even make a reservation by clicking the Online Reservations button.

P A R T 9
Microsoft Publisher 97

MICROSOFT Publisher 97 is one of the easiest-to-use, yet robust desktop publishing applications available. You can publish booklets, brochures, greeting cards, or Web pages and this section helps you accomplish all of that by teaching you the following skills:

IN THIS SECTION YOU'LL LEARN

- How to Install Publisher — 270
- How to Use the Publisher Toolbar — 272
- How to Use the Page Wizard — 274
- How to Create a Text Frame — 276
- How to Add Text to a Text Frame — 278
- How to Format Text — 280
- How to Insert Pages and Navigate Through Pages — 282
- How to Resize and Reposition Clip Art — 284
- How to Wrap Text around Clip Art — 286
- How to Flow Text between Text Frames — 288
- How to Recolor and Add a Drop Shadow to Text Frames — 292
- How to Add a Border to a Frame — 294
- How to Use Gradient Fills and Patterns — 296
- How to Layer Pictures for Special Effects — 298
- How to Group Objects — 300
- How to Insert Page Numbers and Dates — 302
- How to Use Design Gallery to Add Flair to Your Publication — 304
- How to Use the PageWizard for Special Elements — 306
- How to Use Shapes — 308

How to Install Publisher

Installing Publisher onto your Windows 95 computer is very easy. Before you begin, close any software applications that are running. If you have a virus protection program that runs in the background, shut it down.

Insert the CD-ROM or Setup Disk 1 into the appropriate drive. In some cases, depending on your computer, inserting the CD-ROM automatically starts the Publisher Setup program. If that happens, you can move right to step 2.

1 On the Start menu, point to Settings, then click Control Panel. When the Control Panel opens, double-click the Add/Remove Programs icon, then click the Install button.

● Setup spends a few minutes looking through your computer to see if there are any copies of Publisher already installed. If it finds a previous copy, you'll be notified that the installation program will replace it and you'll be asked to confirm that it's okay to do so. Don't worry, your data files (the publications you've prepared) won't be deleted and will be available to you with this new version of Publisher.

● During the installation process you'll be asked if you want to install Postscript printing ability so you can send files to an outside printing service if you ever need to. To do this, you will have to find your original Windows disks to transfer the necessary files. Since you can do this at any time, it's usually better to say No to this query for now, even if you plan to use outside printing services for your publication.

5 When Publisher launches for the first time, the Welcome to Publisher 97 tour appears in the window. You can move through the pages of this mini-manual to get acquainted with the software's features. Just choose Cancel whenever you want to get back to the main window to start working. If you want to peruse it again, choose Introduction to Publisher from the Help menu.

2 As the Setup program begins its work, several screens are displayed. Just follow the simple instructions.

3 Setup wants to know whether you want a Complete Installation or a Custom Installation. It's always safe to choose Complete because if you want to remove or add any features, you can do that at any time. Just click on the appropriate icon to continue. Setup transfers all the necessary files to your hard drive.

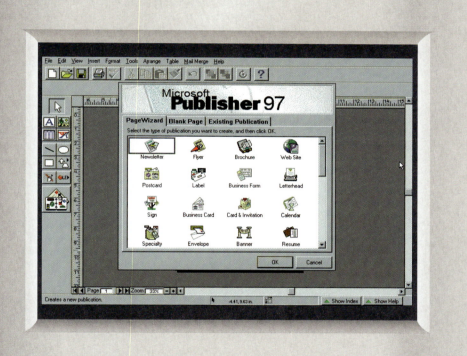

4 After the installation is complete, you can start Publisher. Click the Start button and point to Programs. Then move your pointer to Microsoft Publisher and click on it.

How to Use the Publisher Toolbar

On the left side of the main Publisher window is the Publisher toolbar. The people who use Publisher sometimes call it the Creation toolbar. In the documentation, Microsoft calls it the left toolbar. No matter what you call it, it's quick and handy. The collection of tools is a powerful assistant as you create pages for your publication.

Some of the tools operate as click-and-point, or click-and-drag. That means when you select them, you click on the tool and then point and click at the position on the page where you want to insert the tool's shape (that's click-and-point). You can also click on the tool, then point and drag your mouse pointer on the page to determine the placement and size of the shape. The shape becomes a frame for the tool you selected.

Click the Pointer at the top of the toolbar to turn your mouse pointer back to its normal state after clicking a tool.

1 Click on the Text tool to create a frame that's ready to accept text. You can start typing right away, and if the type is too small to read you can press F9 to zoom in. If you know how to use the Format toolbar, increase the size of the font by using the Font Size button. (Information about the Format toolbar can be found later in this chapter.)

7 Use the Insert Object (OLE) tool to insert an object from another Windows software application. Use the Design Gallery tool to open a catalog of art work you can choose from to add zest to your publication.

- If you're experimenting with some of the tools and don't like the results, select the frame and press Del to make it go away, then try something else.
- WordArt, OLE objects, and the Design Gallery are powerful tools that can satisfy the most creative urges you have, and implement the most complicated projects you design. More information about using these tools is found in other chapters in this book.

Calendar
Ad
Coupon
Logo

6 Click the PageWizards tool and select a special page type to fill a page or part of a page.

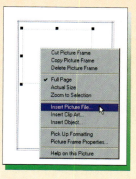

2 Click the Picture tool to put a picture frame on your page. All you see is the frame until you place a picture in it. Right-click in the selected frame and choose a source for the picture.

3 Click the Table tool and then click the page to see the Create Table dialog box. Specify the options to match the format you need. Click OK to put the table on the page, then fill in the figures.

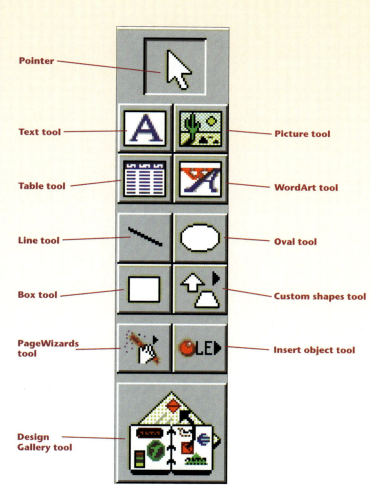

- Pointer
- Text tool
- Table tool
- Line tool
- Box tool
- PageWizards tool
- Design Gallery tool
- Picture tool
- WordArt tool
- Oval tool
- Custom shapes tool
- Insert object tool

4 Click the WordArt tool to enter text, then stretch and bend it for special effects.

5 The shapes are point-and-click easy to put on a page.

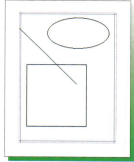

How to Use the Page Wizard

When you first start Publisher, a publication dialog box appears to offer assistance as you create a new publication. Choosing a publication type from the Page Wizard begins a process of answering questions and making decisions.

 To use the PageWizard, choose a publication type and then choose OK. For this example, a brochure is the publication of choice, so the Brochure PageWizard wants to know about your design preferences. Choose Next when you have made a selection.

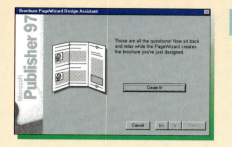

2 Keep moving through the PageWizard, making selections and answering questions. The choices vary depending upon the type of publication you're creating. Some publication types have only a couple of decision windows, others have a great many (and even they change depending upon your decisions in the previous window). Eventually the PageWizard tells you it's time to create the publication. Choose Create It!.

3 The design is ready for you to insert the text and graphics of your choice. The PageWizard even offers to walk you through those tasks a step at a time (you don't have to accept the offer).

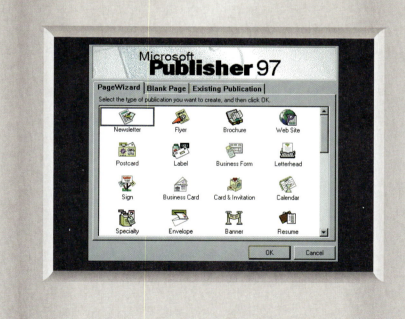

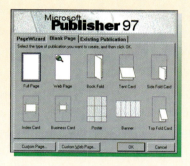

4 If you click the Blank Page tab in the Publication dialog box, you have a choice of styles. Select one and choose OK to begin creating the publication. There aren't lots of choices to make or questions to answer, but the basic layout of the publication style you choose is presented so that you can begin adding text and graphics.

5 If you choose Cancel in the Publication dialog box, the dialog box goes away and leaves behind a standard-sized blank page.

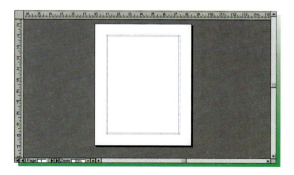

How to Create a Text Frame

It would be very unusual to have a publication that didn't contain text (although it's possible to have one that doesn't involve graphics). No matter what you want to accomplish with your publication—selling an idea, explaining a concept, or announcing something—it's going to take words.

In order to place text onto a page, you have to start with a text frame.

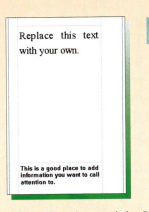

1 If you've used the PageWizard, the design elements for your page (or pages) are preset. Text frames have already been added for you.

● Even if you size the text frame yourself, you can use the handles to resize the frame.

● If you use a corner handle for resizing, the frame will move both of the adjacent sides at the same time.

● To move the frame without resizing it, move your mouse pointer near an edge (but not on top of a handle). When the pointer changes to a moving van, press the left mouse button while you drag in the direction you want to move the frame.

2 To add a text frame to a page, start by clicking on the Text tool.

3 After you've clicked on the Text tool, click on the page. A text frame is placed on the page.

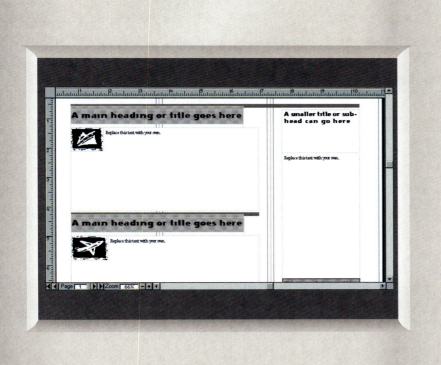

A main heading or title goes here

Replace this text with your own.

A smaller title or sub-head can go here

Replace this text with your own.

A main heading or title goes here

Replace this text with your own.

4 To adjust the size of the frame, move your pointer to one of the handles on the edge of the frame. When the pointer changes to say "Resize," drag the handle inward to make the frame smaller, or outward to make it larger.

5 Another way to position and size the text frame is to click the Text tool and then place your pointer on the page where you want the upper-left corner of the frame to be. Hold down the left mouse button and drag the mouse down and to the right until you've created the frame size you need. Then release the mouse.

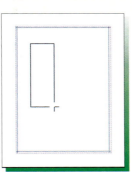

How to Add Text to a Text Frame

Once your text frame is in place, it's time to begin entering the words you need in order to make this publication do the work it's supposed to. When you start, don't worry too much about how the text wraps from line to line, or whether you'll need some text to stand out in some way. You can make those changes later.

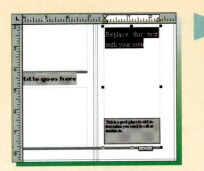

1 If you used the PageWizard to prepare your publication, click on any text frame to select it. When you do, the existing text is highlighted, so that as soon as you enter the first character, the place-holder text is deleted and replaced by whatever you type.

● The F9 key is a toggle switch: Use it to zoom in on a text frame, then use it again to zoom back out so you can see the text frame in relation to the rest of the page.

● If you enter text and it seems to disappear by rolling off the frame, don't worry. It's all there and later you can enlarge the frame or make the font size smaller.

2 Begin typing your own characters where the place-holder text used to be. When you finish, click anywhere on the window outside of the page to take the text frame out of edit mode.

> As soon as I begin to type characters in the text frame, my own words replace the instructions to enter text here
>
> **This is a good place to add information you want to call attention to.**

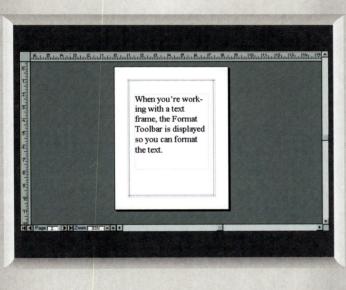

> When you're working with a text frame, the Format Toolbar is displayed so you can format the text.

3 To add text to a text frame you created yourself, select the frame by clicking on it. A blinking insertion point appears in the upper-left corner and you can begin entering characters. (When you first create the frame, it is automatically selected and the blinking insertion point is there, so you only have to take this step if you've left the frame and are now coming back to it.)

4 Many times, when you start entering text you can't make out the characters. They're just too small in relation to the size of the frame or the page.

5 Press F9 to zoom in on your text frame so you can see what you're typing.

> I'm typing like crazy but the text is so small it looks like I'm drawing tiny little worms. That's because I have this large frame on a large page and the font size isn't large. I can make the font size bigger or I can zoom in by using F9. Then I can zoom back out, using F9 again, to see what the text frame looks like in relation to the rest of my page.

How to Format Text

All the buttons on the Text Format toolbar are shortcuts to items that appear in the Format menu. The menu, however, offers a great many formatting options beyond those on the toolbar. In addition, you can fine-tune some of the special formatting effects using the dialog boxes available through the menu items.

If you've been using word processing software, you'll find two big differences in the Format menu in Publisher: There's no Font choice on the menu (use the Character Command instead); and the text formatting items don't even appear on the menu unless you've selected a text frame.

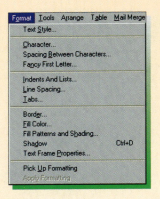

1 Select the text you want to create effects for and choose Format from the menu bar.

● A rule of thumb for professional designers is to limit the number of fonts on a page to just a few. Otherwise the page gets too busy.

● Bold type works best as a headline or a first word in an important paragraph.

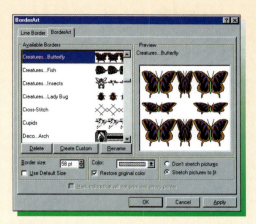

 Choose Format, Character for most of the common formatting tasks. The Character dialog box provides plenty of formatting choices, including fonts and effects.

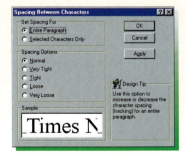

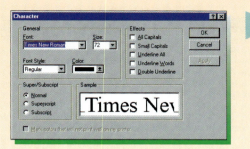

Taking In
Borders

Choose Border to pick a border for your text frame. You can choose a line of varying thickness, and you can choose sides—your border doesn't have to appear on all four of them. Or, pick a fancy design that repeats itself all around the frame.

Choose Spacing Between Characters to tighten up your work—or maybe to loosen it up a bit.

 You can adjust your line spacing (Format, Line Spacing) to give your publication a professional look.

How to Insert Pages and Navigate through Pages

If you used the PageWizard to create your publication and told it you wanted a four-page newsletter or a three-page brochure, what happens if you haven't said everything you want to say when you've filled the publication? Don't worry, you can add a page. In fact, adding a page is so easy that sometimes it's just as easy to begin your project with a one-page publication type and then just add pages as you need them.

Once you've created a multiple page publication, there are some easy ways to move rapidly from one page to another, or to jump over a couple of pages to get where you want to go.

1 To add a page to your publication, choose Insert, Page. This brings up the Insert Page dialog box. Choose the options you need and click OK.

FYI

● To insert a new page quickly, press Ctrl+Shift+N. The new page is created after the current page.

● If you're creating a publication that is printed on both sides or is folded, you may have to add two pages to make everything work. If you can't think of more text to add, grab a piece of clip art to fill in (and amuse your audience).

● An efficient way to use the feature that duplicates objects on each page is to create a page with just the objects you want to duplicate. Then use the Insert Page dialog box to add pages with those objects (choose the Duplicate All Objects On Page Number option). Then go back to the original page and add the objects you don't want to duplicate.

6 If you are working on the last page and need to add another page after it, just click the Next Page arrow (or the Last Page arrow). Publisher figures out what you're trying to do and asks you to confirm that you want to add another page. Click on OK.

2 If you want to reproduce the objects on a page, it's a great way to make a header for every page. Just select Duplicate All Objects On Page Number, and then specify the page you want to duplicate.

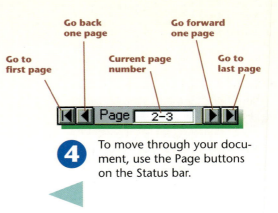

3 If you are working with two pages on your Publisher window, the Insert Page dialog box changes its options so you can be specific about where you want to insert the new page(s).

Go back one page   Go forward one page

Go to first page   Current page number   Go to last page

4 To move through your document, use the Page buttons on the Status bar.

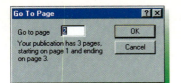

5 To move quickly to a specific page, click on the page number button to bring up the Go To Page dialog box. The current page is selected, so as soon as you type a new page number, the character(s) you type replace the information displayed in the page number box. Click OK. For even faster movement, press F5 to get to the same dialog box.

How to Resize and Reposition Clip Art

Once you've placed clip art on a page, you have to make sure its placement and size are correct. After all, it has to coexist with text, headlines, or even other clip art.

Getting everything "just so" is part of the fine-tuning process that makes the difference between a so-so publication and a slick one.

When you change the size of a clip art frame, the art it contains is resized at the same time.

1 Before you can manipulate a clip art frame, you must click on it to select it. To make the frame and the picture wider, move your pointer to either side handle. When the pointer changes to a Resize double-arrow, click and hold the left mouse button and drag in the appropriate direction. To make the frame taller, perform the same action on the top or bottom handle.

6 Sometimes the best way to make a frame smaller without making the clip art so small you can't see it is to crop the picture. That means you select a portion of the picture to keep and discard the rest. Click the Crop Picture button on the Format toolbar, then move the mouse pointer to one of the frame handles. The pointer changes to the Cropper (scissors). Drag the pointer and watch the grey line that indicates the cut-off point. Release the mouse to crop within the new line. If you want to crop another side of the picture, repeat the process with a different sizing handle. Click the Crop Picture button again to turn it off.

FYI

● To resize an object and keep its proportions the same, hold down the Shift key while you drag a corner frame handle. Be sure to release the mouse button before you release the Shift key.

● To crop a picture on both sides at once, follow the instructions for cropping, but hold down the Ctrl key as you drag the mouse. If you're dragging a side handle, the picture will be cropped equally on the other side. If you're dragging a diagonal handle, the picture will be cropped equally on all four sides.

2 To move two sides at once, move the pointer to a corner handle, and when it changes to a Resize double-arrow, click and drag in a diagonal direction. The two adjacent sides move equally.

3 To reposition clip art, select it and move the pointer anywhere inside the clip art frame. This changes the pointer to a moving van. Click and drag the clip art to its new position on the page.

4 To keep the center of the clip art in the original location as you resize it, hold down the Ctrl key as you drag the sizing handle. Be sure to release the mouse button first, then release the Ctrl key. What this does is force an equal growth or reduction on the opposite side of the sizing handle you're using.

5 To change the size of a clip art frame with more precision, select the frame, then click the right mouse button to display the menu. Choose Scale Object to see the Scale Object dialog box. The numbers that appear reflect the current percentage of size compared to the clip art's original size. Increase or decrease the percentage as you wish. Type the same number in both boxes to resize the clip art proportionately.

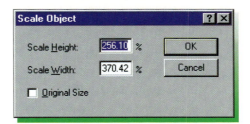

How to Wrap Text around Clip Art

Nothing screams "amateur publication" more than a page that has text in one place, a graphic in another place, and lots of white space between them. While this works fine if the graphic is a logo or some other design that should stand alone, most of the time graphics are used to enhance text and should be married (so to speak) to the text they enhance.

The way this works best, and most professionally, is to wrap text around a graphic. You can do this on a single column page by having the margin next to the graphic move to accommodate the graphic, or in a multiple column page by having the appropriate margins move to make room for a graphic between the columns.

1 Start with a text page, either a regular page full of text or a page of text in columns.

Frame line

5 If the text is a bit irregular when you change the method of wrapping text, you might want to move the graphic a bit. Notice that the frame line is now irregular instead of a rectangle.

● To insert a graphic and have text wrap around it in a page with columns, it's best to put the graphic on one edge of the column or in the middle section between columns. If you do the latter, the right margin of the column on the left will wrap around the graphic and the left margin of the column on the right will wrap around the graphic.

● It is never a good idea to wrap text on both sides of a graphic, because the reader's eye will have to skip over the graphic for every sentence.

2 Click the Picture tool, then create a graphic frame by clicking on the appropriate part of the page and dragging the mouse to create the frame.

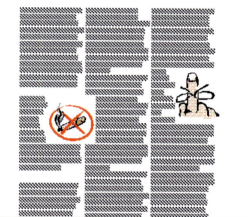

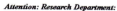

3 Right-click in the graphic frame and select Insert Clip Art. Use the instructions at the beginning of this chapter to choose and insert the clip art you want to use. When the clip art is inserted, the text moves itself around the frame.

4 By default, the text is wrapped around the clip art frame, which is a regular shape. To wrap text around the shape of the clip art itself, right-click in the clip art frame and choose Object Frame Properties from the menu. Then select Picture Only, and choose OK.

How to Flow Text between Text Frames

Picture this: You're typing away and you get near the bottom of the text frame and suddenly you can't see the characters you're typing. You've overrun the text frame. But, unlike a word processor, a new page isn't created automatically so your text can continue. There aren't any error messages, there's no scroll bar to use to move down to where your characters seem to be landing, you can't see what you're typing. Where is all this text you're typing? It's hiding, and Publisher gives you some clues about what's going on.

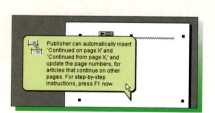

1 When you first create a text frame and begin entering characters, there's a button at the bottom of the frame. The button, which is called a connect button, displays messages about the size of the contents of the frame. It starts out by displaying a diamond. The diamond means that all the text is being held inside the text frame.

FYI

● If your publication is already set up with multiple text pages, you don't have to create a new one, just move to any page with a text frame (or any existing blank page, and use the Text Tool to create a text frame). Then pour the contents of the pitcher into it.

● You can create a new page for the overflow text anywhere; it doesn't have to be the very next page. You might want to move past existing pages and create a new page at the end of the publication. Stories don't have to be on contiguous pages.

6 Before the pitcher empties, Publisher tells you that you might want to consider saying "Continued on page X" on the previous page and "Continued from page X" on this new page. You might want to do that, but not now. Don't worry, we'll cover that soon.

(Continued on next page)

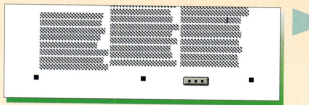

2 As you continue to type and you run out of room in the frame, Publisher stores the characters you can't see. And it announces that it's holding characters in an overflow area by changing the symbol on the connect button to three dots.

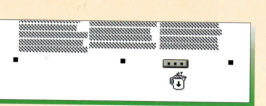

3 Now you have an overflowing text frame and Publisher has the overflow contents tucked away safely. You need to put this extra stuff into a new text frame. That requires two steps: First you must grab the overflow text in its own container, then you have to create a new text frame to accept your container full of text. Start by creating the container, which requires that you click on the connect button (which is displaying three dots). This turns your pointer into a pitcher, which holds the overflow.

Once upon a time, in a land far far away, a little girl named Sarah was waiting for her prince to come.

Sarah was getting really disgusted with all the frogs she'd kissed. *Yuck!*

She'd tried sleeping for a hundred years, but got wakeful and restless after about 8 hours. *Arrgh.*

(Continued on page 7)

Page 6   Zoom 33%

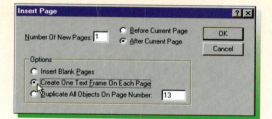

4 Now you need an empty text frame. The quickest way to do this is to insert a new page that's ready to accept the overflow text. Choose Insert, Page and when the Insert Page dialog box appears, specify a new page after the current page and select Create One Text Frame On Each Page. Then choose OK.

5 When you move your pointer onto the new page, the pitcher has tilted, and you can see things spilling out of it. All you have to do is click on the page to put the text on the page. Click quickly before all your words fall on the floor.

How to Flow Text between Text Frames (Continued)

N ow that you've poured your overflow text into a new text page, there are a couple of items to learn about. We'll look at the messages Publisher is giving you with the connect buttons and we'll work on providing a smooth segue for your readers by referring them to the proper pages in order to read your story.

7 Once the overflow text is placed in a new page, you can see if you're finished. Check the button at the bottom of the page. If there's a diamond symbol on it, all the overflow text fit on this page. If there are three dots on it, there's still more text in the pitcher and you have to create or find another blank page with a text frame and pour the overflow into it. Notice that the top of this page has a connect button with an arrow pointing left. If you click on the button, you'll go back to the previous page for this story. (The previous page has a similar connect button, but the arrow is pointing to the right. Click on it to move to the next page of the story.)

Then, one day, Sarah had a brain-storm. She signed up with an ISP and began
(Continued on page 8)

12 If you do eliminate a page in a connected series of pages, go to the blank page and disconnect it. To disconnect, click on the chain link symbol. In fact, you can disconnect a page that isn't blank (the text that was on the page is put into the overflow pitcher) and reconnect your story to a different page if you wish (just pour the text into the text frame of the new page).

● If you accidentally delete the page number when you're editing the "Continued..." message, choose Insert, Page Numbers from the menu bar to replace the code.

● You can also change the font, the font size, and the attributes (bold, italic) for the "Continued..." notice.

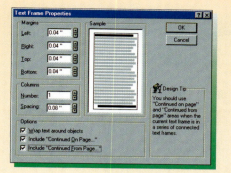

8 When a story or an article spans multiple pages, you'll want to add a notice so your readers can find the next page of your story (or find the beginning of the story if they open to a page that's a continuation). Publisher makes this task extremely easy. Just pick any connected page for your story and right-click. Choose Text Frame Properties. When the Text Frame Properties dialog box opens, check the two Continued options at the bottom. Repeat this step for each page in the connection chain.

9 The pages in your story have the appropriate messages about the continuation scheme for your readers. (Incidentally, the "Continued..." messages are really in small italic type—they've been enlarged in this illustration so you could see them.) If you insert pages in your publication or if you move pages around, the message will make the necessary adjustments to keep everything accurate.

10 You can change the wording of the "Continued..." messages if you wish. Select the text you want to change and insert your new phrase. Notice that on the Text Format toolbar there's a style name for this feature. After you make the change, click the name of the style (there's one for Continued On and another one for Continued From) and press Enter. Publisher displays a message asking if you want to change this style to reflect your changes. Click on OK to do so (click on Cancel if you change your mind). Hereafter your new phrase will be used for that continuation message. Repeat the process for the other (Continued From) message. Be careful not to delete or replace the page number—it isn't really a number, it's a code, and it changes as page numbers change.

11 If the last page of your story is extremely short, you may have a layout problem. For a newsletter, this is no big deal, you just start the next story under the end of this one. But for brochures or other publications, this can leave an awful lot of blank space. Go back to the previous page(s) and see what you can do to eliminate this last page. Make the text frame larger, make the font smaller, make graphics smaller, or even cut some text out of the story.

How to Recolor and Add a Drop Shadow to Text Frames

If you have the ability to print in color, either in-house or because you're using an outside printer, you should take advantage of it. One classic (and classy) way to use color is to put a color border around a text frame. You can make the border elegantly thin, boldly thick, or amusingly decorative.

Another way to add graphical interest to a text frame is to put a drop shadow around it. A drop shadow is an effect that is applied to two adjacent sides of a frame. The best way to picture it is to imagine the sun is on one side of your frame, so on the opposite side your frame is casting a shadow. If you want to put a drop shadow around a text frame, you can have Publisher do it for you or you can do it yourself. The latter is more complicated, but the results are dramatically different. When Publisher creates a drop shadow, it's quite thin (in fact I sometimes have trouble seeing it). And your only color choice is grey. Do it yourself to control thickness and color.

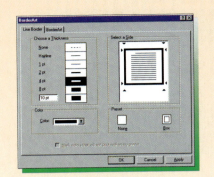

1 To create a color border, select the text frame you want to decorate and click the Border button on the Formatting toolbar. When the Border menu appears, choose More to display the Border Art dialog box. Select a border in the Choose a Thickness section of the dialog box by clicking on it.

● If you added a color border and you also added a drop shadow, make sure they're color coordinated. The shadow should be a deeper shade of the border color (shadows are dark). Technically, shadows should be grey, but there's nothing wrong with having a more colorful approach.

● To enliven the text box even more, bring the shadow's box to the front and choose Format, Fill Patterns and Shading from the menu bar. Then pick a pattern for the color border. This is especially interesting if you are printing in black and white and did have to choose a grey border.

6 Use the Send To Back button on the Standard toolbar to put the colorful box behind the text box. If the shadow is too deep, not deep enough, the wrong color, or there are any other changes you want to make (you might want to imagine the sun is on the other side of the text box, which means the shadow will have to move), use the Bring to Front button to make the changes. Then repeat the steps to make it a shadow.

2 Click the arrow to the right of the Color box to see a color palette and click on the color you want. If you can't find the perfect hue, choose More Colors to see a wider selection. When you have selected the color, choose OK.

3 To create a drop shadow around a text frame, you start by drawing a box on top of the frame. Click the Box tool on the Publisher toolbar. Then place your mouse in the upper-left corner of the text frame and drag the mouse down and to the right to duplicate the size of the frame. I find it easier to work with the box that will become the shadow by making it just a tiny bit wider on the right than the text frame.

4 When you release the mouse, you see only the new box you've created. That's because the box is in front of the text frame. (You can switch their positions, just to reassure yourself that you haven't obliterated the text frame, by clicking the Send To Back button on the Standard toolbar, then clicking the Bring to Front button to put things back so you can work.) Resize the new box to make its bottom edge slightly larger than the text box. If you didn't make the box wider on the right when you first created it, do that now. The bottom and right edges of the box have to show (and are all that will show) when this box becomes the drop shadow.

5 Now you can choose a color for the drop shadow. What you have to do is fill this box with a color. (Remember, only two edges will show when you put it behind the text box.) Choose Format, Fill Color to see the Colors dialog box. Click on the color you want to use for the border. Choose OK.

How to Add a Border to a Frame

You can frame your work with a border that's ornate, spiffy, cool, or elegant. Your choice of style depends on your mood and the objects inside the border. Choosing to use a border means you've decided a frame or a page needs some decorating in order to make it stand out.

Applying the border is easy; it's the decision-making process that's difficult. That picture of your great-great-great-grandfather that's over the fireplace (the one where he's on his steed, holding his saber) needed a thick ornate frame (possibly gilded). But a charcoal drawing needs a thin, more subtle treatment when you frame it. The same thing is true of your frames and pages. Pick a border that does justice to your publication, but doesn't overwhelm its message.

1 To put a fancy border on a frame, select the frame and click the Border button on the Format toolbar. Instead of clicking on a border line and applying a standard border around the frame, choose More from the drop-down menu.

● You can use the choose-a-thickness-per-side feature of line borders to create your own drop shadow effect. Just make two adjacent sides very thick and a dark color.

● To remove a border, select the frame and choose None from the list that appears when you click the Border button on the Format toolbar.

● If you have a clip art frame in which you have set the properties to wrap text around the picture instead of the frame, line borders are placed around the outline shape of the picture (which rarely looks attractive).

5 You can highlight parts of a table to emphasize the contents by placing a colorful border around the specific cells you want to draw attention to. Select the cells you want to use and then apply the border as described above.

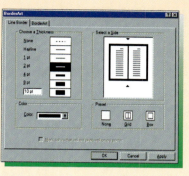

2 The Line Border tab of the BorderArt dialog box lets you create borders of various thicknesses and a variety of colors. You can make your borders a little more interesting by changing the thickness and color of specific sides of the frame. In the Select a Side box, click a side, then click on Border Thickness. You can have a different thickness for each of the four sides of the frame, or a different color for each of the four sides, or any permutation or combination of thickness and color. Choose OK when you have finished clicking away.

3 When you create a border for a frame that has text in columns, you can also make decisions about the border line between the columns. You can place a border line between columns by clicking on the vertical line between columns in the Select a Side box. Then select a border thickness and color.

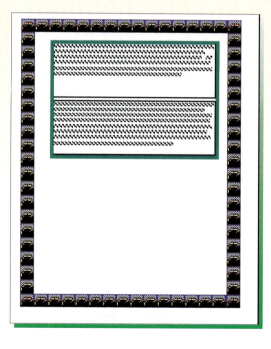

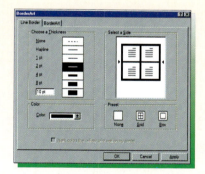

4 Borders for table frames let you manipulate thickness and color for both the horizontal and vertical gridlines. Select either line in the Select a Side box and then choose a thickness and color. To make all the lines the same border style, select a thickness and color and then choose Grid.

How to Use Gradient Fills and Patterns

Add even more zest to the appearance of your publication by using splashes of color to illuminate your message. Publisher provides a way to fill objects with colors and color patterns. Used judiciously, and with taste and common sense, this can make your publication extra special.

A pattern is a way to put texture into color, creating a more interesting eye-catcher than a plain color. It is, however, busier than plain color, so you won't want to use it on a busy frame. A gradient fill changes its depth and texture within the frame, creating an interesting and multidimensional effect. It actually is a graduated fill, moving from dense to thin in its application of dots of color.

1 To use a pattern in a frame, select the frame and then click on the Object Color button on the Format toolbar. When the drop-down menu appears, click on Patterns & Shading.

● When you're putting a pattern or a gradient fill behind a graphic frame, be careful about the choices you make. You don't want to lose the impact of the clip art by having the background overwhelm it.

● Even if you're not printing to a color printer, selecting a color will impact the levels of gray that your black and white printer produces. Picking pastel shades results in lighter shades of gray.

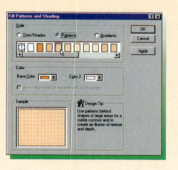

2 Select the Patterns option button and scroll through the display to find a pattern you think suits the frame you're working on. Select suitable colors and choose OK to apply the pattern fill to the frame.

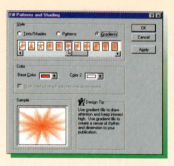

3 To use a gradient fill instead of a pattern, select the Gradients option button. Scroll through the choices to pick the pattern and shape you like, then choose OK to apply them to your frame.

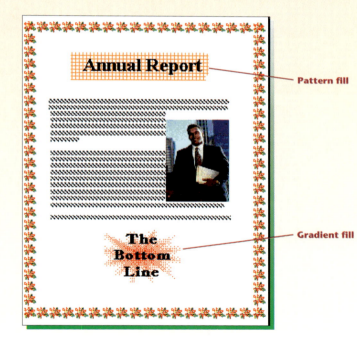

Annual Report — Pattern fill

The Bottom Line — Gradient fill

Headline Here
Sub Headline Here

4 To create a pattern or gradient fill for multiple frames or a page, click the Box tool and draw a box around the elements or the page. Then choose the pattern and color scheme you want to use.

5 To give yourself a larger range of color choices, select the frame, click the Object Color button, and choose More Colors.

How to Layer Pictures for Special Effects

Layering is the process of moving one object over another object so that there is some overlap. In order for both objects to be seen, you don't want to cover either object completely, just overlap them in such a way as to create an interesting effect. You can layer graphics on graphics, or text on graphics.

As with other graphical effects available through Publisher's tools, restraint is the key word. Don't overdo it, or else you'll lose the advantage Publisher gives you of making your publication look as if it were produced by a professional graphics designer.

Time To Practice

1 To layer graphics, create both graphic items on the same page. Select one of the graphic objects (the mouse pointer turns to a moving van) and drag it over the other graphic object.

FYI

● The first time you put one object on top of another, Publisher offers to help you finish the task by showing you a demo on layering objects, or opening the Help files to give you step-by-step instructions. Choose the method of help you prefer, or choose Continue to do it without Publisher's assistance.

● One of the more interesting ways to layer objects is to layer shapes. More information about using shapes is found in Chapter 15.

Game Time
7:00PM

6 To display the text on the graphic cleanly (without the background of the text box) you have to make the text frame transparent so the graphic shows through. Select the text frame and press Ctrl+T.

2 If the graphic that is in the foreground should be behind the other graphic (as in the left page of this illustration), select it and click the Send To Back button on the Standard toolbar. When the graphic moves to the background, the effect you intended is achieved (check the right page of this illustration).

3 You aren't limited to two graphics when you want to use layering. You can use as many items as you need to in order to get the effect you want.

4 When you're layering multiple objects, there's more than the simple "front and back" layering movement available. You can move objects back one or more layers at a time (or move them forward one or more layers at a time) by selecting an object and using the options on the Arrange menu.

 5 You can also move a text frame so that it is on top of a graphics frame.

How to Group Objects

When you've created objects that belong together, you can ensure that whatever you do to one you do to the others. If the objects are meant to be stacked vertically and need to be moved over a bit, if they move as a group you don't have to manipulate them one at a time and you don't have to worry about the relationships changing.

1 To create a group, click the Selection tool on the Publisher toolbar and drag your mouse to draw a box around all the objects you want to place in the group. When the box is around the objects, a group button appears at the bottom. Note that the two connectors of that button are separated.

● Instead of drawing a box to enclose objects in a group, you can hold down the Ctrl key and click on each of the objects. Publisher will create a box containing those objects for you.

● If you want to work on one object in the group, just select the object you want to manipulate. To deselect that object and return to working on the group, click the Group button twice.

● When you have completed your work on the group, click the Group button to ungroup and then click anywhere on the Publisher screen to put things back to normal.

5 You can also move or rotate the group to change the position of all the objects at the same time.

2 Click the group button to connect its two parts. Now your group is firmly connected and you can begin to manipulate the objects as a group. Notice that the group box has its own sizing handles.

3 You can resize every object in the group by using the group box handles to resize the group.

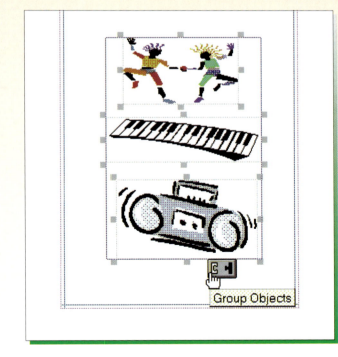

Group Objects

4 If you use the Object Color tool on the Formatting toolbar, the color of all the objects in the group changes. The same thing is true of borders, so that selecting a border for the group really places that border on each of the objects in the group.

How to Insert Page Numbers and Dates

Some publications, such as newsletters, book-lets, or other multipage documents, need page numbering or dates, or both. If you use a word processor, you're probably familiar with using headers or footers to insert these elements so that they appear on every page. In Publisher, you can use the background of the pages of your publication to accomplish the same thing.

However, there is a very large difference between the way headers and footers work in word processors and the way backgrounds work in Publisher. Word processors adjust the page to make room for the headers and footers. Publisher does not. The background is its own page and the only way to use text on the background and have it seen on the page is to clear a spot for it on the page. You have to plan for text backgrounds. Graphic backgrounds (discussed in the next section) are easier to create and they're easier to make visible.

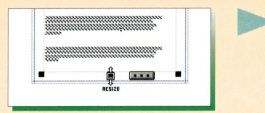

1 To insert page numbers or dates on every page of your publication, first decide where you want the element to fall on the page. Then make sure all the pages of your publication are blank in that spot. For instance, if you want to place a page number at the bottom of every page, make sure the bottom of every frame is above that spot.

● When you're preparing your pages to make room for the background text elements, use a Ruler or Layout guide to be consistent. (See Chapter 5 for more information about using guides.)

● If you don't want your page number to be seen on the front page of your publication, create a blank text frame on that page directly over the text frame on the background. Make sure it's not transparent and it will hide the background text box.

7 Press Ctrl+M to return to your publication page and see the results. Remember that whatever you place on a background page will be seen on every page of your publication.

2 From any page in your publication, move to the background by pressing Ctrl+M. If you started from a blank page, the background page won't look different. Check the status bar—if you're on a foreground page, you'll see the page number and the page controls; if you're on the background, you'll see a double box.

3 To insert either the page number or the date, create a small text box on the background page.

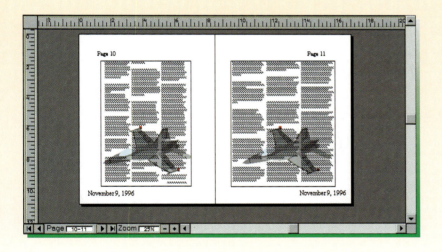

4 To insert a page number, make sure the text frame is selected and choose Insert, Page Numbers from the menu bar. A pound sign appears in the text box. The pound sign is the symbol for a page number on a background page.

6 To insert a date, make sure the text frame is selected and choose Insert, Date or Time from the menu bar. Then choose the date format you want to use. Select Update Automatically if you want the date to change to reflect the current date every time you open this publication. Select Insert as Plain Text if you want today's date to be the permanent date on this publication.

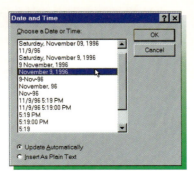

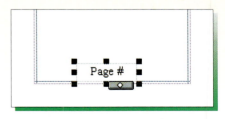

5 You can add additional words to the page text frame. Perhaps you might want to add the word "Page" or the letter P. You can also select the text and change the font, size, alignment, or attributes.

How to Use Design Gallery to Add Flair to Your Publication

S troll through the Publisher Design Gallery to see a wide variety of artwork you can use to add an extra, professional touch to your publication. The ornamental designs are similar to those you've seen in work produced by professional graphic artists.

1 To add an element from the Design Gallery to your publiction, click the Design Gallery tool on the Publisher toolbar.

6 Use the scroll bar to scroll through the designs in the category until you find one you like.

2 The Design Gallery window opens with a list of categories and a variety of designs for each category. The title bar displays the type of designs in this gallery (in this case, Classic Designs).

3 You can choose another gallery by clicking More Designs.

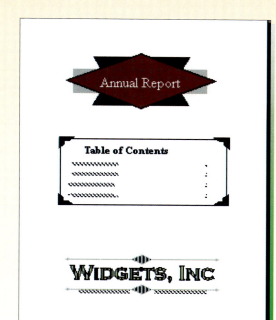

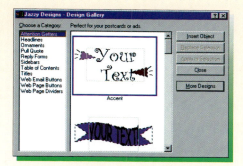

4 When you move to another gallery, you'll see that the design elements have a different look, a different personality. Find the gallery that matches the look you want for your publication.

5 When you decide on the gallery you want to use, choose the category you need for the element you're ready to add to your page.

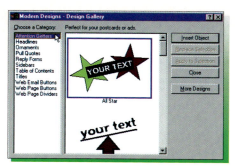

How to Use PageWizard for Special Elements

There are some elements needed occasionally that you could design and create yourself, but it would take quite some time. Publisher has a built-in feature called PageWizard that does the hard work for you when you want to add one of these frames (a calendar, an advertisement, a coupon, or a logo). You get to make the design decisions, but you don't have to do all the work.

The PageWizard elements are multiple frames that have been grouped together to form the final object, so you can fine-tune them by manipulating the individual frames.

1 To use the PageWizard, click the PageWizard tool on the Publisher toolbar, then select the element you want to use.

● The actual questions and design decisions for each type of PageWizard element vary depending upon the choices you make. Responding to a question with one answer will lead to different choices than another answer would have.

● There's a minimum size requirement for the PageWizard elements. A logo must be at least 1" by 1". The other designs require at least 2" by 2".

● Remember that you can disassemble, manipulate, and change any of the PageWizard elements. Then, when it's just right, save your design as explained in the previous sections.

6 For a logo, the style, the shape, the contents (a picture or initials), and text including a slogan are all part of the available design elements.

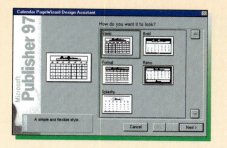

2 Move to the page and put your pointer at the position where you want the upper-left corner of the element to appear. Then press and hold the mouse button while you drag down and right until you have the size you want. When you release the mouse button, the PageWizard window appears. Each PageWizard starts by asking you to select a style. Click the style you like and then click Next.

3 The answers you give and the decisions you make depend upon the element you're adding. For a calendar, you must decide whether you want to spell out the days of the week or use abbreviations; whether you want to have room for note-writing in the date blocks; and whether you want the weeks to begin on Sunday or Monday.

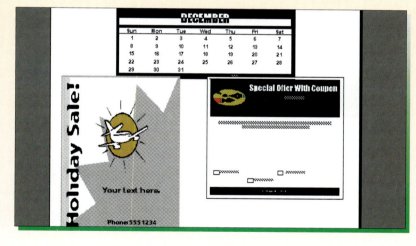

4 For an ad, you can pick the type of ad (classified, product, sale). Publisher will even give you a list of catchy phrases to use if your imagination fails you.

5 If you're inserting a coupon in your publication, you can choose whether it's a mailed-in coupon or a hand-it-over coupon; you can have an expiration date; and you can design the border and title.

How to Use Shapes

Publisher provides a two standard shapes that are frequently useful for adding punch to your publication: the box and the oval. The nice thing about those shapes is that they needn't be standard at all, since you have the opportunity to stretch and bend them to your own taste.

In addition, you can color them and dress them up to make them original and effective.

1 To use a standard shape in your publication, click on it in the Publisher toolbar.

6 To place text on a shape, create a text frame on the shape and enter the text. Then use Ctrl+T to make the text frame transparent.

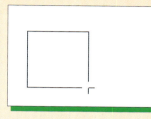

2 To control the placement and shape, place your pointer on the page where you want the shape to appear, then drag the mouse until the shape is the size you need. You can drag the box tool to create a square, a horizontal rectangle, or a vertical rectangle. The oval tool lets you vary the shape in an infinite number of ways, or you can have a perfect circle. (Hold down the Shift key while you're creating the circle to keep it perfectly round.)

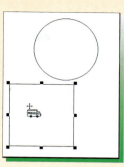

3 For single-click placement of the shape, click on the page in the location where you want the shape. Then, if needed, you can move the shape, or adjust it by using the handles.

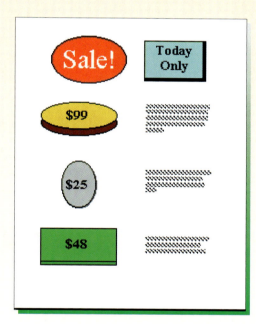

5 You can create a customized shadow for the shape by creating another shape or copying the first one by right-clicking on the shape and choosing the Copy choice from the menu that displays. Then drag one on top of the other, offsetting them just a bit. Color one, then use the Bring To Front and Send To Back buttons on the Standard toolbar to access the other one. Use a contrasting color to create the shadow effect.

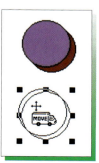

4 To color the shape, make sure it's selected, then choose the Object Color button on the Format toolbar. To add a pattern in addition to color, choose Patterns and Shading after you click the Object Color button, then select Patterns. Choose the pattern design that suits you. To add a gradient, choose Gradients. Then choose a gradient design that matches the look you're trying to achieve.

❶ ❷ ❸ ❹ ❺

A

absolute references, 98–99

Access 97, 119–157. *See also* databases
  adding database fields, 130
  changing database fields, 130–131
  creating a form with Form Wizard, 132–133
  creating a switchboard form, 142–143
  creating a table with Table Wizard, 128–129
  customizing, 156–157
  database queries in, 150
  Database Wizard, 122–123
  data entry in, 136–137
  drawing a text box, 135
  dressing up the switchboard, 144–145
  filtering records, 148–149
  importing data, 152–153
  modifying a form in Design view, 134–135
  modifying a report in Design view, 140–141
  in a network environment, 156
  planning a database, 126–127
  reporting with Report Wizard, 138–139
  sorting data, 146–147
  switchboard menu system, 124–125
  using to export data, 154–155

accounting software add-on (SBFM), 254–263

active cell, 72–73
  border, 82
  making, 74, 76
  and scrolling, 82

active window, 57

Address Book, in Outlook 97, 208–209

adjacent cell, empty but with spilled data, 74

antivirus program, 244

application support on the Web, 246

application window (Excel), 72

appointment book. *See* Outlook 97

appointment tracking (Outlook 97), 220–223

arguments, function, 79, 97

arrow keys, 18, 39, 74–75

asterisks, before and after a word, 26

audio clips, in Office applications, 5

AutoArchive (Outlook 97), 236–237

AutoComplete tips, 25, 80

AutoContent Wizard (PowerPoint), 162–163

AutoDialing contacts (Outlook 97), 230–231

AutoFilter, 102–104

AutoJournal (Outlook 97), 232–233

AutoMap
  finding and marking locations, 264–265
  highlighting a travel route, 266–267

AutoShapes
  using in Excel, 114–115
  using in PowerPoint, 174–175

AutoText entries
  creating and using, 24–25
  deleting, 24
  in headers and footers, 45
  inserting, 25
  list of categories, 24
  modifying, 24
  printing a list of, 24

AutoText toolbar, 24

AVERAGE function (Excel), 96–97

axis titles, chart, 107, 110–111

B

backgrounds
  for database screen and forms, 123
  in Publisher, 302–303

Backspace key, 18, 75

balance sheets, creating, 256–257
bar tabs, 34
Binder (Microsoft Office Binder), 8–9
blank document template, 24
blank document window (Word), 16, 18
blank lines, creating, 18
blocks of text
    copying formatting across, 28
    highlighting, 20
boldfacing text, 26, 28–29
border around a page, creating, 40–41
    line color and width, 41
    line styles, 41
    and paragraph text, 40
Borders and Shading dialog box
    Borders tab, 41
    Page Border tab, 40
    Shading tab, 41
browse buttons (Word), 16
built-in formulas, 76, 78–79, 96–97
bulleted lists
    changing the appearance of, 36
    changing to numbered lists, 37
    creating, 36–37
    separating items with a blank line, 36
    turning on/off automatic, 36

C

calendar. See Outlook 97
Cancel button, Excel worksheet, 75
Caps Lock key, 19
cash flow report, creating, 260–261
categories (database), entering new, 124
Categories form, opening, 125
Category list box number formats, 95
CD-ROM installation, 2–3
CD-ROM installation 11-digit key code, 3
cell A1, moving to, 82
cell addresses, 73–74, 79, 83

cell display
    pound signs (#) in, 74
    scientific notations in, 74
cell range, 79
    average number in, 97
    in a function, 96
    largest number in, 97
    named, 100–101
    smallest number in, 97
cell references, 76–77, 79, 98–99
cells (worksheet). See also Excel worksheets
    avoiding overwriting, 88, 90
    clearing, 86–87
    current cell, 73
    data entry in, 74
    deleting, 86–87
    display of text is cut off, 74, 92
    entering characters as text, 77
    entering labels, 80
    filling automatically, 80–81
    with fixed number or formula, 76
    formatting numbers in, 94–95
    with large number display, 92
    making active, 76
    moving and copying data, 88–89
    moving one that is referenced absolutely, 98
    moving to specific, 83
    naming, 100–101
    spilled data in adjacent empty cell, 74, 92
    text entries spill over, 74, 92
    truncated data in, 74, 92
    viewing contents of, 72, 76
    widening, 74
character formatting (Word), 26, 28–29
chart axis titles, 107, 110–111
chart data (Excel), changing, 112–113
chart features of Office applications, 4–5
chart gridlines, 107
chart legends, 107, 110
Chart menu, 111, 113

chart options, 111
Chart Options dialog box Titles tab, 111
chart shapes, drawing, 114–115
chart sheets (Excel), 106–107, 110, 112
chart titles, 107, 110–111
Chart toolbar, 108
chart type, changing, 108–109
Chart Type dialog box, 109
chart types and subtype, 107
ChartWizard, 5, 106–107
ChartWizard dialog box, 107
clearing cells, 86–87
clip art. *See also* graphics; shapes
    adding to Clip Gallery, 66
    collections on the Web, 242–243
    inserting in a Word document, 66–67
    Publisher Design Gallery, 304–305
    revising categories of, 66
    sizing and positioning in Publisher, 284–285
    using in PowerPoint, 178–179
    wrapping text around, 286–287
Clip Art Connection, 243
Clipboard, 7, 20–21, 90–91, 248
Clip Gallery 3.0, 4, 66–67
closing a document window, 17
closing an Office document, 13, 17
closing a program window, 17
columns (Excel worksheet), 72
    adjusting widths of, 92–93
    deleting, 86
    headings for, 73
    inserting, 84–85
    quickly moving through, 82
    searching for data in, 102–103
    sorting data in, 104–105
columns of labels, entering automatically, 80
common fields (database), 127
common Office applications, 4–5
companies, searching the Web for, 242
company name header (database report), 140
computer virus, 244

connection speeds, Web, 244
contact management in Outlook 97, 226–231
    AutoDialing, 230–231
    sending e-mail, 228–229
cookie conspiracy, 240
cookies, 240
copying
    character formatting, 28–29
    Excel data, 88–91
    formatting across blocks of text, 28
    and pasting, 20–21, 90–91
    text, 21
correcting misspellings, 22–23
COUNT function (Excel), 96–97
Create AutoText dialog box, 25
Create Data Source dialog box, 59
Creation toolbar (Publisher), 272–273
Currency format, assigning automatically, 94
current cell, 73
current date and time, fields for, 45
current page (Word), 16
current record, 136
cursor, 17
    dragging, 20, 29
    moving, 18
Custom Install, 3
customizing Access, 156–157
custom tabs
    deleting, 34
    kinds of, 34
    seeing which are in effect, 34
Cut and Copy toolbar, 91
cut-and-paste, 20–21, 90–91

D
database fields
    adding and changing, 130–131, 133
    deleting, 130–131
    naming, 131
database file, naming, 123

database forms, 120, 123, 132–133
database queries, 132–133
   adding fields for a report, 139
   creating with Simple Query Wizard, 150–151
   naming, 151
database report grouping levels, 139
database reports, 120–121, 123
databases, 58. *See also* Access 97
   basics of, 120–121
   common fields in, 127
   creating, 128
   creating from scratch, 126
   data entry in, 136–137
   determining fields to use, 126–127
   determining tables to include, 127
   entering new categories in, 124
   planning, 126–127
   setting sort order for, 139
   well-constructed, 126
database sorts, 146–147
database tables, 123
database templates, 122
database title, 122
database window
   customizing, 157
   Forms tab, 132, 134
   Reports tab, 138
Database Wizard, 122–123
data entry
   in Access, 136–137
   automatic Excel, 80–81
   chart sheet, 112
   from the Clipboard, 90
   in an Excel worksheet, 74–75, 80–81
   using switchboard, 124–125
data entry forms, 121, 132
data fills, 80–81, 98–99, 176–177
Data Form dialog box, 61
data point, 112
data series, 80, 112

datasheet view, 136–137
data source (mail merge)
   creating, 58–61
   saving, 64
data type choices, list of, 131
Date last modified, 156
dates, inserting, 63, 302–303
date and time, in headers and footers, 45
Date and Time toolbar, 45
days of the week, entering automatically, 80
Decimal tab, 35
decorative line, 19
default margins, changing, 42
default style in Word documents, 24
Default tabs, 34–35
delimited text files, 155
deselecting text, 29
Design Gallery (Publisher), 304–305
Design view
   database report in, 140–141
   form in, 134–135
desktop publishing, 269–309
Details sheet (database), 125
Details window (database), 125
dialog box forms, 132
dictionary, adding words to, 23
Document Map, 46–47
   blank, 46
   change heading levels, 46
   closing, 46
   expanding/collapsing, 46–47
Document Map pane, 46
Document1 (temporary name), 16
document outlines, 46–47
documents (Office)
   adding to a binder, 9
   closing, 13
   copying text to a different application, 20
   opening, 12–13
   printing, 13
   saving, 13

document window (Word), 18
dotted line, 19
double line, 19
double-line border, 40
double quotes, for blank text fields, 150
double spacing, 32
downloading files from the Web, 244–245
downloading software updates/patches, 243
drag and drop (Excel)
    between worksheets and workbooks, 88
    moving and copying cell data with, 88–89
    into an occupied area of a worksheet, 88
drag and drop (Word), 20, 29, 39
Drawing toolbar, 114–115
Draw Table, 38–39
drop shadows, in Publisher, 292–293

E

Edit Formula (=) button in Excel, 77
e-mail (Outlook 97)
    attaching a file to a message, 212–213
    automatic journal recording of, 232–233
    composing and sending, 210–211
    managing received attachments, 218–219
    opening and reading, 214–215
    Personal Address Book, 208–209
    replying to and forwarding messages,
        216–217
    sending to a contact, 228–229
embedded chart, 107, 109
embedded document, 8
embedded object, 6–7
end of file mark, 17
Enter button/key (Excel), 74–75
entering and editing text (Word), 18–19
Enter key (Word tables), 38
Enter key (Word text), 18
Esc key (Excel), 75
Excel ChartWizard, 5, 106–107
Excel menu bar, 73

Excel 97, 71–117. *See also* Excel worksheets
    changing chart data, 112–113
    changing the chart type, 108–109
    chart and axis titles, 110–111
    drawing shapes on a chart, 114–115
    entering data automatically, 80–81
    formula cell references, 98–99
    functions, 76, 96–97
    moving and copying data, 90–91
    named cell ranges, 100–101
    SBFM add-on, 254–263
    searching for data, 102–103
    sorting data, 104–105
    standard and formatting toolbars, 73
    starting, 72
    summing numbers, 78–79
Excel window, 72–73
Excel worksheets. *See also* cells (worksheet);
        Excel 97
    adjusting column widths, 92–93
    applying formatting to groups of, 117
    calculating totals for a group, 116
    clearing and deleting cells, 86–87
    column headings, 73
    entering data, 74–75
    entering formulas, 76–77
    erasing data, 86
    finding which are in use, 73
    formatting numbers in, 94–95
    getting to upper-left corner, 82
    grouping/ungrouping, 116
    inserting columns and rows, 84–85
    moving and copying data, 88–89
    moving to current row beginning, 83
    moving to last nonblank cell in a row, 83
    moving to lower-right cell, 83
    navigating around, 82–83
    quickly moving through, 82
    row headings, 73
    scrolling, 82
    selecting a group of adjacent, 117

title bar, 117
using multiple, 116–117
viewing, 72
Excel worksheet tabs, 73
Excite search engine, 240–241
Explorer (Windows), 12
exporting data using Access, 154–155
Export Text Wizard window, 154

F

field delimiters, text file, 155
Field drop-down list, 134
field label property sheet, 135
Field Options window (importing data), 153
field properties sheet (database), 130–131, 134
fields (database), 120–121
adding and changing, 130–131, 133
deleting, 130–131
determining, 126–127
from different tables for one form, 132
indexed, 153
naming, 131
quick search based on, 148
removing, 135
replacing one with another, 134
report, 139
searching for blank numeric, 150
sizing and positioning, 134
totaling, 151
to use as a grouping category, 139
fields (text), 58
for the current date and time, 45
in headers and footers, 44
files, adding to the Binder, 8
file transfers, 244
fill handle, 80–81, 98–99
filtering database records, 148–149
filtering Excel data, 102–103
filtering a list and then sorting the result, 104

flashing border around selected cells, 91
flashing insertion point, 18
flowing text between text frames (Publisher), 288–291
folders, 3, 13, 56
Font dialog box, 27
font list, 31
Font list box, 31
fonts, 27, 30–31, 141, 280–281
font sizes, 30–31, 141
font style list, 27
font styles, 27
footers, 44–45
adding, 45
AutoText in, 45
fields in, 44
on odd and even pages, 44
page numbers in, 45
in portions of a document, 44
Format Cells dialog box, 95
Format Painter, 28–29
Format Picture dialog box Wrapping tab, 68–69
formatting. *See also* templates
applying to selected text, 30–31
copying, 28–29
a graphic, 68–69
numbers in cells, 94–95
paragraph, 19, 32–33
in PowerPoint, 168–169
text in Publisher, 280–281
text in Word, 26–27
Formatting toolbar (Excel), 73
Formatting toolbar (Word), 17
Form Design view, 134
form detail, 134
form letters
composing, 56–57, 62–63
creating, 56–65
printing, 64

forms
    Access switchboard, 143
    creating with Form Wizard, 132–133
    database, 120, 123
    in Design view, 134–135
    headers and footers for, 134
    layouts for, 133
    sorting, 146–147
    styles for, 133
Forms tab of the database window, 132, 134
form title, 132
formula bar (Excel), 72–74, 76–77
formula cell references, 98–99
formulas
    built-in, 78–79
    and deleting cells, 86
    entering in Excel worksheets, 76–77
    and inserting columns and rows, 84
    mathematical operators for use in, 77
    and moving and copying data, 88
    using named cells or ranges in, 101
Form view, 136–137
Form View toolbar, 149
Form Wizard (Access), 132–133
Form Wizard window, 133
frequently asked questions (FAQs), 247
function arguments, 79, 97
function names, converting to uppercase, 96
functions (Excel), 76, 78–79, 96–97

G

getting help in Office 97, 10–11
Go To dialog box, 82
gradient fills and patterns (Publisher),
    296–297
grammar check, modifying, 22
Grammar Settings dialog box, 22
graphics. *See also* clip art; shapes
    adding to a report, 141
    adding to switchboard, 145
    in database reports, 138
    deleting, 66
    filling with colors and patterns, 296–297
    formatting in Word documents, 68–69
    image control, 68
    image search by keyword, 67
    inserting in Word documents, 66–67
    layering, 298–299
    lightening colors of, 68
    placing behind text, 69
    placing on top of text, 69
    Publisher Design Gallery, 304–305
    selecting, 66
    sizing and positioning in Publisher, 284–285
    as watermarks, 68
    white squares surrounding, 66
    wrapping text around, 68–69, 286–287
graphics files, finding on the Web, 243
graphics sizing handles, 66
gridlines, chart, 107
grouping levels, database report, 139
grouping objects
    in PowerPoint, 184–185
    in Publisher, 300–301

H

handles, on graphics, 66
handles, on label boxes, 135
handouts, creating with PowerPoint, 190–191
header and footer area (Word), 45
Header and Footer toolbar, 45
headers and footers
    AutoText in, 45
    on binders, 9
    fields in, 44
    on odd and even pages, 44
    page numbers in, 45
    for portions of a document, 44
    in Word, 44–45
heading levels, changing in outlines, 46

headings, moving in outlines, 48
headings in documents, outlining, 46–47
help, in Office 97, 10–11
help index, 11
Help Topics window, 11
hiding toolbars, 16
highlighting text, 20
hit, Web page, 241
horizontal scroll bar, 17
hyperlinks, placing within documents,
    248–249

I

I-beam cursor, 17
I-beam cursor with paintbrush, 29
icons, large, 156
ID field
    reads: (autonumber), 137
    refuses to allow entries, 137
ignoring misspellings, 22–23
importing data into Access, 152–153
Import window Tables tab, 152
income statements, creating, 254–255
indenting all the lines in a paragraph, 19
indenting the first line of a paragraph, 19
indexed fields, 153
Insert Hyperlink dialog box, 248–249
Insert Hyperlink feature, 248–249
inserting a document into current, 6
inserting objects from other applications, 6–7
inserting text, 21
insertion point, 16–17
    as an arrow, 89
    as a double arrow, 49
    flashing, 18
    as a four-headed arrow, 49
    as an I-beam, 17
    as an I-beam with a paintbrush, 29
    as a plus sign, 72, 81
    and tabbing, 34

Insert Picture from File, 66
Insert Picture window, 141, 145
Insert Table, 38
installation process, Office 97, 2–3
installing
    Office 97, 2–3
    Publisher 97, 270–271
    Small Business Edition of Office 97, 252–253
Internet addresses (URLs), 242
Internet address (URL) link in a document,
    248–249
Internet Explorer Web browser, 239
Internet features of Office 97, 239–249
italicizing text, 26–29

K

key field, database, 120

L

labels (cell), 80, 101
labels (form), 134
large table, creating, 38
large worksheets, navigating around, 82–83
layering objects, in PowerPoint, 182–183
layering pictures, in Publisher, 298–299
legend, chart, 107
letters, merge, 56–65
line break character, 36
lines, entering, 19
line spacing, changing, 32–33
line styles, 39, 41
linked object, 6
Link to File dialog box, 249
linking objects between applications, 6–7
linking related information, 120
links, hypertext, 248–249
lists, creating, 36–37
Location box, Web address in, 244

M

mail merge, running, 64–65
mail merge data source, creating, 58–61
mail merge document, creating, 56–65
Mail Merge Helper dialog box, 57–58
Mail Merge toolbar, 63, 65
maps of the U.S., 264–267
margins, changing in Word, 42–43
Margins tab, Page Setup dialog box, 43
marquee, 91
mathematical operators, in formulas, 77
MAX function (Excel), 96–97
Maximize button (Word window), 16
maximized window, 16
Memo Wizard, 55
menu bar (Excel), 73
menu bar (Word), 17
menu system, activating, 17
menu system (database). *See* switchboard
merge codes (in chevron brackets), 63
merge letters, creating, 56–65
Microsoft Access 97. *See* Access 97
Microsoft Clip Gallery 3.0, 4, 66–67
Microsoft Clip Gallery 3.0 dialog box, 66–67
Microsoft Excel 97. *See* Excel 97
Microsoft Find It Fast Web page, 241
Microsoft Graph, 4–5
Microsoft Office Binder, 8–9
Microsoft Office folders, 3, 13, 56
Microsoft Office 97. *See* Office 97
Microsoft PowerPoint. *See* PowerPoint
Microsoft Publisher 97. *See* Publisher 97
Microsoft's Best of the Web, 242–243
Microsoft Support page, 247
Microsoft Technical Support menu, 247
Microsoft on the Web, 246
Microsoft Word. *See* Word
MIN function (Excel), 96–97
Minimal Install, 3
minimizing a window, 17

modem speeds, 244
mouse, dragging with, 39, 88–89, 92–93
mouse pointer, 16–17
    as an arrow, 89
    as a double arrow, 49
    flashing, 18
    as a four-headed arrow, 49
    as an I-beam, 17
    as an I-beam with a paintbrush, 29
    as a plus sign, 72, 81
    and tabbing, 34
moving and copying Excel data, 88–91
moving and copying Word text, 20–21
moving the cursor, 18
moving objects in PowerPoint, 180–181
multidocument project, printing, 8
multiple documents, organizing, 8
multiple worksheets, using, 116–117

N

named cells and cell ranges, 100–101
natural language formulas, 100
newsgroups, searching, 240
next page section breaks, 44
Normal (Page Layout) view, 16, 38, 44–45, 48, 66
Normal style, 24
Normal template, 24, 51
numbered lists
    changing the appearance of, 36
    changing to bulleted lists, 37
    creating, 36–37
    separating items with a blank line, 36
    turning on/off automatic, 36
number formats, 94–95
number formatting toolbar buttons, 94

O

Office Assistant, 10–11
Office Assistant character, changing, 10–11

Office 97
   Binder, 8–9
   common applications, 4–5
   getting help, 10–11
   inserting objects, 6–7
   installation process, 2–3
   Internet features, 239–249
   linking objects between applications, 6–7
   opening and closing documents, 12–13
   saving documents, 12–13
   Small Business Edition (SBE), 251–267
OLE (object linking and embedding), 20
one-and-a-half line spacing, 32
online help, 10–11
online help system, 10–11
online support on the Web, 246–247
Open Data Source dialog box, 59–60
Open dialog box, 12
opening and closing an Office document,
   12–13
Outlining toolbar, 49
outlines (document), 46–47
   dragging a heading, 48
   expanding/collapsing, 49
   in plain unformatted text, 48
   moving headings in, 46, 48–49
   promoting/demoting headings in, 46, 48
Outline view (in Word), 48–49
   dragging a heading, 48
   expanding/collapsing, 49
   in plain unformatted text, 48
   moving headings in, 46, 48–49
   promoting/demoting headings in, 46, 48
Outlook 97, 205–237
   AutoDialing contacts, 230–231
   automatic journal recording, 232–233
   composing and sending e-mail, 210–213
   contact management, 226–231
   creating To Do lists, 224–225
   managing received e-mail attachments,
      218–219

opening and reading e-mail, 214–215
opening window, 206–207
Personal Address Book, 208–209
recording manual journal entries, 234–235
replying to and forwarding messages,
   216–217
sending e-mail to a contact, 228–229
tracking appointments, 220–223
tracking recurring appointments, 222–223
using AutoArchive, 236–237

P

Pack and Go (PowerPoint), 202–203
Page Border tab, Borders and Shading dialog
   box, 40
page footer in database reports, 140
page formatting (Word), 26–27. *See also*
   Publisher 97
page header in database reports, 140–141
Page Layout (Normal) view, 16, 38, 44–45,
   48, 66
page margins, changing in Word, 42–43
page numbers
   in headers and footers, 45
   inserting in Publisher, 302–303
   surrounded by dashes, 45
Page Setup dialog box Margins tab, 43
PageWizard (Publisher), 274–275, 306–307
PageWizard special elements (Publisher),
   306–307
Paragraph dialog box, Indents and Spacing
   tab, 33
paragraph mark, 18
paragraphs
   with borders, 40
   ending, 18
   formatting, 19, 26, 32–33
   indenting, 19
   selecting, 32
Paste Name dialog box, 101
Paste Special, 6
Paste Special dialog box, 7

pasting text, 20–21, 90–91
Percentage format, assigning automatically, 94
Personal Address Book (PAB), 208–209
photos, inserting in a Word document, 67
pictures. *See also* graphics
    inserting in a Word document, 67
    using in PowerPoint, 178–179
Picture toolbar, 66, 68–69
PowerPoint, 159–203
    adding shapes, 172–173
    adding text boxes, 170–171
    creating handouts, 190–191
    creating Speaker Notes, 188–189
    formatting and aligning text, 168–169
    grouping and ungrouping objects, 184–185
    inserting/deleting and ordering slides,
        186–187
    layering objects, 182–183
    moving and sizing objects, 180–181
    Pack and Go, 202–203
    running a slide show, 194–197
    self-running slide show, 198–201
    setting up a slide show, 192–193
    slide text, 166–167
    templates, 164–165
    toolbars, 160–161
    using art and pictures, 178–179
    using AutoContent Wizard, 162–163
    using AutoShapes, 174–175
    using sound, 178–179
    using special effects, 176–177
PowerPoint toolbars, 160–161
presentations. *See* PowerPoint
primary key (database), 129, 152
Print dialog box, 12
printing
    form letters, 64
    a list of AutoText entries, 24
    a multidocument project, 8
    an Office document, 13
Print Preview, 44

Print Settings, 8
program files, 3
program window (Word), 16–17
publications. *See* Publisher 97
Publisher Design Gallery, 304–305
Publisher 97, 269–309
    adding text to a text frame, 278–279
    backgrounds in, 302–303
    choosing a publication type, 274–275
    creating a text frame, 276–277
    flowing text between text frames, 288–291
    formatting text, 280–281
    gradient fills and patterns, 296–297
    grouping objects, 300–301
    installing, 270–271
    layering pictures, 298–299
    page insertion and navigation, 282–283
    page numbers and dates, 302–303
    PageWizard, 274–275
    PageWizard special elements, 306–307
    sizing and positioning clip art, 284–285
    text frame borders, 294–295
    text frame colors and shadows, 292–293
    using shapes, 308–309
    wrapping text around clip art, 286–287
Publisher toolbar, 272–273

Q

queries (database), 132–133
    adding fields for a report, 139
    creating with Simple Query Wizard,
        150–151
    naming, 151

R

range of cells, 79
    average number in, 97
    in a function, 96
    largest number in, 97
    named, 100–101

referencing, 79
smallest number in, 97
records (database), 58, 120–121
editing, 136
filtering, 148–149
locked and cannot be edited, 136
that contain blank fields, 150
record selector symbols, 136
record status, 136
referencing cells, 76–77, 79, 98–99
relational databases, 120, 127
relative references, 98
removing text, 26
repeated characters, 19
report detail, 140
report footer, 140
report header, 140–141
reports (Access database), 120–121, 123
avoiding cluttering in, 138
changing font sizes, 141
creating with Report Wizard, 138–139
enlarging sections of, 141
graphics in, 138, 141
layout options, 139
modifying in Design view, 140–141
previewing and saving, 140
removing objects from, 140
styles for printed, 123
switchboard, 143
report sections, 140
Reports tab, database window, 138
report title, 138
report window, 138
Report Wizard, 138–139
Report Wizard window, 139
Restore button (Word window), 16
restoring a window, 16–17
rotating objects, in PowerPoint, 180–181
rows (Excel worksheet), 72
color of, 102
deleting, 86

headings for, 73
inserting, 84–85
quickly moving through, 82
moving to beginning of, 83
moving to last nonblank cell in, 83
ruler (Word), 17, 34–35

S

Save As dialog box, 13
Save As Type drop-down list, 155
Save Table As window, 155
Save To an External File or Database, 154–155
saving a document as a different type, 13
saving an Office document, 13
SBFM (Small Business Finance Manager), 254–263
creating balance sheets, 256–257
creating a cash flow report, 260–261
creating income statements, 254–255
creating a trial balance, 258–259
creating a what-if scenario, 262–263
scientific notation cell display, 92
screen tips, 73
search engine (Web), 240–241
searching for data in Excel, 102–103
searching the Web, 240–243
sections (documents in Binder), 9
selecting text, 20, 26
sending e-mail, 228–229
series of cells, filling automatically, 80–81
series of numbers, producing in cells, 81
shading, in Word, 41
shadows, in PowerPoint, 176–177
shapes
drawing on a chart, 114–115
using in PowerPoint, 172–173
using in Publisher, 308–309
shareware Web sites, 243
sharing data between applications, 6–7
Shift key, 19

Shift+Tab, in tables, 39

Show/hide button, 18, 34, 38

Simple Query Wizard, 150–151

Simple Query Wizard window, 150

single-line horizontal border, 40

slide shows (PowerPoint)
    running, 194–197
    self-running, 198–201
    setting up, 192–193

slides (PowerPoint)
    inserting/deleting and ordering, 186–187
    text on, 166–167
    text boxes for, 170–171

Small Business Edition installation, 252–253

Small Business Edition of Office 97, 251–267

software application support on the Web, 246

software updates/patches, downloading, 243

Sort dialog box, 104

sorting
    in ascending order, 104–105
    a column alphabetically by last name, 104
    a column by financial data, 104
    a column by last and first name, 105
    database data, 146–147
    data in Excel, 104–105
    in descending order, 104–105
    the results of an AutoFilter, 104

sort order, setting, 139

sound files, finding on the Web, 243

Sound Ring, The, 243

sounds
    inserting in a Word document, 67
    using in PowerPoint, 178–179

source data (chart), 112

spacing, changing, 32–33

Speaker Notes, creating, 188–189

special effects, 30

Spelling and Grammar Checker, 22–23

Spelling and Grammar dialog box, 23

spelling suggestions list, 23

spilled data in adjacent empty cell, 74

spreadsheet applications, 71. *See also* Excel 97

spreadsheets, importing into Access, 153

Standard toolbar (Excel), 73

Standard toolbar (Word), 17

status bar (Excel), 72–75

status bar (Word), 16

street maps, U.S., 264–267

styles, 24

Styles window (database report), 138

subsorts, 105

SUM function, 78–79

switchboard, 124–125
    dressing up, 144–145
    sample form, 143
    sample report, 143

switchboard forms, 132, 142–143

Switchboard Manager, 142

Switchboard Manager window, 143

switchboard menu, creating, 142

system menu, opening, 136

T

tab alignment, 35

Tab key
    in Access databases, 137
    in Excel worksheets, 74–75
    in Word, 19, 34
    in Word tables, 39

table border line, choosing, 39

Table Design view (database), 130–131

tables (Access database), 120–121, 123
    creating with Table Wizard, 128–129
    determining, 127
    exporting, 154
    naming, 129
    sorting, 146–147

Tables and Borders toolbar, 38–40

Tables/Queries drop-down list, 132–133, 139, 151

Tables tab, Import window, 152
tables (Word)
  blank line above, 38
  creating, 38–39
  inserting a tab in, 38
  navigating in, 39
Table Wizard (Access), 128–129
tabs, 34–35
  deleting, 34
  with dot leaders, 34
Tabs dialog box, 34
task tracking (with Outlook 97), 224–225
Technical Support menu (Microsoft), 247
templates, 24
  attaching to existing documents, 50
  available, 51
  database, 122
  dummy text to replace, 50
  including instructions in, 50
  modifying, 52–53
  new documents based on, 50–51
  normal blank document, 24, 51
  PowerPoint, 164–165
  using in Word, 50–53
Templates folder and subfolders, 53
text boxes (PowerPoint), 170–171
text files, delimited, 155
text frames (Publisher)
  adding borders, 294–295
  adding text, 278–279
  colors and shadows, 292–293
  creating, 276–277
  flowing text between, 288–291
text (Word)
  deselecting, 29
  entering and editing, 18–19
  formatting, 26–27
  highlighting, 20
  pasting, 21
  placing graphics behind/on top of, 69
  selecting, 20

thick single line, entering, 19
thin single line, entering, 19
3-D chart, 108
3-D effects, using in PowerPoint, 176–177
times, entering automatically, 80
title bar (Excel window), 73
title bar (Word window), 16
Titles tab, Chart Options dialog box, 111
To Do lists, creating with Outlook 97, 224–225
toggle switch, 278
toolbars
  customizing, 157
  Excel, 73
  hiding, 16
  PowerPoint, 160–161
  repositioning, 156
  Word, 16
Tools Options window, 156
top ten values in a list, displaying, 103
total number of pages (Word), 16
travel aid (AutoMap), 264–267
trial balance, creating, 258–259
TrueType (TT) fonts, 30
Typical Install, 3
typing area (Word), 17
typing the same character repeatedly, 19

U

underlining text, 26–29
underscore characters, 26
updates, on the Web, 246
uploading files, 244
URLs, 242, 248–249
utilities, on the Web, 246

V

VCR panel (database), 124
vertical scroll bar, 17

video
 inserting in Office applications, 5
 inserting in a Word document, 67
 using in PowerPoint, 178–179
View buttons (Word), 16
View menu (Access), 137

W

watermarks, 68
wavy line, 19
Web
 blue underlined text, 243
 clip art collections on, 242–243
 downloading files from, 244–245
 finding files on, 242–243
 graphics files on, 243
 online support on, 246–247
 searching, 240–243
 searching for sound files, 243
 viewing Web pages, 241
Web browser (Internet Explorer), 239, 241
Web link, placing within a document, 248–249
Web search engine, 240–241
Web search query, formulating, 241
Web site addresses, 242, 248–249
Welcome dialog box, 2
what-if scenario, creating, 262–263
What's This? help, 10
Windows Clipboard, 7, 20–21, 90–91, 248
Windows Explorer, 12
Windows95.com, 243
Wizard dialog box, 55
wizard-generated documents, 54–55
wizards, 51, 54–55
Word, 15–69
 adding borders and shading, 40–41
 changing fonts and font sizes, 30–31
 changing line spacing, 32–33
 changing page margins, 42–43
 changing tabs, 34–35

copying character formatting, 28–29
copying using cut-and-paste, 20–21
creating lists, 36–37
creating merge documents, 56–65
creating a table, 38–39
entering and editing text, 18–19
formatting graphics in documents, 68–69
formatting text, 26–27
inserting graphics in documents, 66–67
menu bar, 17
program window, 16–17
Spelling and Grammar Checker, 22–23
templates, 50–53
using AutoText, 24–25
using Document Map, 46–47
using headers and footers, 44–45
using Outline view, 48–49
using Wizards, 54–55
WordArt Gallery, 4–5
workbook file title, 73
workbooks
 containing multiple worksheets, 116
 dragging and dropping data between, 88
Word menu bar, 17
word processor, 15
word search feature of help, 11
worksheets. *See* Excel worksheets
Wrapping tab, Format Picture dialog box,
 68–69
wrapping text around clip art (Publisher),
 286–287

X

X-axis and Y-axis titles (chart), 107